An Evangelical Spiritual Theology

Princeton Theological Monograph Series

K. C. Hanson, Charles M. Collier,
and Robin A. Parry, Series Editors

Recent volumes in the series:

Robert A. Hand
Theological Epistemology in Immanuel Kant's Transcendental Idealism and Karl Barth's Theology

Scott P. Rice
Trinity and History: The God-World Relation in the Theology of Dorner, Barth, Pannenberg, and Jenson

Hakbong Kim
Person, Personhood, and the Humanity of Christ: Christocentric Anthropology and Ethics in Thomas F. Torrance

Lisanne Winslow
A Trinitarian Theology of Nature

Matthew T. Prior
Confronting Technology: The Theology of Jacques Ellul

Edmund Fong
Obedience from First to Last: The Obedience of Jesus Christ in Karl Barth's Doctrine of Reconciliation

Chad Michael Rimmer
Greening the Children of God: Thomas Traherne and Nature's Role in the Ecological Formation of Children

Steven Schafer
Marriage, Sex, and Procreation: Contemporary Revisions to Augustine's Theology of Marriage

An Evangelical Spiritual Theology
Donald Bloesch on the Christian Life

JAMIN GOGGIN

◥PICKWICK *Publications* • Eugene, Oregon

AN EVANGELICAL SPIRITUAL THEOLOGY
Donald Bloesch on the Christian Life

Princeton Theological Monograph Series

Copyright © 2025 Jamin Goggin. All rights reserved. Except for brief quotations in critical publications or reviews, no part of this book may be reproduced in any manner without prior written permission from the publisher. Write: Permissions, Wipf and Stock Publishers, 199 W. 8th Ave., Suite 3, Eugene, OR 97401.

Pickwick Publications
An Imprint of Wipf and Stock Publishers
199 W. 8th Ave., Suite 3
Eugene, OR 97401

www.wipfandstock.com

PAPERBACK ISBN: 979-8-3852-4791-2
HARDCOVER ISBN: 979-8-3852-4792-9
EBOOK ISBN: 979-8-3852-4793-6

Cataloguing-in-Publication data:

Names: Goggin, Jamin, 1982–, author.

Title: An evangelical spiritual theology : Donald Bloesch on the Christian life / Jamin Goggin.

Description: Eugene, OR : Pickwick Publications, 2025 | Series: Princeton Theological Monograph Series | Includes bibliographical references.

Identifiers: ISBN 979-8-3852-4791-2 (paperback) | ISBN 979-8-3852-4792-9 (hardcover) | ISBN 979-8-3852-4793-6 (ebook)

Subjects: LCSH: Bloesch, Donald G., 1928–. | Spirituality. | Theology, Doctrinal. | Evangelicalism.

Classification: BT75.2 .G64 2025 (paperback) | BT75.2 (ebook)

VERSION NUMBER 11/19/25

To my parents, Dan and Alice Goggin.

> Evangelical theology is modest theology, because it is determined to be so by its object, that is, by him who is its subject.
>
> KARL BARTH

Contents

Introduction | 1
1. Bloesch as Evangelical Theologian of the Christian Life | 25
2. Defining the Christian Life | 51
3. Distributing the Christian Life | 99
4. Prayer and the Christian Life | 152

Conclusion | 187

Bibliography | 209

Introduction

DONALD G. BLOESCH (1928–2010) was an evangelical theologian whose theological career produced a rich deposit of systematic theology. Best known for his seven-volume systematic treatment of evangelical theology, Bloesch's full corpus of thirty-seven monographs demonstrates a broad range of theological interest. Despite his enormous body of work, Bloesch has been minimally engaged in contemporary systematic theology.[1] Given Bloesch's theological agenda to articulate a fundamental account of evangelical theology as such—the limited engagement by fellow evangelicals is particularly peculiar. At a time when evangelicals are in a process of identity clarification, many seeking to find robust theological resources for constructive theology, attentiveness to Bloesch's body of work will prove not only informative, but also instructive.[2] Toward the end of defining and

1. The lack of engagement with Bloesch's work is perhaps due to his obscure position within evangelicalism specifically and the church more broadly. Bloesch's ecclesial location, in the United Church of Christ, positioned him outside the bounds of normative evangelical ecclesial circles and, in part, outside the bounds of orthodox Christianity. Bloesch remained in the denomination despite what he deemed to be heretical teaching, for the sake of pursuing renewal in the church. His teaching post at Dubuque Theological Seminary positioned him predominantly within mainline and specifically Presbyterian ecclesial circles, but given his ecclesial background, he remained a sojourner in this home. Perhaps more than anything his Pietistic background, appeal to the Reformed tradition, and interest in neo-Reformers such as Barth, provided him with no place to rest his head within the evangelical tent. In many ways, he was a voice crying in the wilderness of his time, not rejected, but perhaps not fully understood. To the more conservative sectors of evangelicalism, Bloesch was too liberal, and to the liberal sectors of evangelicalism, he was too conservative.

2. Two examples of recent volumes that reflect the contemporary debate regarding

describing the nature and goals of a truly *evangelical* theology, Donald Bloesch is an obvious resource.

The present volume seeks to remedy the limited engagement Bloesch's dogmatic project has received in contemporary evangelical theology. His self-identification as an evangelical theologian, his breadth of theological work, and the appreciation he received from his theological peers suggest the credibility of this venture.[3] In what follows, I investigate and interpret the dogmatic contribution of Donald Bloesch for the sake of introducing him into current dialogue regarding evangelical theology. Bloesch's project is worthy of contemporary engagement and appropriation, but first it must be retrieved and articulated.

My thesis, *in nuce*, is that Bloesch provides a vision of evangelical theology marked by a distinctive emphasis on the doctrine of the Christian life. The Christian life is the definitive doctrine shaping Bloesch as a theologian and shaping all his theological work. As the defining doctrine of his dogmatic project, the Christian life functions as a materially distributed doctrine throughout Bloesch's entire system. Consequently, Bloesch's evangelical theology is a theology of the Christian life.

Here, in the introduction, I seek to briefly outline the primary features of my thesis. First, I briefly consider what kind of evangelical theologian Bloesch is. I then move to provide a snapshot of Bloesch's interest in, and emphasis upon, the doctrine of the Christian life. Following this, I outline the basic argument concerning the doctrinal distribution of the Christian life. What is set out in skeletal form in this introduction is fleshed out in the chapters to follow.

Bloesch as Evangelical Theologian

Bloesch began his inaugural address at Dubuque University in 1962 by stating, "The perennial question in systematic theology is the role of the Christian life in our salvation."[4] It is a curious place to begin for a systematic

---

the meaning and identity of evangelicalism are Labberton, *Still Evangelical?*, and Kidd, *Who Is an Evangelical?*

3. One primary example of the appreciation Bloesch received from peers is demonstrated in the monograph *Evangelical Theology in Transition*, edited by Elmer M. Colyer. The entire volume is dedicated to an engagement with Bloesch's theology. Avery Dulles, Millard Erickson, Gabriel Fackre, Clark Pinnock, Thomas Torrance, and other theologians engage Bloesch's doctrinal work.

4. Bloesch, "Christian Life in the Plan of Salvation," 3. Printed independently in

theologian. Yet, perhaps for a theologian with a Pietistic background, this beginning point is not surprising. For Bloesch, the centerpiece of evangelical theology properly constructed is the Christian life. Bloesch represents an underappreciated stream of the evangelical tradition that merits recognition as a distinct and distinctively evangelical theological method. Bloesch's method of emphasizing the Christian life, while remaining firmly rooted in historic Christian faith and affirming common evangelical commitments (Bebbington's Rule), may be of interest to contemporary evangelical theology.[5] So, while definitions of evangelicalism can often be anchored solely in doctrinal commitments, Bloesch would retort, "to be evangelical means to hold to a definite doctrine *as well as* to participate in a special kind of experience."[6] Bloesch would agree doctrine is necessary to defining evangelicalism, but it is insufficient; he would continually assert that a certain spirituality is necessary as well. In casting this evangelical vision, Bloesch asserts, "A new orthodoxy that is both catholic and evangelical will seek the recovery of the 'Christian mind' as well as of Christian spirituality."[7] This is Bloesch's vision for evangelicalism.

There has been a resurgence of interest in spirituality (e.g., the spiritual formation movement) in evangelicalism over the past half of a century, but such a resurgence has often been deemed a niche programme.[8] It has also quite often lacked the theological backbone to stand firmly within evangelicalism's doctrinal boundaries with rootedness and clarity. As a

---

booklet form without date by the Theological Seminary of the University of Dubuque (together with the installation address of C. Howard Wallace) and again in *Theology and Life* in 1962. This subject also formed the topic of his book *The Christian Life and Salvation* (1967). Quotations in this article are taken from the independently printed booklet as found in *The Place of Monasticism in the Thought of Donald Bloesch* by Greg Peters.

5. In chapter 1 I provide a thorough account of Bloesch's evangelical identity. Toward that end, I outline the key features of Bebbington's Rule. I argue that Bebbington's Rule is currently the most agreed upon definition of evangelicalism.

6. Bloesch, *Essentials of Evangelical Theology*, 1:ix, emphasis mine. Bloesch echoes this point elsewhere, stating, "From the evangelical perspective, true Christianity entails doctrine, experience and life. Whenever anyone of these elements is underplayed or denied, something crucial to the faith of the church is lost" (*Future of Evangelical Christianity*, 17).

7. Bloesch, *Ground of Certainty*, 24.

8. A few books that highlight this resurgence of interest include Richard Foster's *Celebration of Discipline* as well as Dallas Willard's *Divine Conspiracy, Renovation of the Heart*, and *The Spirit of the Disciplines*. It is also highlighted by the *formatio* line of books published by InterVarsity, a traditionally evangelical publishing house. The *formatio* line boasts dozens of books all focused on spiritual formation.

result, much of evangelicalism has remained content with focusing on other matters, to the exclusion of the Christian life. Bloesch's criticism then could easily be affirmed today: "Much is said today in evangelical circles about evangelism and church growth but very little on the spiritual life, prayer and asceticism."[9] While Bloesch himself tends to be ignored in conversations about evangelicalism, his account could, in fact, be said to be winning the day. The concern with emphasizing the Christian life as a doctrine of priority finds much contemporary resonance. Thomas Kidd in *Who Is an Evangelical?* writes, "Evangelicals are born-again Protestants who cherish the Bible as the Word of God and who emphasize a personal relationship with Jesus Christ through the Holy Spirit."[10] This emphasis on "personal relationship with Jesus through the Holy Spirit" is precisely the emphasis that Bloesch offers. The two sources of his evangelical identity, Pietism and Reformed theology, suit him well to model this emphasis without a loss of doctrinal rigor.[11]

Bloesch finished his theological career right where it began. In the final years of his life, Bloesch completed his spiritual autobiography *Faith in Search of Obedience*. While the title alone is an apt précis of his prolific theological career, within the first few pages of the text itself Bloesch declares, "The leitmotif of my theology is faith in search of obedience. Conformity to the will of God in daily life has been the motivating force in my vocation."[12] This succinct theological self-attestation bears the marks of repetition if we focus on two key phrases: "faith in search of obedience" and "conformity to the will of God in daily life." Both locutions concern the same doctrinal locus: the Christian life. For Bloesch, evangelical theology is not merely faith seeking understanding, but rather faith seeking obedience. As I demonstrate in chapter 1, Bloesch inherited this emphasis on the Christian life from his pietistic heritage. Here, I show where the journey began in earnest.

---

9. Bloesch, *Evangelical Renaissance*, 25.

10. Kidd, *Who Is an Evangelical?*, 4.

11. Systematic theologian Daniel Treier highlights these two streams, Pietism and Reformed theology, as properly feeding into a true and robust account of evangelical theology. See Treier, *Introducing Evangelical Theology*, 4–8.

12. Bloesch, *Faith in Search of Obedience*, 60.

Faith in Search of Obedience

During his postdoctoral years, Bloesch's understanding of the Christian life as a pilgrimage of faith for obedience took on literal form as he toured a variety of religious communities in Europe.[13] He was on a quest to find communities that embodied "conformity to the will of God in daily life."[14] The formative significance of this pilgrimage on Bloesch as a theologian must not be overlooked. The impact of this experience can be seen in both the body and soul of Bloesch's theology. First, we see its formative impact in the body of his work: two of Bloesch's earliest published works are dedicated to an account and analysis of his experiences in these communities.[15] Second, we see the formative impact on the soul of his work: the emphasis on renewal central to Bloesch's entire theological project was shaped by what he witnessed in these communities.

Within his published account of his pilgrimage, one discovers a rationale for the formative influence of this experience on his thought. Bloesch argues that these communities are one of two legitimate modes of the Christian life. The life of devotion and piety demanded of all Christians can be faithfully endeavored in a *monastic mode* or in a *secular mode*.[16] Regarding the monastic mode, Bloesch states, "some Christians stand under the imperative to fulfill their vocation apart from the world in religious communities or in solitary witness that often entails the renunciation of family, property, and the use of force and violence."[17] In regard to the

---

13. Greg Peters claims, "After completing his PhD, Bloesch spent the following year doing postdoctoral work at Oxford University through a scholarship from the World Council of Churches. While at Oxford, Bloesch exposed himself to the religious life of the Anglo-Catholic monasteries, which, he later said, left a lasting impression on him. Fascinated by these British monastics, Bloesch visited (primarily Protestant) religious houses in Switzerland, France, Italy, and Germany, resulting in his first book, *Centers of Christian Renewal*" (*Reforming the Monastery*, 129).

14. Bloesch, *Faith in Search of Obedience*, 60.

15. The two monographs referenced here are *Wellsprings of Renewal* and *Centers of Christian Renewal*. In *Faith in Search of Obedience* we discover that Bloesch's interest in religious communities remained throughout his theological career: "Besides my fascination with systematic theology, I have continued to engage in research on religious communities and renewal fellowships" (41).

16. Bloesch argues, "In traditional terminology the two types of discipleship are the secular life, i.e., the life of faith in the world, and the religious life" (*Wellsprings of Renewal*, 20). The categories I have developed—"monastic mode" and "secular mode"—are designed to reflect this fundamental distinction Bloesch draws here.

17. Bloesch, *Wellsprings of Renewal*, 20.

secular mode, Bloesch states, "there are those who are called to live wholly in the world for the sake of the Gospel, and this entails family life, property, and participation in the affairs of the state."[18] Despite his great interest in the monastic mode, Bloesch himself chooses the secular, but determines that the monastic mode can and should meaningfully inform the secular mode.[19] Bloesch claims, "My interest in religious communities has been fueled by the concern to make faith real and concrete in daily life."[20] As I show in detail in chapter 1, the seed of interest in the Christian life was already planted in Bloesch's heart through his pietistic upbringing. What he discovers in these European Christian communities is fertile soil from which this pietistic seed can grow and mature.

Bloesch views these communities as bases of *renewal*, equipping "secular Christians" like himself to fight the good fight of faith from their own particular outposts. According to Bloesch, the fundamental resource of renewal identified within these communities is *evangelical piety*.[21] In

18. Bloesch, *Wellsprings of Renewal*, 20.
19. Bloesch, *Wellsprings of Renewal*, 20.
20. Bloesch, *Faith in Search of Obedience*, 61.
21. Perhaps such an emphasis is surprising coming from a Protestant theologian, but Bloesch believes himself to be on solid Reformation ground in arguing his case:

> Religious communities have a definite place in Evangelical spirituality, even though they were censured at the time of the Reformation. It must be recognized that the Reformers protested not against community life as such but against a particular theological understanding of this kind of life in which free grace was supplanted by works-righteousness. In Protestant history, many forms of community life have prospered, and this way of life is being revived today in a remarkable number of new experiments. (Bloesch et al., *Christian Spirituality*, 185)

Bloesch recognizes that Luther and Calvin both opposed the monasticism of their time. And yet, he argues, "despite their aversion to the monasticism of their time the Reformers did not censure the principle of religious community life" (*Wellsprings of Renewal*, 30). He believes in fact that the Reformers maintained a place for the role of religious communities, contingent upon a proper vocational understanding in relation to the church more broadly. And so Bloesch concludes,

> Despite the door that was opened by the Reformation to an evangelical community life, the children of the Reformation have for the most part failed to rise to this opportunity, though, as we shall see, new ventures in this direction are now being made. The secular or ordinary life in the world has generally been regarded as infinitely superior to the religious or cloistered life. Though it is acknowledged that all Christians are called to wholehearted commitment to Christ, sufficient recognition has not been given to the truth that some Christians (besides the clerics) may well be

Centers of Christian Renewal, Bloesch provides an account of eight different religious communities he engaged with directly, and which he believes are "representative types of community life today."[22] More than "representative types," it seems that he chose these eight because they are *ideal types*.[23] What makes these eight communities "ideal types" is that they bear witness to the brand of evangelical piety he himself also seeks to identify and to bear witness to.[24] Bloesch states, "When the world enters the church, not

> called to full-time church service and that this may entail a life of simplicity and renunciation. (*Wellsprings of Renewal*, 32–33)

Consequently, Bloesch believes he is retrieving this properly Reformed openness to religious communities and providing a way forward grounded in Reformed theological commitments and evangelical sensibilities. As Bloesch states, "But once we see that community life can give earnest Christians the opportunity to demonstrate a life liberated by grace as a sign of our gratitude to God for what he has done for us in Jesus Christ, then we can go forward in serving others in a communal venture" (*Faith in Search of Obedience*, 61). Bloesch contends the contemporaneous communal emphasis within Protestant circles that birthed the particular communities he visited can ultimately be traced back to his personal tradition, evangelical Pietism. Perhaps one of the contributing factors in Bloesch's early interest in communities of renewal lies in his understanding of its heritage:

> The revival of interest in community is a well-known fact, but what is not so well known is that Evangelical Pietism is one of the main sources of the new ventures in community life. Pietism (or evangelical revivalism) is presently under a cloud in avant-garde theological circles, but even in its somewhat impure forms it is proving to be a wellspring of new life in the church. Latter-day Pietism has been accused of being reactionary, of bringing the faith into alliance with bourgeois values, and there is some justification for these criticisms; yet today those who come out of this tradition are in the vanguard of what might be considered radical or revolutionary Christianity. (*Wellsprings of Renewal*, 12–13)

22. Bloesch, *Centers of Christian Renewal*, 23.

23. Bloesch, *Centers of Christian Renewal*, 24.

24. This is where Bloesch is surely idiosyncratic within the evangelicalism of his day. As I soon demonstrate, Bloesch views these centers of renewal as funding the renewal of the church. It is this renewal of the church that he is ultimately interested in. However, he turns to religious communities as a necessary "wellspring" of such renewal. His vision of internal ecclesial renewal is predicated on external intervention. Bloesch's outspoken optimism of religious communities in being a source of renewal stands in stark contrast to his silent pessimism of the church's direct role in this endeavor. At the end of his theological career, Bloesch acknowledges his previous silence and subtly signals a shift in his thinking in this regard:

> Today I am inclined to view the local congregation as equally vital for Christian renewal in our time as para parochial fellowships. If the local church can come alive in the power of the Spirit, then the willingness to give

only the world but also the church then stands in the need of lighthouses or signposts that point the way to the goal of man's hope which is 'the holy city, new Jerusalem.'"[25] According to Bloesch, evangelical monastic communities function as "lighthouses" or "signposts" to the church.[26] Bloesch views this as a work of the Spirit to bring spiritual renewal to the bride of Christ.[27] The lighthouse is merely a beacon of that which truly reveals and guides—the light of Christ illumined by the Holy Spirit.

Faith in Search of Renewal

What Bloesch finds in these communities is a model that can serve as a spark of renewal to set ablaze a broader ecclesial renewal in the evangelical church. The renewal Bloesch envisages has a particular trajectory beginning with these ideal evangelical communities, moving to the evangelical church, and ultimately to the church catholic.[28] Even though Bloesch

---

and serve will pervade the entire congregation, and perhaps even the surrounding society. Every local church would then be de facto a community of renewal—a lighthouse in a dark world. (*Faith in Search of Obedience*, 61)

Perhaps it was Bloesch's own experience within the United Church of Christ that left him less optimistic in his early years that the church itself could be a lighthouse and was in need of religious communities to fill this role for the sake of the church. And yet, it is compelling that Bloesch completes his theological career with a turn of optimism, that the church itself can be the lighthouse he believes is so needed for evangelical renewal in our time.

25. Bloesch, *Centers of Christian Renewal*, 17.

26. Bloesch argues, "The evangelical communities that have come into being during this recent period are beginning to fulfill the function of lighthouses for Protestant Christianity much as the monasteries have done for the Roman Catholic communion" (*Centers of Christian Renewal*, 16). Bloesch argues in *The Reform of the Church* that while movements of renewal are needed inside the local parish, part of the renewal of the church entails "para-parochial, extra-ecclesiastical or extra-congregational forms and structures" (99). These communities that Bloesch toured are what Bloesch has in mind here. Forms and structures outside the walls of the parish, that can nevertheless serve the local parish and be a part of a broader ecclesial renewal. However, the need for these "extra-ecclesiastical" communities is not meant to void the critical role of the local congregation. As Bloesch states, "In contradistinction to some of the radical theologians, we hold that the parish church is here to stay. At the same time, one should recognize that it is gravely limited in its outreach. There is a need today for new kinds of structures within the local church as well as apart from the church" (*Reform of the Church*, 97).

27. Bloesch, *Centers of Christian Renewal*, 18–19.

28. "The evangelical community may be defined as a group of persons who are concerned with the renewal of evangelical Christianity and who seek to contribute towards

personally had to leave these communities behind to begin his theological career in earnest, he embraced a vocational calling that stems from what he learned there. Bloesch saw his own location on the evangelical landscape as an outpost of this renewal movement. He writes on the edge of evangelicalism with monastic-like ecclesial obscurity, but always for the sake of wider ecclesial renewal.[29] Neither pastor nor evangelical-monastic, Bloesch was committed to "stay in the churches as long as possible and work for renewal from within."[30] However, he unabashedly argues that North American Protestantism has in part succumbed to enemy invasion.[31] Both conservative

---

this renewal by living the common life under a common discipline" (Bloesch, *Reform of the Church*, 13–14).

29. Bloesch states, "My basic concern is the renewal and reformation of the church in a secular society" (*Theological Notebook*, 2:3).

30. Bloesch, *Faith in Search of Obedience*, 43. Bloesch goes on to state, "Sectarianism is a threat that should be combatted, for it invariably results in the weakening of the church's witness" (43). This bears itself out in Bloesch's personal journey with the church. He remained a member and ordained minister within the United Church of Christ despite what he deemed to be serious deviations from sound Christian doctrine. His continued membership and ordination in the denomination were signs of his firm commitment to pursue renewal (Colyer, "Donald G. Bloesch & His Career," 12).

31. Bloesch states,

> Just as the Barmen Declaration spearheaded a confessing church movement in Germany during the 1930s and 1940s, so I believe a case can be made that with the dissipation of biblical substance in our churches and the unnerving alliance of segments of Christendom with cultural ideologies both left and right, the church is hard pressed to recover its evangelical and catholic identity. It is obliged to bear witness to the faith in a new way in the face of the challenges of our age. (*Church*, 266)

Bloesch echoes this concern in *The Invaded Church*. There we read, "My thesis is that the real division in the church is not between evangelism and social action but between the secular humanism of our technological society, which has infiltrated the church, and the transcendent claims of the holy, catholic faith" (15). He goes on to say:

> In my estimation there is today a need for a confessing church that will testify to its faith before the world and thereby sharpen the distinction between the church and the world. The enemy is not simply collectivism or nationalism or a new Baalism but a secular or worldly Christianity which has accepted at least in part the values and goals of the surrounding society. When secular values however praiseworthy are uncritically adopted by the church as authentically or even potentially Christian, the tension between the transcendent Word of God and human culture is lost sight of, and the result is a compromised version of the faith. In Germany the Barmen Confession was aimed primarily at the German Christians, those who sought to amalgamate the faith and the values and precepts of National Socialism. A confessing church would stand against both a diluted liberalism, which

and liberal, mainline and nondenominational alike, have been infiltrated by a "worldly... spirituality," on Bloesch's assessment.[32]

Bloesch's critical concern with "worldly spirituality" is instructive. Bloesch believes the body of Christ has been sickened by a poisoned account of the Christian life, and as a doctor of the church, Bloesch's theological task is to prescribe a proper account of the Christian life as the necessary remedy. This is what his "renewal" language means to communicate.[33] Despite his sobering assessment of illness in the body of Christ, Bloesch maintains optimism regarding the future health of the church.[34] His hope ultimately lies in the work of the Holy Spirit, the one true physician who can provide the medicine needed to renew the body of Christ. He foresees this Spirit-driven movement of renewal as an "evangelical renaissance."[35]

---

sometimes takes the form of a compulsive social activism, and cultural fundamentalism, which tends toward a privatistic religiosity. (15–16)

32. Bloesch, *Centers of Christian Renewal*, 21. Interestingly, Bloesch argues that this is the downstream effect of the toxic waste of the Enlightenment (20). This insight leads Bloesch to identify, earlier than many of his theological peers, an encroaching cultural condition in North America that can be called "post-Christian" (24).

33. It is worth noting that as Bloesch talks about other modes of reformation and/or renewal in the church, he constantly focuses on the ultimate goal of "piety" (*Reform of the Church*, 22). So, for example, as Bloesch discusses the importance of "liturgical renewal" he states, "If liturgical renewal entails moral renewal, if it prepares the way for a true spiritual awakening, then it will serve the cause of a revitalized Christian church in our time" (34). Ultimately, the value of the liturgical renewal in the church is that it may assist in the renewal most needed—spiritual renewal.

34. Bloesch states,

I must confess to a deepening conviction that both the mainline denominations and the conservative evangelical movement in America are more and more succumbing to the secularism of the technological society. Yet I also sense that the Spirit of God is at work precisely in the midst of the current social upheaval. Even with the collapse of moral and spiritual norms so glaringly apparent in modern society, there is hope for the renewal of the church in our time. (*Crumbling Foundations*, 19)

Bloesch further articulates his concern regarding the secularization of the church in stating, "The secularization of the modern church is painfully evident in the way it routinely follows secular fads" (21). Bloesch goes on to list specific examples of this accommodation to secular fads that has belied both liberal and conservative tribes. He later defines secularism as "a capitulation to the *Zeitgeist*, the 'spirit of the age.' It means not simply an openness to the values and goals of the world but the enthronement of these values and goals. Secularism represents a rival religion, an absolutizing of what had previously been regarded as penultimate concerns: the things that have to do with the maintenance of life in this world" (37–38).

35. Bloesch, *Crumbling Foundations*, 25.

As a theologian of this movement of renewal, Bloesch resolves himself to help to breathe life into the body of Christ, despite his occasional diagnosis of vital organ failure.[36] Like the communities he visited, he seeks to be a "lighthouse theologian," revealing and guiding. He views the theological task as a call to prophetically expose the dark places and at the same time chart a path forward. He believes he is led by the Spirit in this *holy* theological task. What he identifies as the mark of the Spirit's true work in these communities, he wishes to be branded by—evangelicalism. In short, Bloesch is an evangelical theologian, seeking to renew evangelicalism for the sake of renewing the church catholic. Bloesch is so sure that faithful evangelicalism is the hope of the church that he boldly declares: "evangelical Christianity is the true orthodoxy."[37]

The Christian Life as Definitive Doctrine

In mapping Bloesch's early journey as an evangelical theologian, I have demonstrated his unique interest in the Christian life. At its most basic level, the Christian life is, as Reinhard Hütter argues, "life with the triune God made possible by the life, death, and resurrection of Jesus Christ—a life of faith, hope, and charity, exercised by prayer, worship, and discipleship."[38] Bloesch's entire corpus demonstrates a thoroughgoing interest in the material content of the Christian life as broadly defined by Hütter. According to Bloesch, the Christian life is an ongoing, divine-human encounter known in the Christian's life of obedience and made possible by Word & Spirit. This encounter is personal, as it is an ongoing event of fellowship between the Christian person and the tri-personal God of Scripture. The Christian's life of obedience is marked by both personal piety and social action. Through a life of obedience empowered by the Holy Spirit, the Christian fights for and retains his or her salvation.

While Bloesch's project is defined by an emphasis on the subject of the Christian life, his direct use of the language "the Christian life" is limited. When talking about the Christian life Bloesch frequently makes use of language such as "piety," "devotion," "spirituality," and "biblical-personalism"

---

36. This conviction is evident in Bloesch's unwavering commitment to his wayward ecclesial family of origin, the United Church of Christ. It is also evident in the catholic sensibility displayed throughout his entire theological career.

37. Bloesch, *Future of Evangelical Christianity*, 5.

38. Hütter, "Christian Life," 285.

to designate his theme. In light of this, I appeal to the doctrinal language of "the Christian life" as a rubric of both *collection* and *correspondence*. As a collecting doctrine, the Christian life can bring together and organize a wide variety of concepts, motifs, and emphases found in Bloesch's thought. As a doctrine of correspondence, the Christian life can situate unique or idiosyncratic areas of Bloesch's thought within a normative theological idiom. In chapter 2, I accomplish this work of collecting and corresponding. In so doing, I provide an analysis of Bloesch's constructive account of the Christian life.

The present project demonstrates that Bloesch is correct that the "leitmotif" of his theology is the Christian life—"faith in search of obedience."[39] The Christian life is the defining doctrine of his theological career. As it stands, I am not alone in this conviction. Elmer Colyer, a longtime colleague of Bloesch, states,

> Our work has convinced me of the utterly crucial place of the Christian life within Bloesch's theology and his career. It is the hermeneutical key to the interrelationship of Bloesch's early books and to the central Word-Spirit polarity characteristic not only of his theological method but also of his overall theology. Since Bloesch's doctrine of the Christian life is so interwoven in the entire fabric of his theology, it is impossible to give it adequate treatment within a single essay: someone ought to write a dissertation on the subject.[40]

This present project is a response to Colyer's invitation.[41] I argue that a proper investigation and interpretation of Bloesch's thought requires an acute attentiveness to the doctrine of the Christian life within his dogmatic corpus, and this project reveals the fruitfulness of employing that hermeneutical key to interpreting Bloesch's work.

The Christian Life as Distributive Doctrine

As the defining doctrine of Bloesch's dogmatic project, the Christian life applies material pressure throughout his theological system. This material pressure can be effectively identified and investigated through the

---

39. Bloesch, *Faith in Search of Obedience*, 60.

40. Colyer and Weborg, "Bloesch's Doctrine of the Christian Life," 149–50.

41. This monograph is the product of my initial PhD research and dissertation on the theology of Donald Bloesch.

theological concept of "distribution." In chapter 3 of my project, I thoroughly demonstrate the distributive quality of Bloesch's doctrine of the Christian life. Here, in the introduction, I provide a definition of doctrinal distribution and a brief overview of this distribution.

In the first of his two-volume collection of essays *God Without Measure*, the late John Webster argues there are "two distributive doctrines in the corpus of Christian dogmatics."[42] For Webster, the two doctrines of distribution are the doctrine of the Trinity and the doctrine of creation.[43] A distributive doctrine, according to Webster, is a doctrine that is presupposed and pervasive in the construction of all other doctrinal matters. Webster's notion of doctrinal distribution is an apt category to illumine the inner logic of Bloesch's project. For Bloesch, there is a first order and second order doctrinal distribution. The doctrine of revelation can first be identified as the *formal* distributive doctrine in Bloesch's theology, while secondarily the doctrine of the Christian life can be identified as the *material* distributive doctrine for Bloesch. In chapter 3, I argue that Bloesch's formal distributive doctrine—revelation—includes his materially distributive doctrine—the Christian life. The Christian life is materially *presupposed* and *pervasive* in Bloesch's account of revelation, and since revelation is formally distributed throughout Bloesch's entire theological system, it is an assumed and active ingredient in the whole of his dogmatic project.[44]

42. Webster, *God and the Works of God*, 117.

43. Webster states,

> The first (both in sequence and in material primacy) distributed doctrine is the doctrine of the Trinity, of which all other articles of Christian teaching are an amplification or application, and which therefore permeates theological affirmations about every matter; theology talks about everything by talking about God. The doctrine of creation is the second distributed doctrine, although, because its scope is restricted to the *opera Dei ad extra*, its distribution is less comprehensive than that of the doctrine of the Trinity. (*God and the Works of God*, 117)

It is important to note that of the two distributive doctrines Webster does acknowledge, creation is less exhaustive in its theological ubiquity than the Trinity, but nonetheless he names both doctrines as distributive.

44. Interestingly, Bloesch's distributive prioritization of the doctrine of the Christian life in his dogmatic system would have undoubtedly been critiqued by Webster due to its inherit emphasis on the economic operations of the Triune God. Webster states,

> In much of modern exegetical and dogmatic theology, the doctrine of creation does not have this place and function. This may be attributed in part to the way in which in all conceptions of the matter of Christian teaching some doctrines achieve prominence and others contract. Concentration on the

An Evangelical Spiritual Theology

The first place we find evidence of doctrinal distribution within the corpus of Donald Bloesch is in his governing axiomatic idiom of revelation—Word & Spirit—an idiom Bloesch retrieves from the Reformed tradition.[45] Bloesch privileges the language of "Word & Spirit" rather than "Word and Spirit" in defining the nature of this revelatory principle. The ampersand is used by Bloesch to communicate the unbinding relationship of Word and Spirit.[46] The formal distribution of Bloesch's Word & Spirit account of revelation across the whole of his project is readily evident throughout his body of work. It is particularly obvious in his seven-volume dogmatic magnum opus, *Christian Foundations*, where it serves as both an initiator

---

outer works of God, for example, may be such that the first body of dogmatic material on God's infinite perfection *in se* receives only slight attention. (118)

As I noted throughout my project, Bloesch treats God's infinite perfection *in se* with "slight attention." It is not until the third volume of his dogmatic magnum opus that he arrives at an account of the Trinity *in se* and the divine perfections, and even then Bloesch waits until the seventh chapter to do so. Bloesch provides the rationale for this decision in the preface of the volume: "Some who are committed to the faith of Nicaea and Chalcedon might wonder why I do not begin this volume with an excurses on the doctrine of the Trinity. I think the biblical way is to deal first with the mystery of God's self-revelation in Jesus Christ and then find in this revelation allusions to the Trinity" (*God the Almighty*, 14).

45. Bloesch's governing theological construct, Word & Spirit, find their genus in Reformed theology. It is here that Bloesch emphasizes the particular importance of the magisterial Reformers in informing his project, stating, "It will become obvious that my theological approach is strikingly similar to that of the magisterial Reformers (especially Luther and Calvin), who always saw the Word and Spirit together, never one apart from the other" (*Theology of Word & Spirit*, 14).

46. The first volume of Bloesch's mature systematic theology is titled *A Theology of Word & Spirit*. Bloesch's decision to use the ampersand in the title is not incidental or accidental, but intentional and purposeful. While Bloesch uses both "Word & Spirit" and "Word and Spirit" throughout his project interchangeably, his use of the "&" in his initial definition is important. "Word & Spirit" is clearly designed to formally communicate the relation of Word and Spirit that Bloesch wishes to uphold. Bloesch's entire project is formally shaped by the unbinding relation of Word and Spirit, and therefore his use of "&" is designed to signal this unbinding relationship. Consequently, I follow Bloesch's prioritization of the ampersand throughout my project by prioritizing "Word & Spirit" when discussing this axiomatic idiom. It is worth noting that Bloesch is fond of using the ampersand elsewhere to communicate unbinding relations throughout his system. For example, in the subtitles of both the *Jesus Christ* and *Holy Spirit* volumes in his systematic theology Bloesch uses the "&." The subtitle of Bloesch's *Jesus Christ* volume is *Savior & Lord*, and the subtitle of his *Holy Spirit* volume is *Works & Gifts*. In both cases, Bloesch seeks to communicate that these descriptors of the economic operations of the Son and Spirit cannot be separated but must be held together at all times if we are to understand the work of Son and Spirit properly.

giving rise to the project and a persistent theme shaping the whole.[47] It is not provocative to claim that Word & Spirit is *the* governing theological principle that Bloesch "upholds."[48] Yet, at first glance, it is not immediately clear in Bloesch's thought what Word & Spirit references doctrinally.[49] As becomes clear below, central to the Word & Spirit idiom is the doctrine of

47. As just acknowledged, the first volume of Bloesch's *Christian Foundations* is aptly titled *A Theology of Word & Spirit*.

48. Bloesch, *Faith in Search of Obedience*, viii.

49. A theology of Word and Spirit is of course a frequently employed idiom in the Reformed theological tradition. For example, in his letter to Sadolet, Calvin notes, "It is no less reasonable to boast of the Spirit without the Word than it would be absurd to bring forward the Word itself without the Spirit" (Barrett, *Reformation Theology*, 175). Bloesch's account of Word and Spirit is consonant with Calvin and functions as a dialectical safeguard against the dual errors of Word minus Spirit or Spirit minus Word. My sense is that Bloesch has retrieved this Reformed emphasis through the lens of his neo-orthodox mentors, casting his use of Word & Spirit in an epistemological mode. So, for example, Emil Brunner stands as a clear informer of what Bloesch is doing. Brunner states,

> For the God-given power of the Reformation lies in the fact that through it the Church was enabled to escape from this fatal antithesis, Objectivism-Subjectivism, and to find the secret of moving both between and beyond these extremes. Its "epistemological" principle was a dialectic; that is, its form of expression was never the use of one concept, but always two logically contradictory ones: the Word of God in the Bible and the witness of the Holy Spirit, but these understood and experienced, not as a duality, but as a unity. (Brunner, *Divine-Human Encounter*, 20)

Bloesch repeatedly turns to the language of dialectic in describing the nature of his theology of Word & Spirit. For example: "Dialectical theology at its best maintains the object-subject antithesis, and once this antithesis is overcome and paradoxical character of the faith is subverted" (*Theology of Word & Spirit*, 80). Interestingly, it is here that Bloesch appears to privilege Brunner over Barth. So, Bloesch will state, "Indeed, as his theology developed, Barth moved away from both dialectics and paradox without jettisoning these concepts. This perhaps accounts for the fact that he began to lapse into objectivism, thereby failing to hold together the polar opposites of grace and faith, predestination and obedience, heaven and hell" (80). Conversely, we find Brunner speaking of the need for the dialectic of the objective and subjective, Word and Spirit, in much the same manner as Bloesch. Bloesch seeks to strike a similar note of balanced dialectic in regard to Word and Spirit. In Bloesch's mind, these two errors always lurk as real abiding dangers. In the fifth volume of his systematic theology we read:

> In the present theological milieu Word and Spirit are increasingly separated, and this cleavage runs through evangelicalism as well. . . . On the one hand we find those who appeal to Holy Scripture or to the teaching magisterium of the church. The role of the Spirit is to assist the will to assent to Scripture or the teachings of the church. On the other hand, are those who base their case on the universal experience of the Spirit or an all-encompassing Spiritual Presence that is discernible not only in all the world religions but

the Christian life. As the primary theological principle running throughout his work, Word & Spirit carries the Christian life with it, revealing the governing telos of Bloesch's project of renewal. Importantly, Bloesch's use of Word & Spirit is not ontological, but epistemological. This is demonstrated in the ordering of his seven-volume dogmatic work, *Christian Foundations*. The first volume, *A Theology of Word & Spirit*, and the second volume, *Holy Scripture*, materially prioritize the way of knowing over the way of being. In neither volume do we encounter a focused treatment of the doctrine of God as such.[50] Bloesch does not provide an account of the doctrine of God *in se* until the third volume, *God the Almighty*.[51] While he follows this with

> also in the secular world—in politics, economics, the arts and so on. (*Holy Spirit*, 21)

50. Bloesch briefly dips his toe into questions related to the doctrine of God in *Holy Scripture*. In a chapter engaging the impact of Rudolf Bultmann on the nature of revelation and hermeneutics, Bloesch has a short section titled "God Hidden and Revealed." No real constructive work is done here by Bloesch by way of building a doctrine of God, but rather brief engagement with Bultmann's thought. Bloesch sets up this section by stating, "Bultmann held that we can speak of the acts of God but not of the being of God, of God's effects on us but not of God in himself" (*Holy Scripture*, 240).

51. It is telling that Bloesch does not treat the doctrine of God *in se* until *God the Almighty*, which is the third volume in his seven-volume systematic theology, *Christian Foundations*. Clark Pinnock properly identifies a reticence within Bloesch's work to engage the immanent life of the Trinity. Pinnock argues that Bloesch's hesitation to speak of the three persons of the Trinity is in part likely due to the contextual developments in social trinitarianism, which Bloesch was outspokenly opposed to. Consequently, Pinnock argues, "A theologian who cannot affirm three persons in God is not likely to rhapsodize about the triune relationality and its qualities of mutuality, reciprocity and cooperation. No, the emphasis is on God-for-us, not on God-in-himself. The focus rests on the event of revelation in which, by the Spirit, God in his freedom wills to be subjectively present to us" ("Holy Spirit in the Theology of Donald G. Bloesch," 125). Bloesch affirms Pinnock's analysis here in a response later in the edited volume:

> Pinnock raises some important questions in my treatment of the Trinity. He is right that I am not entirely comfortable with the doctrine of the social Trinity. . . . I do not affirm three separate persons in the Trinity, because this implies tritheism. I do affirm three modes of relationship by which God exists within himself, or three agencies of personhood by which God communes with himself and with created humanity. ("Donald Bloesch Responds," in Colyer, *Evangelical Theology in Transition*, 176)

Both Pinnock's analysis and Bloesch's response come prior to volume 5 on the Holy Spirit in Bloesch's systematic theology. Bloesch acknowledges in his response to Pinnock that volume five will develop his answer to these questions more fully. As we turn to volume 5, we read:

> From my perspective it is more felicitous to make the point of departure the unity of God rather than the trinitarian relations. The idea of a social

two more volumes on the Son and the Spirit (*Jesus Christ, The Holy Spirit*), respectively, the emphasis is not on the immanent life of the Trinity but rather the economic operations of Son and Spirit.

In the volume *The Holy Spirit* we begin to get a sense for how the doctrine of the Christian life may be ingredient to his governing axiomatic idiom, Word & Spirit, which reveals how this functions as *the* flavoring agent of Bloesch's entire body of work. Bloesch opens the pages of his *The Holy*

> Trinity, which presupposes three different subjects, leads more often than not into tritheism.... In the contemporary discussion I must confess that I am closer to Karl Barth, Robert Jenson, Eberhard Jungel and John Thompson than to Jurgen Moltmann, Wolfhart Pannenberg, Vladimir Lossky and Clark Pinnock. I prefer to see one God in three events rather than three persons in one nature (though I have no qualms in accepting the latter when rightly interpreted). God remains God, but he is God in a different way in each event. There is one subject but three modalities of action. There is one overarching consciousness but three foci of consciousness. God exists as one self but with three identities. The unity of God is differentiated though not individualized. I hold to one divine being in three modes of existence, not three beings who interact in social unity. (Bloesch, *Holy Spirit*, 269-70)

Despite Bloesch's reticence to speak of the "persons" and his preference for economic talk of God rather than immanent, we do find in Bloesch's earlier work a focused treatment on God *in se*. We find Bloesch's most robust treatment of the immanent life of the Trinity in *The Battle for the Trinity*. Here we do pick up on Bloesch's preference for "mode" language rather than "persons" language once again:

> The church through the ages has confessed one being in three persons, meaning here not separate individuals (this would be Tritheism), but agencies of relationship. Because the meaning of person has changed from an abiding mode of being or activity (*hypostasis*) to an independent or autonomous individual, Karl Barth has rephrased the Trinitarian formula: there is one person in three modes of being. This is not modalism, however, because these three modes of being denote eternal distinctions within God himself and not simply ways by which God relates himself to the world. (Bloesch, *Battle for the Trinity*, 32)

Here we discover that Barth has informed Bloesch's grammatical preference in regard to the Trinity. As we read further in *The Battle for the Trinity*, we do find the most robust treatment of the doctrine of God *in se*. A treatment we do not encounter in his later seven-volume dogmatic project. For example:

> To affirm God as a Trinity means that God not only exists as an absolute being, but also coexists as a fellowship within himself. He not only has the potentiality of love, but he also contains within himself the actual experience of love because he constitutes a community of persons in the pure reciprocity. He does not need the world for fellowship because he has this fellowship of pure love within himself. Trinitarian monotheism affirms that there is one Subject interacting within itself in three ways, one divine consciousness in a threefold self-relatedness. (Bloesch, *Battle for the Trinity*, 31)

Spirit volume by stating, "This is a book on spirituality and historical theology as well as on systematic theology."⁵² It is a work of systematic theology in that it is a project of doctrinal investigation and explication. It is a work of historical theology in that it seeks to survey, with an eye for constructive appropriation, the history of the church in regard to pneumatology. As a theologian, these two emphases, systematic and historical, are not surprising. However, what stands out as unique in the volume is that Bloesch seeks to write not a pneumatology per se, at least not for its own sake, but an account of Christian spirituality. Bloesch hints at what he makes much more explicit throughout the rest of the volume, that to speak of the Spirit is to speak of the Spirit's works, and to speak of the Spirit's works is to speak of the Christian life. In *The Holy Spirit* Bloesch articulates the economic work of the third person of the Trinity. Up to this point in Bloesch's *Christian Foundations* series, readers have been consistently told that Bloesch's theology is a theology of Word & Spirit. It is in his fifth volume that Bloesch explicitly names his emphasis, not on the person of the Spirit, but the work of the Spirit for renewal and Christian formation: "The focus of this book is on the work of the Spirit in renewing the church and shaping the Christian life rather than on his person."⁵³ The telos of the Christian life leads Bloesch away from accounts of the person of the Spirit, or the procession of the Spirit, and to a focus on the Spirit's work in the life of the church and of the individual Christian. With this in mind, it makes sense why Bloesch would write a volume on the Spirit as a work of "spirituality."

By giving doctrinal priority to the Christian life Bloesch articulates the objective basis of the Christian faith for the sake of articulating its subjective application. While Bloesch gives priority to the missions of Son and Spirit, he never does so apart from questions of knowledge and faith. For Bloesch, the objective work of God must always be tethered to the subjective response of the Christian and vice versa. The subtitles of both volumes make this clear: *Jesus Christ* is subtitled *Savior & Lord*, and *The Holy Spirit* is subtitled *Works & Gifts*. Bloesch's emphasis is not on God in himself, but God in action, precisely because Bloesch is writing for the sake of expounding the theological reality of a lived existence for the Christian. This is why Bloesch has little interest in talking about divine action

---

52. Bloesch, *Holy Spirit*, 13.

53. Bloesch states in the foreword to his *Holy Spirit*, "The focus of this book is on the work of the Spirit in renewing the church and shaping the Christian life rather than on his person" (19).

apart from the "divine-human encounter." In *A Theology of Word & Spirit* Bloesch states, "Theology endeavors to present a true picture of the activity and divinity that serves to illumine the pilgrimage of faith. Its purpose is not to give abstract knowledge of God but to direct humanity to its spiritual home for the glory of God."[54] Here, we begin to see signs of how the Christian life is a distributed doctrine in his work. Not only does Bloesch emphasize reflection upon God *ad extra* over God *ad intra*, not only does he emphasize epistemology over ontology, but his epistemological goal is the illumination of "the pilgrimage of faith," which as we have already seen is synonymous with the Christian life.

This emphasis on human experience may strike readers of Bloesch's theology as unbecoming of a theologian claiming Reformed sensibilities. He seems to place more weight upon subjective experience than would be permissible. Bloesch, however, is mindful of this and seeks to avoid too much epistemological weight being given over to human experience. Bloesch claims,

> In the evangelical theology I propose, the focus is neither on divine essence nor on human experience but on divine existence in humanity, as we see this in Jesus Christ. Theology is not the verbalization of religious experience . . . Instead, it is the articulation of a divine revelation that breaks into our experience from the beyond and transforms it.[55]

Bloesch is cautious about collapse into experientialism, but he is equally wary of dogmatic ascendance into divine speculation. Nevertheless, Bloesch moves quickly to categories of the Christian life, referencing revelation, known in human experience, leading to transformation.

The epistemological meaning of Bloesch's recurrent invocation of Word & Spirit is made explicit when he uses it to talk about the two sides of the divine-human encounter: revelation and salvation. We read, "In the theology presented here both revelation and salvation have to be understood as objective-subjective rather than fundamentally objective (as in evangelical rationalism) or predominantly subjective (as in existentialism

---

54. Bloesch, *Theology of Word & Spirit*, 116.

55. Bloesch, *Theology of Word & Spirit*, 117–18. Bloesch echoes his hesitation to invest theological energy into the doctrine of God *in se* as determinative of the dogmatic task in stating, "God has provided a revelation of himself sufficient for us to think deeply and rightly concerning his will and purpose so that we may implement his plan for the world in faithful service. Yet God has not given us an exhaustive knowledge of the inner workings of his Spirit or a direct perception of the essence of his being" (116).

and mysticism)."[56] Bloesch repeatedly employs the paired language of *objective* & *subjective* as parallel with Word & Spirit. The Word is the objective, and the Spirit is the subjective. As Bloesch talks about the Spirit as the subjective component of the divine-human encounter, we find corresponding terminology such as experience and spirituality with reference to the Christian life. Therefore, if one pays attention to this range of terms attached to the Spirit and the "subjective," one begins to taste the distributive spread of the Christian life. In the end, Bloesch baldly asserts, "pneumatology becomes spirituality" in his constructive project.[57] What becomes clear is that Bloesch's theology of Word & Spirit is foundational and operative throughout the whole of his theological corpus, and this emphasis carries with it a distributive ingredient: the Christian life. As Bloesch succinctly and clearly states in the foreword to the inaugural volume in his seven-volume systematic theology, "To speak of a theology of Word and Spirit or Spirit and Word is to reintroduce into theology the critical role of the experience of faith."[58] Bloesch's driving doctrinal interest in the Christian life is imbedded in the defining framework of his entire theological system.

---

56. Bloesch, *Theology of Word & Spirit*, 15. Bloesch is opposed to an epistemological subjectivism in which "autonomous human reason or experience becomes the determinant of Christian thinking or practice" (130). At the same time, he is opposed to an epistemological objectivism in which the "human mind is called to submit to a purely external authority" (131). For Bloesch, objectivism and subjectivism result in divergent, yet equally dangerous, modes of divine knowledge—rationalism and mysticism. Bloesch refers to these two failed modes of divine knowledge as "rationalist and spiritualist theologies" (*Holy Spirit*, 21). In response to this Bloesch argues, "The biblical theologian contends that our knowledge of God is neither clear and distinct (as in rationalism) nor abstruse and recondite (as in mysticism) but dialectical and paradoxical. It is a knowledge that is on the way to comprehension rather than one that claims comprehension" (*Theology of Word & Spirit*, 80). Bloesch uses other terms to signal the same distinction. For example, "In contrast to both a spiritualism that makes light of the particularities of sound doctrine and a credalism that underplays the role of experience in the drama of faith, I uphold a theology of Word and Spirit, which brings together the normativeness of Holy Scripture and the decisiveness of the Holy Spirit" (*Faith in Search of Obedience*, viii).

57. Bloesch, *Holy Spirit*, 33. While it would be accurate to argue that his pietistic background gives him this impulse, the same would be true of his commitment to Reformed theology. In Bloesch's mind, he is carrying on the best of what John Calvin had in mind in *The Institutes*: a theology of Word and Spirit whereby regeneration is viewed not merely as an objective reality tied to justification, but a subjective reality pointing forward into a "lifelong sanctifying process" (31).

58. Bloesch, *Theology of Word & Spirit*, 14.

Conclusion

Donald G. Bloesch is an uncommon evangelical theologian. His unique theological contribution has yet to be robustly engaged, analyzed, and appreciated. The peculiarity of his theological upbringing and development, coupled with his catholic and irenic disposition, undoubtedly contributed to his underappreciation. Bloesch refused to commit exclusively to a theological tribe which resulted in a certain degree of theological isolation in his own time.

Bloesch remains underappreciated and for this reason alone, a serious and sustained excavation of his theological corpus is a worthy enterprise. Further, the current climate of North American Christianity makes Bloesch a valuable figure to engage. In an age of disconnect and division between theological tribes and ecclesial traditions, Bloesch stands as a "bridging figure" providing a historically rooted, ecumenical way to navigate these divisions.[59] Bloesch operated with the conviction that the church was in need of renewal, and that evangelical theology at its best could be the source of such renewal; he was theologically committed to the renewal of evangelicalism for the sake of the renewal of the wider church.

The central thesis of this monograph is that Donald G. Bloesch is a distinctly important evangelical theologian well-suited to provide a *renewed vision* for contemporary evangelicalism. His central theological axiomatic idiom, Word & Spirit, and its abiding doctrinal ingredient, the Christian life, give Bloesch an important voice in evangelicalism. As Bloesch himself states:

> A discerning student of my theology will note that my particular emphasis is not the very same as that of modern evangelicalism. The preoccupation of the evangelical mainstream is igniting a commitment to Christ through both sharing one's personal story and apologetic argumentation. In my brand of evangelical theology—which is consonant with the awakening movements after the Reformation—it is not enough simply to believe in Jesus: we must follow him in faith and obedience.[60]

Bloesch's brand of evangelical theology is uniquely concerned with the Christian life—faith seeking obedience. As Bloesch himself states, "From the evangelical perspective, true Christianity entails *doctrine, experience*

---

59. George, "Evangelical Theology in North American Contexts," 286.
60. Bloesch, *Faith in Search of Obedience*, 61.

and *life*. Whenever any one of these elements is underplayed or denied, something crucial to the faith of the church is lost."[61] The present project engages in a thorough investigation and consideration of the doctrine of the Christian life within Bloesch's body of work. I argue that Bloesch's entire theology is and must be understood and appreciated as a theology of the Christian life arising from the work of the divine Word and Spirit.

Project Overview

The central argument of this project is that Bloesch's commitment to the doctrine of the Christian life is the defining feature of his uniquely *evangelical* theology. Put differently, Bloesch's theological identity and work are most fundamentally formed by his commitment to the Christian life. The way this shows up in his theology is that the Christian life is materially distributed in his theological system, and is, therefore, presupposed throughout the whole of his dogmatic work. It is the purpose of this volume to demonstrate this to be the case in Bloesch's thought, and to draw out the implications of this move as a core feature of his brand of evangelical theology.

In chapter 1, *Bloesch as Evangelical Theologian of the Christian Life*, I identify what it means for Bloesch to be an *evangelical* theologian. Employing the most commonly agreed upon definition of evangelicalism, Bebbington's Quadrilateral, I locate Bloesch within the bounds of evangelical theology, comparing and contrasting his emphases with that of Bebbington. On Bebbington's approach, there are four primary tenets of evangelical identity—conversionism, activism, crucicentrism, and biblicism. While Bloesch would recognize each of these features as necessary to evangelicalism, he refuses to see these as sufficient, adding the centrality of the Christian life as essential to naming the evangelical identity. Consequently, I argue it is this emphasis on the Christian life that distinguishes Bloesch on the landscape of evangelical theology.

In chapter 2, *Defining the Christian Life*, I excavate Bloesch's constructive account of the Christian life. Initially, my analysis focuses on a critical survey of his primary vocabulary of the Christian life—devotion, piety, spirituality, and biblical-personalism—all of which Bloesch readily employs. Nonetheless, he gives priority to the concept of biblical-personalism to articulate the core of the Christian life—a divine-human encounter between the God of Scripture and the Christian. According to Bloesch, the

---

61. Bloesch, *Future of Evangelical Christianity*, 17.

divine-human encounter occurs in and through a life of personal and social obedience. *Personal* obedience is marked by piety, devotion, and prayer, while *social* obedience is marked by ethics, action, and mission.

Continuing my analysis of Bloesch's constructive account of the Christian life, chapter 2 demonstrates how the distributed feature of the Christian life has real material import in his doctrine of salvation. I demonstrate that the Christian life is doctrinally integrated with the doctrine of salvation. According to Bloesch, the Christian life is the arena of salvation—the place where salvation is fought for and retained. This begins to unveil the implications of the distributive role of the Christian life in Bloesch's theological system. To develop and clarify this feature of Bloesch's account, I explore his concern with a deviant account of the Christian life—mysticism. I provide a detailed analysis of Bloesch's concern regarding the spirituality of mysticism. Bloesch identifies two forms of mysticism as competing with his view of spirituality: *classical* mysticism and *new* mysticism. By analyzing Bloesch's concerns with classical and new mysticism I contrastively highlight the distinctive features of Bloesch's brand of evangelical spirituality.

In chapter 3, *Distributing the Christian Life*, I advance the notion of a "distributive doctrine" to demonstrate the ubiquitous and formative character of the Christian life in Bloesch's systematic project. I argue that, for Bloesch, the Christian life is materially distributed throughout his theological system in and through his doctrine of revelation. The influence of the Christian life on Bloesch's account of revelation is demonstrated by his description of revelation as a divine-human encounter. According to Bloesch, this encounter is a transhistorical event that has happened *objectively* in the incarnation, and continues to happen in the believer's *subjective*, Spirit-led communion with Christ. Ultimately, Bloesch refers to this subjective-objective dialectic of revelation as a theology of Word & Spirit. I argue that, for Bloesch, the subjective-Spirit pole of revelation *just is* the Christian life. At the close of this chapter, I apply my reading of the formal and material distribution of revelation and the Christian life to explain why the Christian life shows up unexpectedly in doctrinal loci such as the doctrine of God and the doctrine of the atonement, giving further justification for my proposal.

In chapter 4, *Prayer and the Christian Life*, I provide a concrete example of Bloesch's account of the Christian life by investigating Bloesch's theology of prayer. Focusing on Bloesch's theology of prayer serves as a meaningful case study in his theology of the Christian life, because of how Bloesch locates prayer in relation to the Christian life. Prayer is the central location of personal encounter between the Triune God and the Christian. In prayer, the Christian comes to know the divine-human encounter through dialogue and struggle—the Christian fights for and retains his or her salvation in prayer. Prayer is the heart of the Christian life for Bloesch, precisely because of the nature of how the divine-human encounter governs the Christian life all the way down.

I conclude this project by weaving together the threads of this argument to demonstrate that Bloesch is an evangelical theologian of the Christian life worthy of engagement in contemporary evangelical theology. I situate Bloesch on the current landscape of evangelical theology, exploring some contemporary examples to show that his project not only anticipated lines of inquiry and emphasis, but to highlight how his project still uniquely advances a vision for evangelical theology. I end by proposing further lines of inquiry from his theological corpus that can be developed to retrieve his project and contribute to current areas of interest in evangelical theological discourse.

I

Bloesch as Evangelical Theologian of the Christian Life

THE FOCUS OF THIS project is an investigation and interpretation of the central role of the doctrine of the Christian life in the theology of Donald Bloesch. Bloesch's account of the Christian life ultimately defines him as an evangelical theologian. While I briefly highlighted Bloesch's evangelical identity in the introduction, more must be said to establish the nature of Bloesch's evangelical identity. In the present chapter, I argue that Bloesch can rightly be identified as an evangelical theologian, and I demonstrate that the Christian life is indeed the distinguishing doctrine of his brand of evangelical theology. Subsequent chapters provide an account of Bloesch's constructive work on the doctrine of the Christian life, and I demonstrate how Bloesch's focus on the Christian life has formal and material impact on his dogmatic project.

Defining Evangelicalism

To identify and properly locate Bloesch as an evangelical theologian, it is necessary to do some broad mapping of the various approaches and definitions of evangelicalism. I do this simply for the purpose of locating Bloesch's theological project and method in light of his self-defined *evangelical* emphases. In engaging with the contemporary discussion of evangelicalism, the goal is not to anachronistically apply these definitions to Bloesch, but to get a sense of the movement of which Bloesch was a part and to locate him within this movement.

Lamenting the difficulty in defining evangelicalism is so ubiquitous that it has become cliché. Yet, there is good reason for this lament, and the battle to define evangelicalism shows no sign of waning.[1] The debate does not merely revolve around proposed definitions but begins with contrasting views of method, often depending upon the disciplinary lens utilized to try to construct a proper formulation (i.e., theology, history, sociology, etc.).[2] The volume of definitions available in the contemporary discussion is dizzying, making agreement seem impossible and even clarity itself a challenge.[3] In what follows, I do not attempt to map all potential definitions of evangelicalism but instead engage issues salient to this project. First, I acknowledge the challenge in defining evangelicalism. In particular, I focus on the debate regarding the unity and diversity of evangelicalism. Second, I identify unifying characteristics of evangelicalism. In particular, I highlight the most broadly affirmed definition of evangelicalism—Bebbington's Quadrilateral.

The Unity and Diversity of Evangelicalism

The difficulty in defining evangelicalism lies within the source history of the movement itself: Evangelicalism is a child of diversity.[4] Some would argue it is this diversity that is the defining characteristic of evangelicalism. There are those who believe evangelicalism to be an essentially diverse movement marked by a variety of ecclesial expressions that cannot be streamlined without undue reduction of the movement itself. Donald Dayton affirms this perspective, stating, "For this reason, the category 'evangelical' remains an 'essentially contested concept,' and any effort to obscure these lines of difference implicitly resolves the conflict in favor of one or another basic

---

1. Bauder et al., *Four Views on the Spectrum of Evangelicalism*. This is merely one recent example of the ongoing debate over the definition of evangelicalism.

2. Bloesch himself recognizes the different lenses with which to define evangelicalism in his article, "Evangelicalism," in Musser and Price, *New Handbook of Christian Theology*.

3. Roger Olson states, "Like many good terms and categories, then, *evangelical* and *Evangelicalism* have broad semantic range, one that is so variegated that the terms seem to lose all shape" (*Westminster Handbook of Evangelical Theology*, 6).

4. Alister McGrath states, "Evangelicalism also has historical roots in the sense that there have been significant movements in Christian history that have prepared the way for it and on whose resources it may draw. Several such movements may be recognized, and this complex mutual interaction of sources has led to a number of tensions within modern evangelicalism" (*Evangelicalism & the Future of Christianity*, 23).

sets of connotations."⁵ Elsewhere, Dayton seeks to explain this definition of diversity through an historical lens. He examines church history and identifies three types of evangelicalism. Type one is "Protestant/Lutheran Evangelicalism," type two is "Revivalistic Evangelicalism," and type three is "Fundamentalist Evangelicalism."⁶ Because of the diversity and complexity of evangelicalism, he rejects what he calls "easy generalizations," opting instead for naming different movements that acknowledge "a diversity that is compromised from the beginning by any effort to find a common label."⁷ Dayton's argument is situated within a broader claim, namely, that the word "evangelical" is the result of a defused generalization of a variety of unique expressions within the church. Consequently, Dayton believes "evangelical has lost whatever usefulness it once might have had and . . . we can very well do without it."⁸ On this account, there are no meaningful and definable core commitments that hold evangelicalism together as a cohesive theological movement, but rather evangelicalism is pushed into the sphere of the manifold contingencies of social history. Ironically, while Dayton himself continues to use the word, he appears to reject its value going forward.⁹

While some advocates of the diversity perspective hold to a kind of definable evangelicalism, the more extreme voices completely reject any possibility of definition. Gerald R. McDermott speaks to this reality, "Some years ago, evangelical historian Nathan Hatch said, 'there is no such thing as evangelicalism.' By that he probably meant that evangelicalism and its attendant theologies constitutes a many-headed monster that regularly transforms itself into new shapes."¹⁰ In objection to Hatch's call to void the term "evangelical," McDermott states, "But historic evangelicalism does

5. Dayton, "Some Doubts," 245.

6. Johnson, "American Evangelicalism," 254.

7. Dayton, "Some Doubts," 248.

8. Dayton, "Some Doubts," 248.

9. Dorrien argues that Dayton does reject the use of "evangelical" and yet fails to practice said rejection. He states, "While sharing his sense of its deeply conflicted nature, I do not accept Dayton's verdict (which even he fails to practice) that use of the term *evangelicalism* should therefore be discontinued. Rather, I use the term in a way that carefully bears in mind the different kinds of gospel Christianity that evangelical Protestantism has engendered" (Dorrien, *Remaking of Evangelical Theology*, 4).

10. McDermott, "Emerging Divide in Evangelical Theology," 373. This quote from Nathan Hatch is found in *Evangelical Affirmations* which is a compilation of papers from a conference at Trinity Evangelical Divinity School. Hatch's paper is given in response to Carl Henry. Henry opened the conference with a paper titled "Who Are the Evangelicals?" Here Henry argued,

have a recognizable character."[11] In defense of this claim McDermott enlists William Abraham for support:

> "It would be a mistake . . . to dismiss evangelicalism as a useless category for understanding Christianity; without it we would have to invent a functional equivalent immediately." It represents a network of Christians "bound together by a loose but identifiable cluster of convictions and practices that have been and continue to be a potent religious force."[12]

It is noteworthy that Abraham's response to the diversity position's rejection of definition does not go to the opposite extreme. Abraham does not turn a blind eye to the reality of diversity but argues that within the diversity there are core "convictions and practices" that hold the movement together. In other words, there is *unity within diversity*. The argument for unity within diversity is buttressed by George Marsden who asks, "Is there one evangelicalism or many? The answer, of course, is both. This means that no one part can be equated with the whole. On the other hand, it affirms that there is a whole, even if sometimes it is difficult to define precisely."[13] Evangelicalism is a movement of undeniable diversity, and yet what McDermott, Abraham, and Marsden argue is such diversity does not render evangelicalism indistinguishable. Robert K. Johnston agrees and posits that within the diversity of the evangelical movement there remains "a family resemblance."[14] There

---

> Evangelicals, in summary, are spiritually regenerate sinners who worship the supernatural self-revealing God as the sovereign source, support and judge of all creaturely life. They affirm that on the ground of the substitutionary life and work of Jesus Christ, the holy Lord mercifully delivers the penitent from spiritual death and its dire consequences and restores them to fellowship and service. This God does, moreover, in accord with the inspired Scriptures that comprise his authoritative Word and Truth constitute the rule of faith and doctrine by which the risen Christ through the Holy Spirit governs the regenerate church. Evangelicals are a people of the Bible and of the risen Redeemer; historically speaking, consistent evangelicals have never been cognitively constrained either to demean the Savior or to demean the Book in order to be wholly faithful to one or both. (94)

Hatch does not reject the value of Henry's definition but rejects the idea that the commitments held in Henry's definition are unique to evangelicals. Hatch does reject the very premise of a definition for evangelicalism on the grounds that it is fundamentally marked by "rampant pluralism" (Henry, "Who Are the Evangelicals?," 96–97).

11. McDermott, "Emerging Divide in Evangelical Theology," 373.

12. McDermott, "Emerging Divide in Evangelical Theology," 373.

13. Marsden, "Fundamentalism and American Evangelicalism," 24.

14. Johnston, "American Evangelicalism," 254. McGrath echoes this terminology

are degrees of familial resemblance; siblings differ from cousins, and yet defining characteristics remain that identify everyone within the same family. If this is the case, it begs the question: Are there commonly agreed upon unifying characteristics that distinguish evangelicalism?

The Unifying Characteristics of Evangelicalism

The diversity of evangelicalism results in a diversity of opinions regarding the unifying characteristics of the movement. That being said, one definition has broken through the debate and has been met with broad and steady affirmation: Bebbington's Quadrilateral. Bebbington's definition provides a means of identifying family resemblance. It provides a set of unifying characteristics that distinguish evangelicalism.

Bebbington's Quadrilateral (otherwise known as Bebbington's Rule) was enumerated in his monograph *Evangelicalism in Modern Britain: A History From the 1730s to the 1980s* and offers a definition of evangelicalism as a unified reality.[15] As Larsen states, "Bebbington's definition is routinely

---

employed by Johnston when stating, "There is, to use Wittgenstein's helpful term, a clear 'family resemblance' among the various types and styles of evangelicalism" (McGrath, *Evangelicalism & the Future of Christianity*, 27).

15. Bebbington's definition is not immune to disagreement and debate, but of all the definitions available it has been met with the widest approval amongst scholars. Timothy Larsen highlights the widespread support and far-reaching impact that Bebbington's definition has had (Larsen, "Reception Given to Evangelicalism," 21–29). While flagging the danger of narrowing the meaning of "evangelical" and recognizing the diversity of self-definition within the movement itself, the edited volume *New Perspectives for Evangelical Theology* acknowledges Bebbington's Rule as a helpful baseline definition (Greggs, "Introduction," 5). The influence of Bebbington's definition is also on display in other edited volumes focused on evangelical theology. For example, it is repeatedly referenced and often affirmed in *Four Views on the Spectrum of Evangelicalism*. In recent volumes such as *The Future of Evangelical Theology: Soundings from the Asian American Diaspora*, Bebbington's definition serves as a base of operation for discussing evangelicalism (Yong, *Future of Evangelical Theology*, 33). Another scholar who consistently upholds Bebbington's definition is Mark Noll. In fact, in his most recent (there are many) monographic discussion of evangelicalism, he recites Bebbington's Quadrilateral as the "key ingredients" of evangelicalism (Noll, "Defining Evangelicalism," 20). Amidst the affirmation of Bebbington's Rule, three critiques are worth noting. First, Bebbington's Rule is critiqued for a lack of continuity between evangelicalism and orthodox Christianity historically. As Timothy George states, "While such a list is helpful in pointing out major emphases, it can also obscure the basic continuities linking evangelicals with other orthodox Christians on such key doctrines of the faith as the Holy Trinity and the classic Christology of the early church" ("If I'm an Evangelical," 62, quoted in Larsen, "Reception Given to Evangelicalism," 24). Timothy Larsen himself affirms this critique of Bebbington's

employed to identify evangelicalism; no other definition comes close to rivaling its level of general acceptance."[16] Explaining the methodological import of Bebbington's Rule, David Bundy avers,

---

Quadrilateral but emphasizes that what should be added is a commitment to "Protestant Orthodoxy" (Larsen, *Advent of Evangelicalism*, 1). Second, George Marsden argues that Bebbington's definition is lacking an emphasis on evangelicalism as a "transdenominational movement":

> Evangelicalism can designate a more organic movement. Religious groups with some common traditions and experiences, despite wide diversities and only meager institutional interconnections, may constitute a movement in the sense of moving or tending in some common direction . . . within evangelicalism in these broader senses is a more narrow, consciously "evangelical" transdenominational community with complicated infrastructures of institutions and persons who identify with "evangelicalism." (Marsden, *Evangelicalism and Modern America*, ix)

The final critique is offered by Bebbington himself, stating, "There was a higher degree of continuity with the Puritans than the book of 1988 recognizes" (Bebbington, "Response," 427–28). Now, years removed from the initial argument, Bebbington believes he could have established a greater continuity with the Puritan tradition and evangelicalism, and he argues the chronology of the "early stages" of evangelicalism could have been expanded (428). It is worth noting that all three of these critiques are suggested additions to the definition, not rejections of the definition's central tenets.

16. Larsen, *Cambridge Companion to Evangelical Theology*, 1. Larsen elaborates on the pervasive acceptance of Bebbington's definition when he states, "A decade on, Bebbington's 'magisterial study' was being used in the *American Historical Review* as a gauge by which to judge new works" (*Advent of Evangelicalism*, 21–23). An explicit affirmation of Bebbington's definition is found with Reformed evangelical scholar Mark Noll. Noll states, "In one of the most useful general definition of the phenomenon, the British historian David Bebbington has identified the key ingredients of evangelicalism" (*Scandal of the Evangelical Mind*, 8). On the other side of the evangelical aisle, Wesleyan scholar Kenneth Collins affirms Bebbington's definition without explicitly citing him:

> More to the point, the similarities expressed among American evangelicals, the common elements that foster a spirit of community that transcends denominational affiliation, geography, and even at times theological tradition, can best be explored in terms of four major concerns: (1) the normative value of Scripture, (2) the significance of the atoning work of Christ, (3) the necessity of conversion, and (4) the imperative of evangelism. (*Evangelical Moment*, 41)

Larsen is right in stating that, like Collins,

> many other sources engage in much hand-wringing and hedging, emphasizing that evangelicalism is a complex and diverse phenomenon difficult to define. Nevertheless, when one examines carefully what has been said in such discussions it is generally noticeable that, in the midst of all these declaimers, the Bebbington quadrilateral is the only definition that has actually been offered. (*Advent of Evangelicalism*, 26–27)

> This functional definition of Evangelicalism allows Bebbington to provide an evenhanded scholarly approach to the range of phenomena normally understood as Evangelicalism and helps him avoid the ideological pitfalls into which many American scholars fall. This phenomenological approach cannot be too highly praised.[17]

As Bundy states, Bebbington's Rule is "phenomenological" in its approach. It is a definition arising from historical observation of evangelicalism as a movement, and to employ Abraham's categories, it focuses less on "practices" and more on "convictions," seeking to identify unifying characteristics. Bebbington's approach is not ideologically governed in that he seeks to describe what he sees in the movement throughout its history without vying for the priority of any particular camp within evangelicalism. Bebbington argues for what he calls a "quadrilateral of priorities," offering a succinct explanation of these priorities:

> There are four qualities that have been the special marks of Evangelical religion: *conversionism,* the belief that lives need to be changed; *activism,* the expression of the gospel in effort; *biblicism,* a particular regard for the Bible; and what may be called *crucicentrism,* a stress on the sacrifice of Christ on the cross. Together they form a quadrilateral of priorities that is the basis of Evangelicalism.[18]

Bebbington articulates four characteristics to look for in determining evangelical family resemblance. The first marker of evangelicalism is "conversionism." According to Bebbington, "the call to conversion has been the content of the gospel. Preachers urged their hearers to turn away from their sins in repentance and to Christ in faith."[19] Bebbington argues that "conversionism" is established on the ground of two primary theological commitments: justification by faith and assurance of salvation. "Activism," the second characteristic of evangelicalism, is a commitment to share the good news of the gospel for the sake of conversion. This commitment to evangelism and the communication of the gospel lends itself to an undeniable pragmatism at the heart of evangelicalism. This activist impulse also resulted in an emphasis on campaigns against slave trade, work for public health, etc. As Bebbington notes, "Activism often spilled over beyond

---

17. David Bundy quoted in Larsen, *Advent of Evangelicalism,* 26.
18. Bebbington, *Evangelicalism in Modern Britain,* 2–3.
19. Bebbington, *Evangelicalism in Modern Britain,* 5.

simply gospel work."[20] The third marker is "biblicism," which highlights the Bible-centric focus of the evangelical family. He baldly notes, "Evangelicals revered the Bible."[21] The authority of Scripture is a (if not *the*) foundational principle for evangelicalism. Bebbington argues that within evangelicalism there is a range of understanding regarding Scripture's authority but a common commitment to its authority. This commitment to authority does not merely have doctrinal value but pragmatic value in the Christian life as well. The final marker of evangelicalism in Bebbington's Quadrilateral is "crucicentrism." At the center of evangelical faith stands the cross. Here, the doctrine of the atonement is given particular emphasis.[22] According to Bebbington, "the atonement eclipsed even the incarnation among Evangelicals."[23]

These four markers of evangelicalism provide an effective means of identifying the unity within diversity of evangelicalism. According to Bebbington, "conversionism," "activism," "biblicism," and "crucicentrism" are the unifying characteristics of evangelicalism. Bebbington acknowledges certain doctrinal commitments inherent to each of these four priorities, such as justification by faith and the atonement. Nevertheless, he argues that these four priorities are the fundamental defining features of evangelicalism.

Bloesch the Evangelical Theologian

In the previous section I briefly explored the debate regarding the unity and diversity of evangelicalism. I appealed to Bebbington's Rule as the most commonly accepted definition of evangelicalism in order to establish a set of unifying characteristics for evangelicalism. With this in mind, I now turn my attention to Bloesch specifically. Following the same movement as the previous section, I investigate Bloesch's view of the unity and diversity of evangelicalism, and then I establish Bloesch's evangelical identity by reference to Bebbington's Rule. In conclusion, I identify the distinguishing features of Bloesch's account of evangelicalism.

---

20. Bebbington, *Evangelicalism in Modern Britain*, 12.

21. Bebbington, *Evangelicalism in Modern Britain*, 13.

22. Bebbington states, "What Evangelicals agreed on seemed of infinitely greater importance than their disagreements, and their pre-eminent ground of agreement was the cruciality of the cross" (*Evangelicalism in Modern Britain*, 17).

23. Bebbington, *Evangelicalism in Modern Britain*, 15.

Unity in Diversity

Donald Bloesch acknowledges there is theological and cultural diversity in evangelicalism's external expression. Bloesch is not naïve to the challenge of constructing an effective definition in the face of glaring diversity. In his context he concedes there is a lack of "consensus" in defining "evangelical."[24] Yet, Bloesch rejects the idea that such diversity ought to relegate evangelicalism into ambiguity, stating, "I believe that the term 'evangelical' needs to be rehabilitated and restored rather than abandoned."[25] Bloesch remains optimistic at the prospect of establishing a unifying definition: "Although there are centrifugal forces pulling evangelicals apart, there is also a unifying power bringing them back together."[26]

Bloesch posits an evangelicalism marked by unity in diversity. In this way he stands with McDermott, Abraham, and Marsden rather than Dayton. Bloesch believes there are a set of core theological tenets that cohesively bind the evangelical movement. Bloesch states, "First, I wish to defend the thesis that evangelicalism today exists as a cohesive, growing movement and must therefore be taken seriously by the church at large, both Catholic and Protestant. Despite its tensions and schisms, it has an inner theological unity in the midst of external theological and cultural diversity."[27] This "inner theological unity" of evangelicalism is marked by a set of core theological distinctives.[28] In what follows I argue these theologi-

24. Bebbington, *Evangelicalism in Modern Britain*, 9.
25. Bloesch and Eller, "Evangelical," 9.
26. Bloesch, *Future of Evangelical Christianity*, 5.
27. Bloesch, *Future of Evangelical Christianity*, xix.

28. It is worth noting, Bloesch is so thoroughly committed to the unity of evangelicalism that he invests significant energy in his constructive doctrinal work arguing for an expanded list of theologically binding distinctives. Bloesch believes part of his vocation as an evangelical theologian is to advance the unity of evangelicalism. While Bloesch limits his list of core distinctives to those which he believes are most fundamental in establishing unity within evangelicalism, he nevertheless argues for a more exhaustive list of distinctives fit to mature the movement in its unity. The first place such an endeavor is set forth is in *The Evangelical Renaissance*, where he exposits what he calls the "hallmarks of evangelicalism" (48). Bloesch articulates ten hallmarks of evangelicalism: the sovereignty of God, the divine authority of Scripture, the total depravity of human persons, the substitutionary atonement, salvation by grace, faith alone, the primacy of proclamation, Scriptural holiness, the church's spiritual mission, and the return of Christ. Moving to Bloesch's two-volume work *Essentials of Evangelical Theology*, he includes these ten hallmarks once again with five additions—the deity of Christ, the new birth, the priesthood of all believers, two kingdoms, and heaven and hell. Bloesch presents these fifteen

cal distinctives clearly locate Bloesch within the space mapped by Bebbington's Quadrilateral.

Bloesch's Evangelical Identity

An examination of Bloesch's definition of evangelicalism demonstrates his affirmation of Bebbington's Rule. Not surprisingly Bloesch's starting point for defining evangelicalism is the gospel. He states, the "Gospel is the very heart and soul of evangelical theology."[29] Elsewhere Bloesch argues, "The word 'evangelical' is best reserved for that segment of Christianity that makes the proclamation of the biblical gospel its chief concern, that appeals to this gospel in its biblical setting as the final arbiter of faith and practice."[30] Bloesch's emphasis on the gospel being "biblical" and being cast in its "biblical setting," is an immediate affirmation of one of Bebbington's four unifying characteristics—biblicism.

According to Bloesch, the gospel is the material norm of evangelical theology.[31] He baldly asserts that the essence of the gospel is "justification by grace through faith alone."[32] Nevertheless, Bloesch wishes to make clear

---

total doctrinal loci as fit for establishing the theological unity within evangelicalism. In many respects, these fifteen doctrines are hallmarks of the historic Christian faith, not merely evangelical faith (*Essentials of Evangelical Theology*, 1:ix). That is precisely why Bloesch chooses them. He acknowledges that these fifteen loci have been historically contested areas of debate in the church. With that in mind he states, "It will be noticed that the format of this book is somewhat innovative, since it does not follow the traditional outline in general works of systematic theology. The chapter headings focus on controversial themes that have proven barriers to Christian unity in the past" (1:xi). Somewhat ironically, Bloesch seeks to find theological unity at the very points where unity has been hard to find. At these points of historical tension, Bloesch's goal is to "build bridges between the various strands within the evangelical spectrum" (2:235). This two-volume systematic theology is designed to provide a constructive account of these doctrines that is distinctively evangelical, and as a result, it is designed to nurture the unity of evangelicalism.

29. Bloesch, *Essentials of Evangelical Theology*, 1:4. Bloesch states elsewhere, "Our ultimate standard must be the gospel of God that brings all human experience and cultural values into radical question" (*Theology of Word & Spirit*, 42). This emphasis on the gospel has not gone unnoticed by fellow theologians in Bloesch's theological project. Torrance states, "What I like here and throughout his work is the studied fidelity of Bloesch to the gospel" (Torrance, "Bloesch's Doctrine of God," 138).

30. Bloesch, *Future of Evangelical Christianity*, 4.

31. Bloesch, *Essentials of Evangelical Theology*, 1:4.

32. Bloesch, *Holy Spirit*, 15. Bloesch reiterates this point in the fourth volume of his systematic theology. There he states, "Luther rediscovered the heart of the

that while justification by grace through faith is the essence of the gospel, it is not the whole of the gospel. He states,

> As a Reformed theologian I would argue that the gospel cannot be reduced to either justification or election. The gospel is the good news that Jesus Christ came into the world to save sinners by placing them in right relationship to God through his substitutionary sacrifice on the cross and by engrafting them into the righteousness of Christ by the purifying work of his Spirit. The gospel needs to be received in faith and repentance and demonstrated in a life of lowly service, faith working through love. It also needs to be manifested in the practice of the spiritual gifts, which both build up the church and empower the church to reach the spiritually lost for the gospel. The life of the Christian should be one of unstinting devotion to Jesus Christ in the freedom that comes to us through the outpouring of the Spirit, whose generosity is evidenced in the proliferation of spiritual gifts and an abundance of fruits of love and obedience.[33]

Here, Bloesch offers a more developed definition, rejecting reductionism and stressing the depth and complexity of the gospel. In short, the essence of the gospel, justification by grace, is necessary but not sufficient to account for the gospel's breadth and depth. It is noteworthy that this more robust definition of the gospel highlights the other three characteristics of evangelicalism as defined by Bebbington. Bloesch places an emphasis on salvation, the atonement, and faith in action; the markers of "conversionism," "crucicentrism," and "activism" are clearly on display in Bloesch's articulation of the gospel.

There is no question that Bloesch affirms the four markers of evangelicalism as developed in Bebbington's Rule. At several points Bloesch brings all four commitments together as he seeks to define evangelicalism. For example,

> At this point it is appropriate to define *evangelical* more precisely: An evangelical is one who affirms the centrality and cruciality of Christ's work of reconciliation and redemption as declared in the Scriptures; the necessity to appropriate the fruits of this work in

---

gospel—salvation by free grace alone and sacrificial service through the power of agape love" (*Jesus Christ*, 191).

33. Bloesch, *Holy Spirit*, 111–12. Perhaps there is a shorthand version of this longer gospel enunciation by Bloesch in his final work, *Faith in Search of Obedience*, wherein defining the evangelical gospel, Bloesch states, "I am thinking of the message of free grace through faith in the atoning death and glorious resurrection of our Lord Jesus Christ" (55).

one's own life and experience; and the urgency to bring the good news of this act of unmerited grace to a lost and dying world. It is not enough to believe in the cross and resurrection of Christ. We must personally be crucified and buried with Christ and rise with Christ to new life in the Spirit. Yet even this is not all that is required of us. We must also be fired by a burning zeal to share this salvation with others. To be evangelical means to be evangelistic. We are not to hide our light under a bushel but manifest this light so that God might be glorified in the world.[34]

In this definition all four of the evangelical markers appear. First, there is an emphasis on "crucicentrism," as Bloesch emphasizes the importance of Christ's reconciling and redeeming work. For Bloesch, this marker of evangelical identity is most fundamental. As he says elsewhere, "The evangel is none other than the meaning of the cross."[35] Evangelicalism, according to Bloesch, emphasizes the uniqueness of Christ and therefore emphasizes the uniqueness of his work upon the cross.[36] Second, there is an emphasis on what Bebbington calls "biblicism." For Bloesch, the unique work of Christ is made known only because it is "declared in the Scriptures."[37] Elsewhere, Bloesch refers to this evangelical distinctive as the "supreme authority of the word of God."[38] Third, Bloesch emphasizes the priority of "activism"

---

34. Bloesch, *Jesus Christ*, 17.

35. Bloesch, *Jesus Christ*, 15. Elsewhere Bloesch places such emphasis on the cross that he identifies it as *the* definitive feature of evangelicalism:

> It is appropriate at this point to consider what is *the hallmark* of evangelical faith. We affirm that the watershed of evangelicalism is not the inerrancy of Scripture, not even its divine authority, nor is it the person of Christ or the Trinity. Instead, it is the cross of Christ, the doctrine of salvation through the righteousness of Christ procured for us by his sacrificial life, death and resurrection. It is the cross that gives authority to Scripture, and it is the cross that reveals and confirms the Messianic identity of Jesus as the Son of God. (*Essentials of Evangelical Theology*, 2:238, emphasis mine)

36. Bloesch, *Essentials of Evangelical Theology*, 2:247.

37. Bloesch, *Jesus Christ*, 17.

38. Bloesch, *Essentials of Evangelical Theology*, 2:239. In a sense, it is ill-fitting to use "biblicism" to describe Bloesch's emphasis on the authority of Scripture. Bloesch would certainly bristle at a Biblicist notion of the Word of God. Rather, as I demonstrate in chapter 3, he seeks to uphold Barth's threefold understanding of the Word as living, written, and proclaimed. As Bloesch states, "This Word is not simply a past event but a living reality that meets us as we encounter Scripture and the kerygmatic proclamation of the church" (2:239). As I argue in chapter 3, for Bloesch, the Word of God is primary authority as the source of revelation rather than experience or intellect. Indeed, the Word of God calls these things into question and refurbishes them. Likewise, the Word of God stands over church tradition (2:239–41).

when he states, "We must also be fired by the burning zeal to share this salvation with others."[39] Bloesch's account of activism stresses the importance of evangelism. Lastly, "conversionism" is emphasized in Bloesch's definition when he discusses the believer's need to be personally "crucified and buried with Christ and rise with Christ to new life in the Spirit."[40] Bloesch's language of death and resurrection is informed by his commitment to what he calls the "radical pervasiveness of sin."[41]

Bloesch follows the contours of Bebbington's Quadrilateral as the defining characteristics of evangelicalism. He firmly plants his feet on the soil of evangelicalism himself, calling this land home and allowing its strictures to guide his theologizing. However, in Bloesch's above definition of evangelicalism he stresses one more key characteristic not captured with Bebbington's Rule. There he articulates this other theological distinctive as "the necessity to appropriate the fruits of this work [the cross] in one's own life and experience."[42] Elsewhere, Bloesch echoes this emphasis, arguing that a unified account of evangelicalism is marked by a commitment to the "pursuit of holiness in thought and life."[43] Herein lies Bloesch's distinguishing mark as an evangelical theologian. Beyond, an emphasis on the authority

---

39. Bloesch, *Jesus Christ*, 17.

40. Bloesch, *Jesus Christ*, 17.

41. Bloesch, *Essentials of Evangelical Theology*, 2:244. In succinct fashion, Bloesch repeatedly affirms the Reformed doctrine of total depravity. He does, however, provide further explanation regarding what he means by the "radical pervasiveness of sin": "Sin signifies not simply outward acts but a restless egoism that moves in the secret, hidden depths of the personality. Man is both good and evil, but the good within him is poisoned by the evil. The sinner can choose the natural good but not the spiritual good. Man sins inevitably but not from natural causality or ontological necessity" (2:244). According to Bloesch, as evangelicalism embraces total depravity, it rejects the notion that the human will can ascend to God. As such it stands against Neo-Catholic and existentialist optimism regarding the capacity of the human will. Evangelicalism also rejects moral optimism regarding the human persons capacity for doing good. This does not mean that evangelicalism has lost hope for humanity. Bloesch states, "Our hope lies not in what man in and of himself is able to do but in what God has done for man in the person of Jesus Christ" (2:246). This is why Bloesch also emphasizes *sola Christus*, *sola gratia*, and *sola fide* as essential evangelical doctrines (2:250). As Bloesch states, "Our hope lies not in what man in and of himself is able to do but in what God has done for man in the person of Jesus Christ. Evangelical religion looks beyond man the sinner to Christ the Redeemer, and this is why evangelicalism is essentially a religion of hope" (2:246).

42. Bloesch, *Jesus Christ*, 17.

43. Bloesch, "Evangelicalism," 172.

of the Bible, the cruciality of the cross, the call to actively bear witness to Christ, and the need for conversion, Bloesch stresses the need to pursue holiness. Bloesch goes beyond Bebbington's Rule, emphasizing the doctrine of the Christian life as essential to evangelical identity. For Bloesch, the Christian life is a "key doctrine" of evangelical theology.[44]

Bloesch the Evangelical Theologian of the Christian Life

Bloesch's agreement with Bebbington's Rule is clear. What is of particular interest is the way in which he adds to the definition. There is one key characteristic that Bebbington's Rule neglects that Bloesch believes is paramount, namely "the necessity to appropriate the fruits of this work in one's own life and experience."[45] This emphasis on the Christian life is stressed throughout his corpus, particularly as he seeks to define evangelicalism. So Bloesch asserts, "If asked to list the key elements in a vital Christian faith, an evangelical in the classical sense might well reply: biblical fidelity, apostolic doctrine, the experience of salvation, the imperative of discipleship, and the urgency of mission."[46] Once again, an emphasis is placed on markers of Bebbington's Quadrilateral but in addition to these characteristics is the "imperative of discipleship." The Christian life of discipleship is the distinguishing feature of Bloesch's definition of evangelicalism.

As I demonstrated in the introduction, Bloesch holds that evangelicalism not only has a distinctive spirituality, but it is by nature a "movement of spiritual renewal."[47] The Christian life is not merely a doctrine of *interest*, but a doctrine of unique defining *influence* in Bloesch's understanding of the nature of evangelicalism. Consequently, for Bloesch, evangelical theology is ever a theology of the Christian life. Bloesch's distinguishing emphasis on the Christian life demands further investigation. In what follows I explore both the formative *source* and the formative *impact* of Bloesch's focus on the Christian life. First, I argue that Bloesch's pietistic upbringing is the formative source of Bloesch's Christian life focus. Bloesch's pietistic impulse informs his theological project. Second, I contend that Bloesch's focus on the Christian life formatively impacts his theological method. As an evangelical theologian Bloesch is a theologian of the Christian life.

44. Bloesch, "Evangelicalism," 172.
45. Bloesch, *Jesus Christ*, 17.
46. Bloesch, *Jesus Christ*, 17.
47. Bloesch, "Evangelicalism," 168.

Formative Source: Bloesch the Pietist

The source of Bloesch's "evangelical" identity leads him to prioritize the Christian life. In the foreword to his early work *The Future of Evangelical Christianity,* Bloesch states, "I identify myself as an evangelical because I definitely share in the vision of the Reformers, Pietists."[48] The "because" of Bloesch's self-identification is instructive. What is found throughout his corpus is a retrieval of two streams of evangelicalism—the Reformed and Pietistic traditions. Bloesch arrived at the shores of evangelicalism by the convergence of these two streams. His journey began in the experiential waters of Pietism, but he was carried along by the doctrinal currents of the Reformed tradition to appropriate the "experimental divinity" of Puritanism. As the progeny of these two streams, Bloesch can be difficult to locate on the landscape of evangelicalism. As Roger Olson rightly states, "Undoubtedly, Bloesch's exact place on the landscape of contemporary evangelical theology is difficult to pinpoint."[49] The temptation is to singularly identify him with either the Pietist stream or the Reformed stream; however, to locate Bloesch properly, it is essential that attention be paid to the formative nature of both streams.

Bloesch's evangelical identity is sourced in the tradition of Pietism. In his spiritual autobiography Bloesch states, "The church in which I was baptized (in 1928) was the Evangelical Synod of North America... The Evangelical Synod of North America had its origin in the union church established by King Frederick William III of Prussia in 1815. This church reflected the irenicism of German Pietism."[50] Bloesch's pietistic heritage emerges in his disposition as an evangelical theologian. As Olson and Winn note,

> Bloesch's whole theological career in the bosom of both evangelicalism and "mainstream Protestantism" was driven by a passion for the spiritual renewal of the church and the individual. And his debt to Pietism is both explicit... and implicit, as in his hundreds of quotations from and positive references to the historical prototypes of Pietism from Spener to Blumhardt.[51]

---

48. Bloesch, *Future of Evangelical Christianity*, vii.
49. Olson, "Locating Donald G. Bloesch," 30.
50. Bloesch, *Faith in Search of Obedience*, 1.
51. Olson and Collins Winn, *Reclaiming Pietism*, 166. One such example of this point appears early in Bloesch's writing career in *Crisis of Piety*. There Bloesch employs the language of "devotion" to discuss the Christian life and signal his indebtedness to the tradition of Pietism in doing so: "The deepest affinities of a theology of devotion are to

Bloesch repeatedly identifies evangelicalism as defined not only by a particular doctrine but also by a particular experience. For example, in the sixth volume of Bloesch's systematic theology it reads, "The truth of the gospel must be discovered anew, not simply in abstract thought but in personal experience."[52] Bloesch strikes a familiar contemporary evangelical emphasis on the need to emphasize the gospel, but he does so with a unique pietistic emphasis on experiencing the gospel. This pietistic impulse is showcased in his theological method. In his analysis of Bloesch's doctrine of salvation theologian Fred Sanders notes,

> The family resemblance that becomes undeniable in Bloesch's soteriological method is his position in the theological tradition of Protestant Pietism. Pietism resonates with evangelicalism in countless ways, and since its classic expression in the seventeenth and eighteenth centuries it has exerted a positive pressure on Christian theology and life: it curbs rationalistic tendencies, insists on application to life, and it centralizes and integrates the otherwise disparate set of truths that make up a theology, connecting them all in a vital way with the experience of communion with God.[53]

Sanders rightly observes Bloesch's Pietistic heritage. Bloesch would no doubt agree with Sanders on the "positive pressure" Pietism has applied to "Christian theology and life." His emphasis on experience is indeed wedded with the other areas of pietistic emphasis that Sanders identifies here—a curtailing of rationalism and an emphasis on life application. As is demonstrated throughout this project, Bloesch's pietistic emphasis shows up most

---

Lutheran and Reformed Pietism. Spener, Francke, Zinzendorf, and in more recent times Christian Spittler, Kierkegaard, and the Blumhardts also affirmed the need for personal devotion to Jesus Christ" (*Crisis of Piety*, 18).

52. Bloesch, *Church*, 14.

53. Sanders, "Saved by Word and Spirit," 90. Bloesch himself defines the movement of Pietism:

> A comparable force of renewal was Pietism, which signaled the rekindling of experiential religion in the Lutheran and Reformed churches in Europe. Its heyday was the seventeenth and eighteenth centuries, but the movement as a whole has continued into the nineteenth and twentieth centuries, constituting a major core element in the wider constellation of evangelicalism. The key emphasis of the Pietists was on the need for a new birth (*Wiedergeburt*) through the power of the Holy Spirit. (*Holy Spirit*, 119)

He goes on to provide a brief snapshot of key Pietist theologians—Johann Arndt, Philip Jacob Spener, August Hermann Francke, Nicholas Count Zinzendorf, Gerhard Testeegen, and Johann Christoph Blumhardt. See Bloesch, *Holy Spirit*, 119–25.

fundamentally in his dogmatic project by way of his unique prioritization of the doctrine of the Christian life.

In contemporary theological discourse, "pietism" is often a term of derision, so it is helpful to note how Bloesch qualifies the term. While he is concerned that Pietism can tilt toward "perfectionism,"[54] most of all he is concerned with what he refers to as "neo-Pietism" which is "characterized by an emphasis on religious experience over doctrine."[55] Fundamentally, Bloesch refuses to allow an emphasis on subjective spiritual experience to overshadow the objective work of Christ upon the cross. Bloesch states,

> The "new Pietism" reflected in the Faith at Work and higher life movements falls short of genuine evangelicalism because of its focus on regeneration and sanctification to the virtual exclusion of justification. We need to remember that the essence of the Gospel is not Christ coming into our hearts but Christ coming into the world to save sinners. Inner renewal by the Spirit is part of the Gospel when it is related to and grounded in the obedience and death of Jesus Christ, but when presented as the Gospel itself, it can only lead to heresy and confusion.[56]

Elsewhere, Bloesch warns that "pietism invariably fades into latitudinarianism and liberalism unless it is informed by the wisdom of orthodoxy."[57] Therefore, as a theologian with a pietistic impulse, his is not a blind-pietism, unfamiliar with its dangers. Bloesch is a theologian committed to an orthodox, creedal confession of the Christian faith, sourcing and appropriating the Christian tradition but doing so with a practical end in mind. As Olson notes, "The claim that Pietism ignored doctrine and theology today is completely falsified by the example of American Pietism's leading evangelical theologian—Donald Bloesch."[58] Bloesch consciously chose to correct a pietistic propensity to minor on doctrine by majoring on doctrine himself.

The commitment to Christian doctrine and its historical precedents is sourced in the second stream of his evangelical identity, Reformed theology.[59] Bloesch's evangelical theology was formed not only by his Pietis-

---

54. Bloesch, *Christian Life and Salvation*, 31.
55. Bloesch, *Essentials of Evangelical Theology*, 1:1.
56. Bloesch, *Essentials of Evangelical Theology*, 1:236.
57. Bloesch, *Crisis of Piety*, xii.
58. Olson, "Pietism," 13.

59. I have just noted that Olson presents the theological work of Bloesch as a defense against the notion that Pietism minored on doctrine. While I have no doubt Bloesch

tic upbringing but also by his commitment to the Reformed theological tradition.[60] In his spiritual autobiography, Bloesch narrates:

> At my ordination, I made a public pledge to be guided by the Augsburg Confession, Martin Luther's Small Catechism, and the Heidelberg Catechism. . . . Later, when I was inaugurated as a professor of theology at Dubuque Theological Seminary where I started teaching in 1957, I made a pledge of allegiance to the Westminster Confession of Faith.[61]

In his mid-career, two-volume, systematic treatment of Christian doctrine, Bloesch states, "A true Evangelicalism will be Reformed in the theological as well as the historical sense in that it will include many emphases associated with Reformed Christendom."[62] While Bloesch clearly commits himself to the Reformed tradition, it remains somewhat unclear what this really means. He provides greater specificity earlier in the same volume where it says, I "seek to stand in the Reformed tradition, but Reformed is to be understood more broadly than Calvinistic, since I look to Luther as well as Calvin, to evangelical Pietism as well as Reformed orthodoxy, to the neo-Reformation theology of Barth and Brunner as well as the neo-Calvinism of Hodge and Warfield."[63] Bloesch's definition of "Reformed" is broad rather than narrow, holding within its borders not only the magisterial Reformers

---

would agree with this argument, albeit with hesitating humility, it would be accurate to state that Bloesch's development as a systematic theologian owes more to his study of Reformed theology than his pietistic upbringing.

60. Bloesch signals his particular doctrinal affinity for the Reformed tradition in *The Holy Spirit*:

> I basically speak out of the perspective of the Protestant Reformation, but I do not see the Reformation as encompassing the whole counsel of God, though it did indeed recover the essence of the gospel—justification by grace through faith alone. Where I fully concur with the Reformers is in their emphasis on the complementarity of Word and Spirit, the priority of grace over works, including works of faith and repentance, and the practice of Christian love as the cardinal sign and evidence of genuine faith. (15)

61. Bloesch, *Faith in Search of Obedience*, 6.

62. Bloesch, *Essentials of Evangelical Theology*, 1:11. The vagueness of Bloesch's meaning regarding "Reformed" arises throughout his project. He will often establish an argument as "Reformed," but not always clarify what that means. For example, in *The Church* volume of his seven-volume systematic theology it reads, "In the Reformed view that I am enunciating . . ." (*Church*, 59).

63. Bloesch, *Essentials of Evangelical Theology*, 1:4.

but also including Barth, Brunner, Hodge, and Warfield.[64] In some locations Bloesch emphasizes his particular "indebtedness" to Luther and Calvin,[65] while in others he includes "evangelical Pietism" as a feature of embracing "Reformed" theology.

Bloesch's peculiar decision to include the first stream, Pietism, in the second stream, Reformed, is worthy of analysis. The inclusion of Pietism reveals something about Bloesch's primal theological emphasis. Bloesch believes that Pietism fills a doctrinal lacuna left by the tradition of Reformed theology. Bloesch argues:

> It was the Protestant Reformers, Luther and Calvin, who recovered the decisive significance of the kerygmatic proclamation, although their primary concern was right doctrine rather than the Christian life. It remained for the post-Reformation movements of Pietism, Puritanism, and Evangelicalism to give the proper attention to the need for a reformation in life as well; in this respect, they signify the fulfillment of the Protestant Reformation.[66]

A pietistic vision for the *reform of life* was necessary, in Bloesch's mind, to fulfill the vision of Reformational theology. To be sure, Bloesch believes

---

64. In his posthumously-published spiritual autobiography, Bloesch states, "I regard myself as a Reformed theologian, but not in the sense of a narrow or sectarian stance. I adhere to the creeds of the Reformation, not as infallible pronouncements but as gateways to deeper understanding" (*Faith in Search of Obedience*, 45).

65. Bloesch, *Essentials of Evangelical Theology*, 1:xi.

66. Bloesch et al., *Christian Spirituality*, 165. Bloesch repeatedly makes this point throughout his corpus:

> Our position is in line with the main thrust of the Protestant Reformation. The sole foundation of the Christian life must be regarded as the justification of the ungodly (*justification impii*). The free grace of God is the basis of our salvation, and faith is the necessary response. At the same time, we seek to move beyond the Reformation by giving a more positive appraisal to the Christian life in the working out of our salvation. The Reformers talked much of "a holy gospel" and a "holy faith" but very little of holy persons. (*Christian Life and Salvation*, 15–16)

> There is no doubt that the spiritual movements of purification subsequent to the Reformation (Pietism, Puritanism, Evangelicalism) brought new life and vigor to the churches of the Reformation. In one sense, they signaled the fulfillment of the Reformation, since a reform in life is just as necessary as a reform in doctrine. (*Essentials of Evangelical Theology*, 1:39)

Interestingly, Herman Bavinck uses almost identical language to talk about the contribution of Pietism: "Though the term is variously used, Pietism seeks to move the church beyond reformation of doctrine to the reformation of life" (*Reformed Ethics*, 274).

An Evangelical Spiritual Theology

the roots of such an emphasis are to be found in the initial soil of the Reformation, but that those roots had yet to develop into the doctrinal and experiential growth called for. As Bloesch argues,

> In the polemics that followed the Reformation right doctrine came to be viewed as more important than right living, and the call to holiness, which was present in the original Reformation, receded more and more into the background. It remained for the movements of Pietism and Puritanism to recover this dimension of the Christian faith for the mainline churches within Protestantism. The Christian life was seen not simply as a by-product of salvation (as in later Protestant orthodoxy) but as the arena of salvation, the field in which salvation is recovered and renewed.[67]

Bloesch does not believe the Reformers were wrong, but rather that they did not go far enough in the application of Reformed doctrine in regard to the Christian life. While indebted to the foundation laid by the magisterial Reformers, Bloesch seeks to emphasize the additional building blocks Pietism provides. Reform of doctrine is not enough; a reform of life is also necessary, and this is what Pietism delivers.[68] Reformed doctrine must be

---

67. Bloesch, *Essentials of Evangelical Theology*, 2:36–37. Bloesch appears to draw a distinction between the magisterial Reformers he looks to primarily in Luther and Calvin, and the tradition that followed them in this regard. Bloesch believes that Luther and Calvin provide rich soil for developing a Word & Spirit theology that gives due attention to the Christian life. Echoing the sentiment of Bloesch, a more recent scholar summarizes the history of the relation between theology and spirituality by noting a similar movement. Philp Sheldrake states:

> A second reason why classical Protestantism did not develop an explicit spiritual theology concerns the Reformed understanding of the fundamental relationship between spirituality and theology. The major sixteenth century reformers, most notably Martin Luther, were inherently opposed to the kind of divisions that late medieval scholasticism brought about between spirituality and theology, especially doctrine and ethics. From the very beginning, Lutheran and Calvinist theologies had at their heart a concern for what we now think of as spirituality. That is, the primary task was to describe the nature of the divine-human relationship and ways in which this should be expressed in the life of the individual Christian and the Church. Understood in these terms, Luther's *The Freedom of a Christian* (1520) and Calvin's *Institutes of the Christian Religion* are fundamentally essays in "spiritual theology." (*Spirituality and Theology*, 46)

68. In the quote just provided which this statement is referencing, Bloesch acknowledges the Puritan tradition and the Evangelical tradition as companions in providing a needed emphasis on the Christian life post-Reformation. While Pietism certainly takes center stage in influencing Bloesch, these companions couple with references to Pietism

"united with a call to holiness and discipleship."[69] For Bloesch, this emphasis on a reform of life is essential to evangelical theology and practice.

Formative Impact: Bloesch the Spiritual Theologian

Donald Bloesch's Pietistic emphasis on the Christian life shapes his theological identity and self-understanding as a Christian theologian. As I demonstrate throughout this project, the Christian life shapes the content of Bloesch's theology from start to finish. Significantly, it also is enlisted as a formative constituent in his theological methodology. Theology is fundamentally a spiritual endeavor for Bloesch; the life of devotion and the theological task are one and the same. In the prologue to his final work on the Christian life, *The Paradox of Holiness,* Bloesch states, "This is a book of devotion as well as theology. It is a venture into the theology of the spiritual life . . . which flows out of a theology of the Word of God."[70] This statement could serve as the prologue to Bloesch's entire theological career. Bloesch labels his brand of evangelical theology "a theology of devotion,"[71] and the theological task is governed by "the life of obedience."[72]

It is worth considering Bloesch's vocational vision as a theologian a fulfillment of what Hans Urs von Balthasar argues must be reclaimed in the field of theology when he states,

> In the whole history of Catholic theology there is hardly anything that is less noticed, yet more deserving of notice, than the fact that, since the great period of scholasticism, there have been few theologians who were saints. We mean here by theologian one whose office and vocation is to expound revelation in its fullness, and

---

all throughout Bloesch's work. For example, in *Spirituality Old & New*, it says:
> A convergence between mysticism and biblical faith is clearly discernible in Pietism, a movement of renewal within Lutheran and Reformed churches in Europe beginning in the seventeenth century and continuing to our own day. An analogous movement grew up in Britain: Puritanism. Evangelicalism in the eighteenth century built upon both Pietism and Puritanism. (21)

69. Bloesch, *Jesus Christ,* 11.

70. Bloesch, *Paradox of Holiness,* xxii–xxiii.

71. Bloesch, *Theological Notebook,* 2:100. This language shows up elsewhere in Bloesch's writing: "We therefore conclude that doctrinal theology (*theologia dogmatica*) should be held in balance with a theology of spiritual life or devotion (*theologia vitae spiritualis*)" (*Crisis of Piety,* 4).

72. Bloesch, *Theological Notebook,* 2:101.

> therefore whose work centers on dogmatic theology. If we consider the history of theology up to the time of the great scholastics, we are struck by the fact that the great saints, those who not only achieved an exemplary purity of life, but who also had received from God a definite mission in the Church, were, mostly, great theologians.[73]

Bloesch takes up this call to a saintly life as a dogmatic theologian but does so in an evangelical register. In a collection of his intimate devotional reflections, Bloesch provides a window into this saintly vocation: "I often pray to God: 'Make me a saint before a scholar; grant me piety before academic proficiency.'"[74] Bloesch fittingly concludes his theological career by publishing his spiritual autobiography *Faith in Search of Obedience* as a mode of demonstrating the telos of his *theological* vocation. Within this capstone monograph, Bloesch shies away from talking about his "theological career" and instead opts to speak of his personal "pilgrimage of faith." Bloesch defines the Christian life as a "pilgrimage of faith that is never completed while we are still in mortal flesh."[75] In summary, Bloesch believes a true evangelical theologian is a theologian—but even more a practitioner—of the Christian life.

For Bloesch, theology and spirituality are mutually informing realities integrated into one stated theological initiative: "faith in search of obedience."[76] Bloesch avers, "Spirituality is inseparable from theology. Indeed, it could be defined as the living out of theology."[77] Spirituality

---

73. Balthasar, *Word and Redemption*, 49.
74. Bloesch, *Theological Notebook*, 3.
75. Bloesch, *Faith in Search of Obedience*, vii.
76. Bloesch, *Faith in Search of Obedience*, vii.
77. Bloesch, *Spirituality Old & New*, 13. Bloesch develops this point further a couple of chapters into the volume:

> The breadth of the meaning of spirituality can also be partly grasped when we see it in its ineradicable relationship with theology. Spirituality is the way we live out our religious commitment. Theology is the way we reflect on God and on life in the light of the knowledge of God. Theology is oriented about *logos*, spirituality about *praxis*. The focus in theology is on the truth of faith and the confession of faith. The focus in spirituality is on the life and experience of faith. The hallmark of theology is the endeavor to know the truth. The hallmark of spirituality is striving for holiness. Theology's task is to maintain the integrity of faith in the midst of an unbelieving world. Spirituality consists in making our faith concrete in deeds of love. Dogma and praxis are inseparable; one leads into the other. (28–29)

and theology's inseparable relation is repeatedly emphasized throughout Bloesch's writing.[78] This integration of theology and spirituality reflects the sentiment of Philip Sheldrake who articulates a similar sort of vision: "Spirituality without theology runs the danger of becoming private or interior. Theology, however, needs the corrective of spirituality to remind us that true knowledge of God concerns the heart as well as the intellect."[79] Bloesch believes spirituality is utterly dependent upon theology, heeding both von Balthasar's and Sheldrake's worries, such that there can be "no vital spirituality without a sound theology."[80] The spiritual life can be properly directed only by a commitment to theology which funds an "integrity of faith."[81]

Yet, this must not run in one direction. Theology, likewise, is dependent on spiritual experience: "doctrine is important, but it becomes lifeless apart from the experience of the Spirit, the life of obedience and the adoration of the true God in prayer and thanksgiving."[82] Theology done properly is theology done in devotion to Christ and in pursuit of holiness. In short, theology must be done prayerfully. Bloesch states, "Theology that is biblical and evangelical will always be nurtured by prayer. Moreover, it will give special attention to the life of prayer, since theology is inseparable from spirituality."[83] Theology provides an anchor to spirituality, and spirituality is the proper expression of theology.

---

78. In *Crumbling Foundations* Bloesch states:

> We may well be entering a new church struggle (*Kirchenkampf*) in which the fundamentals of the faith are increasingly called into question. Purity of doctrine is as essential as purity in worship. In fact, the reason for the erosion of a biblical spirituality today is the erosion of the apostolic and doctrinal substance of the faith. Right worship (doxa) is grounded in right doctrine (dogma). But right doctrine cannot be maintained apart from the practice of the spiritual life. Only theologians in daily contact with the Spirit of God can successfully discriminate between truth and error and thereby produce sound theology. (137)

79. Sheldrake, *Spirituality and Theology*, 32.

80. Bloesch, *Crumbling Foundations*, 111.

81. Bloesch goes on to state, "When spirituality is divorced from theology it speedily deteriorates into sentimentality" (*Spirituality Old & New*, 31). In *Essentials of Evangelical Theology*, Bloesch is critical of what he calls a "neo-Pietism" within evangelicalism which values experience above doctrine: "It is well to bear in mind that faith is deeper and wider than a spiritual experience: it is an acknowledgement of the claims of Jesus Christ and an obedience to his commands" (1:2).

82. Bloesch, *Theology of Word & Spirit*, 129.

83. Bloesch, "Prayer," 946.

An Evangelical Spiritual Theology

The integration of theology and spirituality, objective and subjective, is how Bloesch understands the task of a properly *evangelical* approach to theology. Bloesch states, "True Evangelicals will be concerned for right doctrine as well as the right way of living. And yet Evangelicalism, because it values a personal faith in Jesus Christ over loyalty to creeds and dogma, cannot simply be equated with or subsumed under Protestant Orthodoxy."[84] Notice once again the particular emphasis placed on the Christian life as *the* distinguishing feature of evangelicalism. What makes evangelicalism distinct within Protestantism more broadly is its commitment to the notion of personal faith. For Bloesch, this does not signal any rejection of the central role and responsibility of doctrine in evangelicalism. Bloesch notes that evangelicalism must embrace both the Reformation contribution of core doctrine (namely the *solas*), while at the same time embrace the contribution of Pietism in regard to spiritual experience. He concludes by stating, "Evangelicalism must give due appreciation to both religious experience and doctrinal integrity, and certainly also to the call to ethical obedience, if it is to become a viable option for the church of the future."[85]

According to Bloesch, to be an evangelical theologian is to be a spiritual theologian.[86] In light of this, it is not surprising that Bloesch's academic

---

84. Bloesch, *Essentials of Evangelical Theology*, 1:11.

85. Bloesch, *Essentials of Evangelical Theology*, 1:5.

86. I refer to Bloesch as a spiritual theologian in a broad sense. Simon Chan argues, "Spiritual theology can be defined both broadly and narrowly. In the broad sense it refers to a certain way in which all theological reflections ought to be undertaken. In the narrower sense it refers to a distinct branch of theological studies concerned with the principles and practices of the Christian life" (Chan, *Spiritual Theology*, 16). The "narrow" definition of "spiritual theology" that Chan refers to is given more specificity by theologian Jordan Aumann, who states, "Spiritual theology is that part of theology that, proceeding from the truths of divine revelation and the religious experience of individual persons, defines the nature of the supernatural life, formulates directives for its growth and development, and explains the process by which souls advance from the beginning of the spiritual life to its full perfection" (Aumann, *Spiritual Theology*, 22). As I demonstrate throughout the course of this project, Bloesch could fit within Chan's "narrow" definition of "spiritual theology" as he expends vocational energy exploring the specific dynamics of the Christian life, such as prayer. For example, this is demonstrated in his monograph *The Struggle of Prayer*. However, if Jordan Aumann's narrowed definition of "spiritual theology" is considered as a field of theological inquiry, Bloesch does not engage in this kind of sustained focus on the dynamics of the spiritual life. Bloesch himself does not wish to narrow his vocation to a specific field of theological study called "spiritual theology" but rather sees himself as a systematic theologian doing theology spiritually. As such, I am inclined to use the term "spiritual theology" as a descriptor of Bloesch's theological posture in the broader sense that Chan references.

career is bookended with monographs focused on the Christian life.[87] As concomitantly a point of departure and destination, the Christian life formally defines Bloesch's theological corpus. Likewise, it is not surprising that the Christian life is a materially distributed doctrine, presupposed and pervasive throughout his entire corpus. If evangelical theology is for the sake of spiritual renewal, then the whole doctrinal system must be in service of this telos. As the defining doctrine of Bloesch's thought, the Christian life shapes the formal and material content of his dogmatic work.

Conclusion

The task of defining evangelicalism is fraught with debate and difficulty. Amidst a sea of competing views and complex analysis, one definition of evangelicalism has been the most commonly appealed to and affirmed—Bebbington's Quadrilateral. Bebbington stresses four central tenets of evangelical identity—conversionism, activism, crucicentrism, and biblicism. My investigation of Donald Bloesch's self-identification and description of evangelicalism has clearly demonstrated Bloesch's alignment with Bebbington's qualification of evangelical identity. While Bloesch stresses commonly held hallmarks of evangelicalism, his unique emphasis lies in his focus upon the doctrine of the Christian life. Evangelicalism, according to Bloesch, is defined not only by Bebbington's four marks but also by a fifth mark—a particular account of the Christian life. This emphasis on the Christian life is shaped by Bloesch's pietistic background. It has formed him into an evangelical spiritual theologian whose driving doctrinal concern is the Christian life. In other words, Bloesch's commitment to the Christian life formally shapes his theological project.

Thus far, I have not specified what makes for a distinctively evangelical account of the Christian life according to Bloesch. I take up that task in the next chapter. In chapter 2 I explore the material content of Bloesch's *evangelical* doctrine of the Christian life by investigating Bloesch's variegated terminology for the Christian life. As a collecting doctrine, the Christian life allows us to gather Bloesch's diverse vocabulary of the Christian life in service of establishing a definition of the doctrine according to Bloesch. I also analyze the primary constructive development of the Christian life

---

87. Bloesch begins his writing career with *The Christian Life and Salvation* and *The Crisis of Piety*, and he ends his writing career with *Spirituality Old & New* and *The Paradox of Holiness*.

in Bloesch's theological corpus. This provides further clarity regarding Bloesch's definition of the doctrine of the Christian life and begins to demonstrate its distributive material force in his theological system.

2

Defining the Christian Life

AS THE DISTINGUISHING DOCTRINE of his dogmatic project, it is critical that I establish the substance of Bloesch's account of the Christian life. This is the task before us in this chapter. However, locating this doctrine within Bloesch's thought is not an easy assignment. As a doctrine it is woven into the entire tapestry of Bloesch's theological system. As a result, it can easily blend in. To see the thread throughout the whole tapestry, we first need to identify its starting point.

One might expect to find a focused treatment of the doctrine within his seven-volume, dogmatic magnum opus, *Christian Foundations*. However, such a constructive presentation of the doctrine is conspicuously absent.[1] This does not mean the doctrine has gone completely missing. As I argue in chapter 3, the Christian life can be located in Bloesch's mature, dogmatic work by way of its distributive embeddedness.

A search to identify Bloesch's definition of the Christian life requires a different starting point. Bloesch's earlier work provides a definition of the Christian life, which is the focus of this chapter. My investigation begins with a survey of Bloesch's primary vocabulary of the Christian life and then moves to an analysis of his primary constructive account of the Christian life. Through this conceptual and constructive analysis, I argue that according to Bloesch, the Christian life is a divine-human encounter marked by personal and social obedience. As such, the Christian life is the arena of

---

1. As presented in the next chapter, its hiddenness is in part the consequence of its distributive character within Bloesch's theological system.

salvation. Through a life of obedience, the Christian fights for and retains his/her salvation.

The Language of the Christian Life

As a doctrine diffused throughout his corpus, the Christian life is implicitly everywhere in Bloesch's thinking even when it is not explicitly named. This presents a challenge. While Bloesch speaks of the Christian life often, he does so by employing a variety of terms.[2] To understand his unique account of the doctrine, one first needs to become attuned to his distinctive idiom. I focus attention here on four key terms—piety, devotion, spirituality, and biblical-personalism. As I explore Bloesch's primary vocabulary of the Christian life, the meaning of this critical doctrine begins to take form. As I demonstrate, for Bloesch the Christian life is a life of obedience. The gospel sets a human person free to obey God's law.[3] While the believer is never "totally free from the presence of sin" he or she "can have freedom from every particular sin" as he or she seeks to "keep the law through the grace of God."[4] According to Bloesch, obedience comes in two forms—*personal*

---

2. I prioritize Bloesch's primary terminology in the section below, and I prioritize terminology that is weighted with the most material content in his corpus. That being said, there are other terms used in his corpus, like "discipleship" (Bloesch, *Spirituality Old & New*, 30) and "evangelical obedience" (Bloesch et al., *Christian Spirituality*, 168). Likewise, Bloesch uses the language of "the Christian life" directly.

3. Bloesch, *Freedom for Obedience*, 131. Bloesch's manner of defining the Christian life with a particular emphasis on obedience echoes Karl Barth's definition of the Christian life:

> "Christian life" as we use it here means the life of Christians. We are not now thinking of Christians in their quality as members of variously ordered and directed Christian fellowships, nor of Christians as the more or less devout and convinced representatives of personal Christian piety, let alone of Christians as representatives of a so-called Christian outlook and practice. What we have in view are Christians in that which in fact makes them such, in their relation to Jesus Christ, and especially in the obligation and commitment that derives from this relation. What we have in view is their life in its relation to the divine command as it is given to them as those who are thus obligated and committed to Jesus Christ. We are asking in what sense and measure their life can be understood as one of obedience to this command. (Barth, *Christian Life*, 81–82)

4. Bloesch, *Crisis of Piety*, 54. Bloesch defines sin as "positive rebellion, not simply a privation of goodness or being" (*Essentials of Evangelical Theology*, 2:92). He goes on to state, "The essence of sin is unbelief, which appears as both idolatry and hardness of heart" (2:92). "Sin," argues Bloesch, "is both an act and a state. It entails separation from God as

and *social*. The Christian life is about personal obedience in that it is a life of private piety, but likewise it is about social obedience in that it is a life of public ethics. This life of obedience is grounded in a divine-human encounter.

In charting the vocabulary of the Christian life in Bloesch's theology, it is fitting to begin with the term "piety." In *The Crisis of Piety* Bloesch provides a collection of "essays toward a theology of the Christian life."[5] This endeavor is undertaken in light of what he believes to be a "loss of piety."[6] Bloesch defines piety as "fear and trust in the living God."[7] He then briefly outlines what he calls "hallmarks of biblical piety."[8] Here we get a more developed sense of the contours of "piety" as Bloesch conceives it. In contrast with Friedrich Schleiermacher's attempt to recover piety, Bloesch asserts a piety not principally focused on "resignation and surrender" but rather "obedience."[9] For Bloesch the obedience of piety comes in two

---

well as a deliberate violation of his will" (2:93). Regarding sin and the Christian life, Bloesch argues that while the believer is regenerated his or her "bias toward sin lingers on" (2:96). Therefore, the Christian must "daily put off the old nature and put on the new" (2:96).

5. This is the subtitle of *The Crisis of Piety*.

6. Bloesch, *Crisis of Piety*, 1.

7. Bloesch, *Crisis of Piety*, x. Just a few pages later Bloesch states that piety is "the fear of God" (1). In *Essentials of Evangelical Theology* this same definition is repeated as Bloesch states, "The biblical meaning of piety is fear of the Lord" (Bloesch, *Essentials of Evangelical Theology*, 1:32). We read also in Bloesch's *Theological Notebook*, "True piety entails both fear of the Lord and zeal for his glory" (*Theological Notebook*, 3:136). Again, we read, "We should be concerned with saving souls as well as building the holy community. Both personal salvation and social holiness are necessary in the drama of redemption" (2:84).

8. Bloesch, *Crisis of Piety*, 4. Bloesch often uses the language of "biblical" to describe his constructive theological project. Here, he has in mind an account of piety that is "biblical." What does Bloesch mean by "biblical"? We get something of an answer if we turn our attention to his *Holy Scripture*. There Bloesch tells us, "In biblical religion error means swerving from the truth, wandering from the right path, rather than defective information" (*Holy Scripture*, 107). He goes on to say, "The Bible is normative as the unique instrument of the Spirit and as the original witness to God's special revelation fulfilled in Jesus Christ" (117). For Bloesch, "biblical" piety is a mode of piety anchored in the normative authority of Scripture. It is a form of piety that is true, as it accords with God's revealed truth.

9. Bloesch, *Crisis of Piety*, 5. Bloesch's concern with Schleiermacher is that piety is unmoored from any meaningful sense of relation to God in which we are called to know God and obey God, and is instead collapsed into a kind of existential experience. In *The Christian Faith* Schleiermacher states, "The piety which forms the basis of all ecclesiastical communions is, considered purely in itself, neither a Knowing nor a Doing, but a modification of Feeling, or of immediate self-consciousness" (Schleiermacher, *Christian Faith*, 5). As David Ford notes, Schleiermacher's emphasis on "immediate self-conscious

forms—"inward devotion" and a dedication to "the will of Christ" in "every area of life, including the public or political sphere."[10] For Bloesch this is an important twofold reality of the Christian life that must not be lost; inner devotion must be combined with outward action. To state it differently, there is both an interior and exterior pole to the Christian life.[11]

Where Bloesch talks about "piety," one frequently finds him talking about "devotion." In his definition of piety just observed, the word "devotion" is used to talk about the interior pole of the Christian life. This formula of relating "piety" and "devotion" is echoed elsewhere in his writing. For example, Bloesch states, "Piety in the Christian context essentially means heartfelt devotion and consecration to the God who has revealed himself in Jesus Christ."[12] Here, "heartfelt devotion" is used in a similar sense as "inward devotion," as it represents the believer's personal fellowship with God. However, Bloesch does not remain consistent in his use of "piety" and "devotion." The inconsistency shows up in his ordering of these two terms.[13] Bloesch completely reverses their roles in relation to one another, giving priority to "devotion" as the primary category under which "piety" is one facet.

While this may appear to simply be a linguistic variation in Bloesch, I believe there are two reasons for his shift in language. First, piety lacks an emphasis on the human commitment which Bloesch wishes to infuse into

---

or feeling of absolute dependence on God" assumed "God is present in the immediate dynamic relationship that grasps our whole being" (Ford, "Introduction to Modern Christian Theology," 8). The effect of this error, as Bloesch would describe it, regarding piety, plays itself out in Schleiermacher's theological methodology. He goes on to argue, "The doctrines in all their forms have their ultimate ground so exclusively in the emotions of the religious self-consciousness, that where these do not exist the doctrines cannot arise" (Schleiermacher, *Christian Faith*, 78). We see Bloesch's concern with a subjectively oriented Schleiermacherian approach in *The Holy Spirit*: "As Christians we are not to try to make ourselves pious in the sense of spiritually superior, but true piety will be seen in our lives by others if we strive to obey God's commandments. Our task is not to become self-consciously holy, for then our focus is on our own supposed holiness rather than on Jesus Christ" (*Holy Spirit*, 330).

10. Bloesch, *Crisis of Piety*, 4.

11. To demonstrate the diversity of language Bloesch uses to make this distinction it is worth noting he also refers to these two poles of the Christian life as "spiritual but also ethical" (*Crisis of Piety*, 5).

12. Bloesch, *Crisis of Piety*, 26.

13. Bloesch uses mirror language to define devotion in *Spirituality East & West*: "Devotion for the Evangelical does not mean worship *per se*, but rather heartfelt consecration to Christ. It is not adoration so much as commitment, a commitment which pervades all spheres of man's life" (*Spirituality East & West*, 168).

his account of the Christian life.[14] Second, the term "piety" is fraught with variegated meaning and tied to criticisms of "Pietism" as a historical movement, both of which Bloesch wishes to transcend in his own articulation of the Christian life.[15] Bloesch does not completely avoid the term "piety" because he still believes its underlying historical and theological commitments are of use in developing an account of the Christian life. Nevertheless, he finds "devotion" to be a more resourceful word to postulate the robust and nuanced account of the nature of the Christian life he wishes to uniquely espouse.[16] Ultimately, Bloesch departs from the word "piety," finding it insufficient to fully articulate his evangelical theology of the Christian life, and in its place, he posits what he calls "evangelical devotionism."[17]

With the terminology of "devotion" and "piety" now reversed, we read, "Devotion entails piety, that is, the fear of God, but it also includes mercy, service to our fellow humanity."[18] Here again, we encounter the two components of the Christian life. Bloesch wields the term "devotion" to articulate the two-fold account of obedience, personal and social, for which he has been vying all along. This time, personal obedience is "piety" and social obedience is "mercy."[19] Evangelical devotionism entails a personal

---

14. Bloesch claims as much in *The Crisis of Piety*: "I have chosen the term 'devotion' rather than 'piety' because the former term connotes a commitment of the will as well as an attitude of the mind" (*Crisis of Piety*, 15). Colyer notices this shift: "The term *piety* does not connote enough of commitment and will, whereas *devotionism* makes commitment and will paramount" (Colyer, *Evangelical Theology in Transition*, 165).

15. Bloesch, *Crisis of Piety*, 25–27.

16. Bloesch, *Crisis of Piety*, 15. There is a hint of Bloesch's linguistic logic in his *Theological Notebook* when he states, "Just as Pietism saved the church in the seventeenth and eighteenth centuries, so 'evangelical devotionism' is needed to save the church in our time." Bloesch goes on to state, "An evangelical theology of devotion is to be contrasted with revivalistic fundamentalism by its emphasis on a life of obedience under the cross rather than on a crisis experience of conversion" (*Theological Notebook*, 2:100–101). In this we see Bloesch's commitment to the Christian life. His emphasis is not placed on the experience of salvation, but rather on the life of obedience and in that the priority of the Christian life is demonstrated clearly.

17. Bloesch, *Crisis of Piety*, 15. Bloesch uses "devotion" as a synonym for the Christian life. We read in *The Crisis of Piety*, "A theology of devotion or Christian life" (*Crisis of Piety*, 33).

18. Bloesch, *Crisis of Piety*, 16.

19. With a different governing terminology, Bloesch echoes this point in *Faith & Its Counterfeits*: "True religion has an ethical as well as a spiritual dimension. It will inevitably issue in both works of piety (prayer, meditation, devotion) and works of mercy. It will strive to give honor to God as well as meet both the spiritual and the legitimate material needs of an ailing and despairing humanity" (*Faith & Its Counterfeits*, 113).

obedience expressed in "a deepening concern for prayer and meditation," and at the same time a social obedience expressed in "a passionate concern for the outcasts and unfortunates in our world, those who have been made homeless by war and famine, the victims of racial apartheid, and the diseased and forsaken."[20] For Bloesch, a theology of devotion secures an ordered emphasis on the inner life of the Christian and the ethical life of the Christian. Obedience in the Christian life begins in "spiritual passion" that informs "ethical action."[21] Fear of the Lord leads to love of neighbor. In the end, devotion is a properly ordered "total commitment to Jesus Christ."[22]

As we turn to another Christian life term, "spirituality," we again find the same double emphasis on personal and social obedience. At a fundamental level, Bloesch defines evangelical spirituality as seeking "to bring the whole person—including the full range of secular activities—into relationship with God."[23] Bloesch briefly outlines the features of what he calls "true spirituality" (evangelical) in *Spirituality Old & New*.[24] First, Bloesch stresses that "true spirituality" is "anchored in a vital faith in the God and Father of our Lord Jesus Christ."[25] It is about "fellowship with the living God."[26] Second, Bloesch stresses "true spirituality" involves loving one's neighbor through concrete acts of service. He states, "True spirituality entails the sacrifice of the self for the good of our neighbor and for the glory of God."[27] Bloesch goes on to say that "true spirituality involves living in the midst of the world's afflictions for the greater glory of God."[28] Bloesch frames these two features of true spirituality with familiar categories—personal and social. However, here in *Spirituality Old & New*, Bloesch specifically appeals to John Wesley's notion of "personal" and "social holiness" as a helpful device for articulating his vision of true spirituality.[29] For Bloesch, holiness

---

20. Bloesch, *Crisis of Piety*, 3.

21. Bloesch, *Crisis of Piety*, 15.

22. Bloesch, *Crisis of Piety*, 16.

23. Bloesch, *Theological Notebook*, 2:132.

24. Bloesch follows his short section on "True Spirituality" by referring to "true spirituality" as "biblical, evangelical spirituality" (*Spirituality Old & New*, 31).

25. Bloesch, *Spirituality Old & New*, 29.

26. Bloesch, *Spirituality Old & New*, 30.

27. Bloesch, *Spirituality Old & New*, 29. Echoing this point Bloesch argues that "authentic spirituality will be a holiness that is not removed from the travail of the world, but one that is lived out in the midst of it" ("Call to Spirituality," 156).

28. Bloesch, *Spirituality Old & New*, 30.

29. Bloesch, *Spirituality Old & New*, 30. Bloesch refers to Wesley's account of "social

is the fruit of obedience. As Bloesch writes elsewhere, "Holiness indeed is the goal of the Christian life."[30] The goal is not merely individual holiness, but a social holiness, which is expressed in "our thoughts and actions."[31]

---

holiness" again (Bloesch et al., *Christian Spirituality*, 177). He is consistent on this emphasis through to his much later dogmatic work *The Holy Spirit*, where we read, "Biblical, evangelical spirituality also sounds the call to social holiness" (Bloesch, *Holy Spirit*, 320). Bloesch attributes the phrase "social holiness" to John Wesley. It is a phrase Bloesch employs throughout his writing to articulate a distinction between a kind of individual or private holiness, and a corporate or social holiness. Whether or not Bloesch has specifically excavated the phrase "social holiness" from the writing of Wesley or from the broader Wesleyan tradition is not clear, but in the interest of following his stated source, it is helpful to locate Wesley's original use of the phrase. Wesley uses the phrase "social holiness" only once, in fact. The phrase is found in Wesley's preface to his 1739 edition of "Hymns and Poems." It is there that Wesley states, "Directly opposite to this is the gospel of Christ. Solitary religion is not to be found there. 'Holy solitaries' is a phrase no more consistent with the gospel than holy adulterers. The gospel of Christ knows of no religion, but social; no holiness but social holiness. 'Faith working by love' is the length and breadth and depth and height of Christian perfection" (Wesley, *Works of John Wesley*, 13:321). Andrew C. Thompson provides us with helpful analysis of Wesley's use of the phrase "social holiness." Thompson argues Wesley is communicating three things here: "First, *social holiness* names the environmental context in which Christians are progressively transformed by grace, which is a fundamentally social one" (Thompson, "From Societies to Society," 162). Second, "to note is that, while social holiness refers foundationally to the environmental context of sanctification, the concrete community that finds its life within that context does not exist as an enclosed sphere separated from the outside world" (163). Finally, "social holiness refers neither to the historically later concept of social justice nor to a counterpart for personal holiness, whether understood as a bifurcated way persons can exhibit holiness or to an individual/public division of the means of grace" (164). It is also important to note that Andrew Thompson argues the distinction often made between "personal" and "social" holiness has been improperly sourced in Wesley's thought. Rather, the corresponding or contrastive form of holiness Bloesch has in mind in relation to social holiness is "solitary holiness" (165). Bloesch himself appeals to this distinction between "personal" and "social" holiness, and therefore this is a helpful note of resourcement criticism that we can be mindful of as we encounter Bloesch's use of this distinction throughout his thought.

30. Bloesch, *Paradox of Holiness*, xxi.

31. Bloesch, *Paradox of Holiness*, 30. We pick up on a similar note in Bloesch's *Theological Notebook*: "Hand in hand with piety must go morality. We have obligations not only to God but also to our neighbor" (*Theological Notebook*, 2:66). Bloesch makes a similar point in a short section titled "Holy Worldliness" in *Spirituality Old & New* when he states, "The commandment that we hear in Scripture is not that the people of God withdraw from the world into a hermitage or monastery but that they permeated the world with a message of healing and redemption" (*Spirituality Old & New*, 92).

The Christian life is a "road to holiness."[32] It is a pilgrimage of faith seeking obedience unto holiness.

Perhaps a more peculiar term in Bloesch's idiom is "biblical personalism."[33] This term is used throughout his body of work to signal an *evangelical* vision of the Christian life.[34] In *Spirituality Old & New*, Bloesch provides a single chapter treatment of "biblical personalism,"[35] beginning his account with "the self-revealing God who calls people to fellowship with himself."[36] In so doing, he seeks to draw a distinction between "biblical" and "philosophical" personalism. The primary difference is an emphasis on a personal self-revealing God, as opposed to a generic God defined by universal tenets of theism.[37] This self-revealing God is the God of biblical faith who is sovereign Creator of all things. The God of biblical-personalism is a God "above" humanity.[38] He is a God who has chosen to descend to humanity. "This God," Bloesch states, "is ever active and ever working."[39] For Bloesch, beginning with the self-revealing, sovereign, Creator God of action means that an evangelical spirituality begins, not with humankind's

---

32. Bloesch, *Paradox of Holiness*, 1.

33. Bloesch claims that this language stems from Brunner but does not provide specific reference in this regard. As I demonstrate later in the book, Bloesch's use of the language "divine-human encounter" does come directly from Brunner. Since these two terms "biblical personalism" and "divine-human encounter" are bound together conceptually for Bloesch, it seems he credits Brunner for the notion as broadly appropriated in his own constructive work. Bloesch states, "Evangelical devotion is wholly biblical, being grounded in the Old Testament as well as the New. This kind of spirituality has also been called biblical personalism (E. Brunner) in order to distinguish it from a monistic mystical religion in which personality is negated or transcended" (*Crisis of Piety*, 82).

34. For example, in *Spirituality East & West* Bloesch states, "The Evangelical point of view, therefore, might be denominated a 'biblical personalism' as over against a monistic mysticism" (170).

35. Bloesch states that biblical personalism can also be properly called "prophetic religion, evangelical piety, revelational religion and Puritan spirituality" (*Spirituality Old & New*, 77). These proposed synonyms are instructive as we consider Bloesch's unique posture as an evangelical theologian. Once again, a Pietistic impulse is signaled. We see this linguistic connection made elsewhere in Bloesch's work. He states, "What is needed today is a piety grounded not in religious enthusiasm but in biblical personalism" (*Theological Notebook*, 2:90).

36. Bloesch, *Spirituality Old & New*, 77.

37. Bloesch, *Spirituality Old & New*, 77.

38. Bloesch, *Theological Notebook*, 5:341.

39. Bloesch, *Spirituality Old & New*, 78.

quest for God, but God's personal pursuit of humankind.[40] God's mission is not undertaken to meet a divine need, but to meet human needs; God is fully satisfied within His divine life, but "in acting to fulfill human need he gives glory to himself."[41]

According to biblical-personalism, the Christian life is a tangible encounter with this gracious and glorious self-revealing God.[42] Bloesch regularly refers to this personal encounter as a "divine-human encounter."[43] As I show more fully in chapter 3, this "divine-human encounter" is "personal" because it is an encounter of the human person with the person of the Word by the person of the Spirit. "Biblical personalism" will become the dominant rubric for Bloesch as he endeavors to bring his doctrine of the Christian life to its full maturity in his systematic work in *Christian Foundations,* which is explicitly framed by his Word & Spirit taxonomy of revelation.

This divine-human encounter of biblical-personalism is first known in the incarnation of Jesus Christ and then known by individual Christians in their discipleship to Christ.[44] On Bloesch's account, the human person's encounter with God is an encounter of grace alone.[45] It is an encounter with a loving and holy God that in turn forms the Christian in and for love and holiness.[46] As one might expect, this encounter is worked out in a life of obedience, both personal and social. The divine-human encounter is experienced in the interior life of prayer and expressed in the exterior life of mission (great commission).[47] As the defining feature of the Christian life, this encounter is not a singular event but rather is an ongoing experience. The Christian life is a running personal encounter between God and the believer.

I have surveyed Bloesch's primary vocabulary of the Christian life—piety, devotion, spirituality, and biblical-personalism. In so doing, I established a basic definition of Bloesch's account of the Christian life. The Christian life is a divine-human encounter initiated by the Triune God of Scripture. In this encounter the Christian comes to know and be formed by a loving and holy God. This encounter is experienced by way of personal

---

40. Bloesch, *Spirituality Old & New*, 79.
41. Bloesch, *Spirituality Old & New*, 80.
42. Bloesch, *Spirituality East & West*, 170.
43. Bloesch, *Spirituality Old & New*, 80.
44. Bloesch, *Theological Notebook*, 5:183.
45. Bloesch, *Spirituality Old & New*, 87.
46. Bloesch, *Spirituality Old & New*, 89–94.
47. Bloesch, *Spirituality Old & New*, 94–97.

obedience—piety, devotion, and prayer, and it is expressed by way of social obedience—ethics, action, and mission.

2.2 The Christian Life as The Arena of Salvation

While Bloesch uses a wide-ranging vocabulary to discuss the Christian life, he does also directly employ the language of "the Christian life." Therefore, having identified some of the key vocabulary of the Christian life, I now analyze Bloesch's direct discussion of the doctrine. This constructive account of the Christian life is found in his early monograph *The Christian Life and Salvation*. In this volume we find the most focused treatment of the doctrine in Bloesch's entire body of work—it is the only monograph in which Bloesch specifically privileges the language of "Christian life" when speaking of the doctrine.

In *The Christian Life and Salvation*, Bloesch moors his discussion of the Christian life in salvation. The two doctrines are inextricably bound together in his system. Bloesch clearly believes this is an idiosyncratic feature of his constructive project. As Bloesch states in another early monograph *The Crisis of Piety*, "In contrast to the mainstream of current Protestant thought I maintain that the Christian life must be viewed as being integrally related to salvation."[48] The uniqueness of Bloesch's view lies in the "integral" role of the Christian life in salvation. For Bloesch the Christian life is the arena of salvation. Salvation is fought for and retained in the personal and social obedience of those who have encountered God.

At the outset of *The Christian Life and Salvation*, Bloesch tells the reader his goal is to "re-examine the role of the Christian life in our salvation."[49] He quickly identifies two potential errors in such an endeavor: (1) the "separation of the Christian life from salvation" and (2) "to make the Christian life the foundation or ground of our salvation." The separation of the Christian life and salvation would be "to divorce ethics from religion." Conversely, to ground salvation in the Christian life would be to capitulate to a kind of works righteousness. For Bloesch this would betray an evangelical commitment to justification by faith as foundational for salvation and the Christian life.[50] With these two errors in view, Bloesch summarizes his approach:

---

48. Bloesch, *Crisis of Piety*, 115.
49. Bloesch, *Christian Life and Salvation*, 14.
50. Bloesch, *Christian Life and Salvation*, 15.

> Our position is that the Christian life is the arena or theater of our redemption and not simply an effect or sign of this redemption. It is the battleground on which our salvation is continually fought for and recovered. The Christian cannot earn his salvation, but he is called to retain and defend it. The Christian life is not the basis or source of our salvation, but it is an integral element in our salvation. It is the necessary fruit of our justification and a means to our final salvation.[51]

Here we encounter two metaphors to express this integral approach. First, the image of warfare, in which salvation is fought for in the arena or theater of battle.[52] Bloesch states elsewhere, "I affirm that the life of devotion is the battleground on which our salvation is fought for and continually recovered."[53] Second, Bloesch appeals to an agricultural metaphor to discuss faithfulness in the Christian life as the fruit of God's work in justification. The notion that the Christian life and salvation are to be held in an organic relationship to one another is repeated multiple times in the early chapters of *The Christian Life and Salvation*: "A life of faithful obedience must be viewed as having an organic relation to our salvation."[54] With these two metaphors of warfare and agriculture, Bloesch seeks to stave off the two errors he initially has identified—separating the Christian life from salvation

---

51. Bloesch, *Christian Life and Salvation*, 17. Bloesch directly anchors this position in Pietism as he states, "It remained for the movements of Pietism and Puritanism to recover the dimension of the Christian Faith for the mainline churches within Protestantism. The Christian life was seen not simply as a by-product of salvation (as in later Protestant orthodoxy) but as the arena of salvation, the field in which salvation is recovered and renewed" (*Essentials of Evangelical Theology*, 1:37). This language carries all the way through into his later dogmatic work. In *Jesus Christ* Bloesch states, "The Christian life is not simply the fruit and consequence of a past salvation accomplished in the cross and resurrection of Christ but the arena in which Christ's salvation is carried forward to fulfillment by his Spirit" (*Jesus Christ*, 11).

52. Bloesch echoes this imagery later. "The Christian life is not simply a by-product or fruit of faith but the field or arena in which faith is worked out amid much tribulation and opposition" (*Essentials of Evangelical Theology*, 2:207).

53. Bloesch, *Crisis of Piety*, 4. We read also in *The Holy Spirit*, "The metaphor that most clearly describes the living out of a Christian life is 'battle,' a motif that pervades the New Testament. Faith does not lead us beyond conflict but right into conflict, for the devil fights for our souls as we try to remain steadfast in our determination to give glory to Christ" (*Holy Spirit*, 321).

54. Bloesch, *Christian Life and Salvation*, 18. We read later on, "The Christian life must be viewed as being organically related to and rooted in this other crucial sphere of action" (29). Similarly, we read, "In our view the fruit is organically related to the root" (30).

and grounding salvation in the Christian life. Bloesch's agenda is clear—to imbue the doctrine of the Christian life with theological weight, while also ensuring it is kept in fitting proportion to the doctrine of salvation.

Bloesch seeks to thread the needle carefully as he weaves the Christian life into an account of salvation. At times it appears he may miss his mark and fall prey to the second error he warned against—making the Christian life the foundation of salvation. For example, Bloesch declares, "The Christian life must be recognized as being equally indispensable for our salvation."[55] Bloesch echoes this conviction with a more robust argument in *The Crisis of Piety*, where he declares,

> We need also today to perceive the integral relationship between the life of devotion and Christian salvation. Is consecrated devotion only a sign and mirror of a salvation procured for us in the past? Or is it not the means by which this salvation is realized and made concrete in our lives? I hold to the latter position. I affirm that the life of devotion is the battleground on which our salvation is fought for and continually recovered. It is not the cause of our justification, but it is a major factor in the implementation of justification in the world. It is a means by which the fruits of Christ's past sacrifice are appropriated in the present. Not on account of our works, and yet not apart from our works.[56]

As a reminder, Bloesch's language of "devotion" is a synonym for the Christian life. With that in mind, the trajectory of Bloesch's argument here regarding the indispensability of the Christian life in salvation is compelling. Bloesch refers to the Christian life as the "battleground" of salvation, echoing his earlier metaphor from *The Christian Life and Salvation*. However, he presses the critical role of the Christian life with even stronger language, referring to it as the implementer of our justification and the means of appropriating Christ's atoning work.

---

55. Bloesch, *Christian Life and Salvation*, 29.

56. Bloesch, *Crisis of Piety*, 4. We encounter a similar tone in Bloesch's *Theological Notebook*: "Evangelical theology conceives of God as the sole cause of our salvation, and our obedience as the means by which God accomplishes his saving work. It is permissible in Evangelical theology to regard our obedience as an instrumental cause of salvation, but this does not mean that we play a positive role in procuring our salvation. It means only that we receive it from God and retain it by the power of his Spirit" (*Theological Notebook*, 2:87). The language Bloesch uses here of "instrumental cause" necessitates explanation, which Bloesch clearly acknowledges. While continuing to anchor salvation in God's action, he does not want to rid man of participatory engagement in God's action. We do "retain" salvation, of course by the power of the Holy Spirit.

The indispensable role of implementation and appropriation comes rather close to grounding salvation in the Christian life. Indeed, Bloesch makes it clear that he believes the Christian life is the "means by which . . . salvation is realized and made concrete in our lives."[57] To be sure, some safeguards are in place here. While the Christian life is "a major factor" in the "implementation" of our justification, he is quite clear that it is not the "cause." For Bloesch, nothing can displace the central role of the justifying work of Christ upon the cross. While human "works" are a necessary expression of salvation, they nevertheless follow Christ's work in the organic order of salvation.[58] Christ's work comes first and is foundational to salvation. Bloesch clearly seeks to watch his step: as an evangelical theologian he remains committed to a traditionally Protestant account of justification, whereby "God declares the sinner righteous by virtue of faith" in the person and work of Christ.[59]

Bloesch's willingness to flirt with the line he himself has drawn makes a strong statement regarding the depth of the integral relationship he envisions between the Christian life and salvation. Bloesch flirts with his second error because he is determined to counterbalance a corresponding error he sees within the Reformed tradition. As I highlighted in the introduction, Bloesch believed the Reformed tradition did not give sufficient dogmatic weight to the doctrine of the Christian life. Regarding the classical Reformed view of the Christian life, Bloesch states, "The Christian life is conceived primarily as an effect or fruit of salvation rather than a vital contributing factor in our salvation. . . . The struggle to remain true to our faith is not taken seriously, since according to this point of view election and salvation are predetermined."[60] As we might expect, Bloesch turns to Pietism for a solution to this error. He states, "The German Pietists rightly saw that salvation is not only something done for man but also something done in man. They properly discerned the integral relationship

---

57. Bloesch, *Crisis of Piety*, 4.

58. We read in *Freedom For Obedience*, "The evangelical Christian does not believe that one can merit salvation by good works but that good works will flow spontaneously out of a joyful heart" (Bloesch, *Freedom For Obedience*, 32).

59. Bloesch, *Jesus Christ*, 177. As Bloesch says in *The Crisis of Piety*, "An evangelical devotionism must be grounded in the biblical message of justification of the ungodly. Christ died for us while we were yet sinners—this was the fundamental doctrine of the Protestant Reformation" (*Crisis of Piety*, 16).

60. Bloesch, *Christian Life and Salvation*, 30.

between sound thinking and repentance and obedience."[61] While Bloesch goes on to critique the Pietists for neglecting the Reformed emphasis on the accomplished sanctification of Jesus Christ, the primary point remains. Bloesch seeks to retrieve a pietistic emphasis on the "integral relationship" between the Christian life and salvation. Bloesch is critical of any account of the Christian life in which it is viewed as merely an outcome or verification of salvation. Interestingly, while he initially posited an organic analogy as one way to articulate the role of the Christian life in salvation, Bloesch has clearly placed greater emphasis on his first analogy of battle. His primary language of arena intends to press into service the vital role of the Christian life in salvation.[62] The Christian must fight for his/her salvation in a life of personal and social obedience. Consequently, the Christian life is not only the arena of salvation but is also the arena of salvific assurance.[63] As Bloesch states, "Faith brings us assurance of our salvation, but this assurance needs to be renewed and confirmed in Christian practice."[64] Assurance begins with the objective work of Christ, but it is brought to completion in the subjective experience of the Christian life.[65]

61. Bloesch, *Christian Life and Salvation*, 30.

62. Bloesch, *Christian Life and Salvation*, 30–31.

63. Bloesch states, "The Christian life is the field of certainty, the arena in which we constantly renew our assurance. The assurance of faith and hope is not something gained once for all but something that must be realized in the practice of Christian living (Heb 6:11; Rev 2:10). We are summoned to make our calling and election sure as we engage in the struggle of faith, for only in this way will we remain in the faith (2 Pet 1:10; Heb 10:23, 35, 36)" (*Essentials of Evangelical Theology*, 1:239–40). Here Bloesch stresses the importance of perseverance in the Christian life to the point of suggesting a person can lose his/her salvation. Bloesch counterbalances this in stating, "The Christian is called to work out his salvation without any doubt as to the outcome, since he knows that the gifts and the call of God are irrevocable (Rom 11:29)" (1:242). Bloesch wishes to uphold the priority of divine action, but the force of his argument on the whole affords the struggle of the Christian life a critical role in upholding one's salvation.

64. Bloesch, *Theological Notebook*, 5:65. Bloesch goes on to say later in the same volume, "We cannot be sure in any finalized sense that we are saved. But we are always becoming sure as we take up the cross and follow Christ in faith. Christian assurance is a process of continually becoming sure of God's mercy as we go forward in obedience" (5:107).

65. Bloesch's account of assurance is built upon his theology of Word & Spirit, which is explored in further detail in the next chapter. As with Bloesch's entire project, he is concerned with avoiding both an objectivist and a subjectivist account of assurance. On the objectivist side he is concerned with a view of assurance that is focused solely on the objective historical work of Christ affirmed with a kind of rational certainty. On the subjectivist side he is concerned with a collapse of assurance into the Christian's spiritual

Nevertheless, Bloesch himself acknowledges that this flirtation with error merits some shifts in linguistic emphasis. In a short response to Elmer Colyer's recognition of the central role the Christian life plays in his theology, Bloesch acknowledges,

> Colyer rightly perceives the crucial role I assign to the Christian life in salvation. The Christian life is not simply a byproduct but a concrete sign and witness of Christ's passion and victory in his struggle against the powers of darkness. But it is more than that: it is the arena in which the implications of our salvation are unfolded as we strive to appropriate the fruits of Christ's cross and resurrection victory. In my early writings I sometimes gave the impression that the Christian life is a contributory agent in the effecting of our salvation. I would now contend that our works of obedience mirror and proclaim Christ's work of obedience unto death, but they do not render his death and resurrection efficacious.[66]

Bloesch repeats his fundamental emphasis on the critical role of the Christian life, but he acknowledges the danger in viewing the Christian life as "contributory" in salvation and signals a desire to guard this more carefully later in his theological career. This is exhibited in his mature theological work, where his abiding emphasis on the crucial place of the Christian life is tempered by more cautious language. For example, later in his theological career Bloesch declares, "a holy life is not an appendage to our salvation but the sign and evidence of the authenticity of our salvation."[67] Again he argues, "Our salvation is based on the extrinsic righteousness of Christ that is imputed to us in faith, but our salvation is manifest in our striving for personal holiness."[68] And yet, his primary emphasis is not lost. We read, "Salvation is not only a gift to be received but also a task to be performed."[69]

---

experience. Here, Bloesch seeks to thread the needle, guarding against both errors, while upholding a "divine-human encounter" view of assurance. Assurance for Bloesch is known in both the objective and subjective poles of this divine-human encounter.

66. Bloesch, "Donald Bloesch Responds," in Colyer, *Evangelical Theology in Transition*, 200.

67. Bloesch, *Jesus Christ*, 12.

68. Bloesch, *Holy Spirit*, 323.

69. Bloesch, *Holy Spirit*, 330. While Bloesch did not directly engage with or affirm covenantal nomism, one might detect a commonality of emphasis between his view of justification and that of covenantal nomism, which traces its roots to E. P. Sanders's monograph *Paul and Palestinian Judaism*. In his groundbreaking work Sanders "questioned the idea that first-century Judaism taught a religion of merit and works righteousness. He described it rather as 'covenantal nomis,' according to which we enter the

In succinct conclusion Bloesch argues, "We are justified *by* grace, but we are justified *for* holiness."[70] What does it mean to be justified for holiness? Bloesch states, "While the righteousness that redeems lies outside us in Jesus Christ, this righteousness does not remain outside us but is reflected in our thoughts and actions."[71] For Bloesch, the viability of salvation is inextricably bound to the vitality of the Christian life. This does not mean that a person earns his or her salvation, but it does mean that he or she plays a real part in keeping it.[72] The Christian life is not the progenitor of salvation, but it is the preserver and protector of salvation. The Christian's call to holiness is a call to live the salvation he or she has been given.[73]

The Material Influence of the Christian Life in Salvation

Up to this point in my analysis of Bloesch's constructive account of the Christian life, I demonstrated the integral role of the Christian life in

---

covenant by grace but remain in it by obedience to the law" (Lane, "Justification by Faith" 418). There is no evidence to suggest that Bloesch is influenced by Sander's view directly, nor that he engages the downstream discussion around Pauline theology from scholars such as James Dunn or N. T. Wright. However, it is worth noting the familiarity of description regarding a biblical account of justification.

70. Bloesch, *Holy Spirit*, 323–24. Similarly, we read in *Freedom For Obedience*, "We are justified not by a holy life, not by sincerity or zeal, not even by good intentions, but only by the perfect righteousness of Jesus Christ that covers our sins and presents us blameless before the throne of God. But once justified we then are moved irresistibly to zeal for the honor of God and love for our neighbor for whom Christ died" (*Freedom for Obedience*, 32).

71. Bloesch, *Holy Spirit*, 325.

72. Bloesch's emphasis on retaining salvation in the Christian life brings to the surface questions of the efficacious nature of grace. Bloesch is aware of this. Therefore, in *Essentials of Evangelical Theology* Bloesch affirms that grace is irresistible "in the sense that it is efficacious, that once it enters into the life of man it will penetrate his inner being and alter his will" (*Essentials of Evangelical Theology*, 2:205). And yet, he argues for a genuinely subjective component to salvation, the Christian life. As the arena of salvation, the Christian life is the location in which saving faith is worked out (2:206). As such, Bloesch seems to hold to some form of human rejection of grace, or perhaps we might say he holds to the notion of human responsibility to retain such grace. Nevertheless, he wishes to maintain an account of irresistible grace "even in the case of the one who falls from grace" (2:206). According to Bloesch, "grace still triumphs but now in the form of wrath and judgment" (2:206).

73. Bloesch frequently describes the relationship of the Christian's objective holiness and the Christian's subjective holiness as the "paradox of holiness": "Holiness is a paradox. It is both a crown to be won and a gift to be received" (*Theological Notebook*, 4:42).

DEFINING THE CHRISTIAN LIFE

salvation. According to Bloesch, the Christian life is an indispensable part of salvation; it is the arena of salvation, the location where salvation is fought for and kept by the believing Christian. Bloesch casts the Christian life in this integral role in order to avoid the separation of the Christian life and salvation. Nevertheless, what remains to be seen is the degree to which this integral role materially influences Bloesch's doctrine of salvation. In what follows, I show that the influence of the Christian life on soteriology is not doctrinally superficial for Bloesch, by demonstrating the influence of the Christian life on Bloesch's definition of salvation. I then turn to a more substantial analysis of Bloesch's account of the *ordo salutis*, demonstrating the material pressure of the Christian life in his development of this critical piece of soteriological machinery. This material pressure is an early sign of what I identify in chapter 3, the distributed role of the Christian life in Bloesch's theological system.

Turning back to his early work, *The Christian Life and Salvation*, we read, "Salvation in its deepest sense refers to the rectifying or restoration of the broken relationship between God and man, a restoration which entails a transformation of the being of man."[74] Here, we get a brief definition of the doctrine of salvation independent of direct consideration of the doctrine of the Christian life. However, what is striking is the subtle lingering Christian life influence present in the definition. Bloesch is not content with an account of salvation primarily focused on the rectification and restoration "of the broken relationship between God and man" but pushes salvation into the register of "transformation of the being of man."[75] The enduring connection to the Christian life is evident in this rudimentary definition. The restoration of right relationship, the divine-human encounter, requires "transformation," or holiness. This implicit note of Christian life influence in Bloesch's definition of salvation is the first fruits of what is to come. It is a whisper of the material pressure applied by the Christian life on Bloesch's doctrine of

---

74. Bloesch, *Christian Life and Salvation*, 33. Elsewhere Bloesch claims, "Biblical Christianity defines salvation first of all as redemption—being bought back or delivered from the slavery to sin" (*Jesus Christ*, 176). Here, "redemption" seems to be the fundamental notion, rather than restoration. The emphasis being "redemption" from enslavement to sin, which Bloesch defines as "unbelief or hardness of heart" (44). It is this notion of sin that points us toward Bloesch using the concepts of redemption and restoration interchangeably. The problem to be overcome is a "hardness of heart" to God. In other words, a rebellious estrangement from the God of love is the problem, and therefore as Bloesch will state, "sin can be overcome only by radical love" (49). In short, restoration to right relationship with the God of love is at the heart of God's work of redemption.

75. Bloesch, *Christian Life and Salvation*, 33.

salvation. As we analyze Bloesch's constructive account of the *ordo salutis*, we find further evidence of the material influence of the Christian life.

The order of salvation, in Bloesch's scheme, is properly understood as two corresponding orders—temporal and eternal—each containing four dimensions.[76] These "orders" are not to be seen as separate realities, but are two sides of one coin, accounting for the divine and human aspects of salvation. He visually outlines these two orders:

Temporal Order	*Eternal Order*
seeking for help	predestination
repentance and faith	justification
obedience in faith	sanctification
perfect love	glorification[77]

Bloesch understands the order of salvation to be *paradoxical, correlative,* and *transhistorical*. All three of these unique features of his account highlight the material pressure the Christian life applies on Bloesch's doctrine of salvation.[78]

On Bloesch's account of a two-fold order, the divine and human side are held together *paradoxically*, according to the dialectic that Bloesch employs under that grammar.[79] Every part of the *ordo salutis* is integral to and necessary for salvation.[80] Importantly, while Bloesch's eternal and temporal

---

76. Bloesch, *Christian Life and Salvation*, 25.

77. Bloesch, *Christian Life and Salvation*, 26.

78. Bloesch stresses the importance of the *ordo salutis* in establishing a proper priority on the Christian life in *The Crisis of Piety*:

> The order of salvation (*ordo salutis*) will play a major role in any theology that seeks to take the Christian commitment with the utmost seriousness. It is fashionable in contemporary theological circles to speak only of various facets of the one great event of our salvation rather than of an order of salvation. Yet this kind of thinking fails to do justice to the biblical testimony that salvation has a definite beginning and that it progresses through a series of stages towards a final culmination. I affirm that the Christian life plays a decisive role in the divine plan of salvation, although it is not its base or source. (*Crisis of Piety*, 33–34)

79. Bloesch, *Crisis of Piety*, 25. A few pages later Bloesch articulates what this paradoxical marriage means. He states, "This means that the predestined can be properly described only as those who seek for help. The sanctified can be understood only as those who obey. The inverse of these two propositions can also be affirmed and are equally in accord with biblical thinking" (28).

80. It is worth noting that according to Bloesch, these two sets of corresponding dimensions are correlative in the process of salvation, but not strictly chronological. Bloesch stresses that this diagram does not establish a strict chronology of the order

ordo seeks to uphold the critical role of both God and humanity in the work of restoring their relationship, he does give priority to God's action. At its most fundamental level "our salvation is *in* the Son . . . *from* the Father and *through* the Holy Spirit."[81] Bloesch is concerned to emphasize this divine priority in the paradoxical marriage of his two orders when he states,

> This position must not be confused with synergism. In our view God not only takes the initiative, but He also follows through. Yet man is active also from the beginning to the end. The temporal order describes man's activity; the divine order refers only to God's activity. But it is important to note that man's activity is grounded in God's activity. Predestination is nothing else but divine election through human decision. Yet man's decision rests not on free will but rather free grace.[82]

Bloesch's concern to ground human activity in divine activity is intended to safeguard against an error he named earlier: grounding salvation in the Christian life. Bloesch resists this error by giving priority to God's action in the *ordo*. Salvation is grounded in God.

With proper priority given to divine action, Bloesch now turns his attention to human activity. According to Bloesch, both sides of this two-sided, four-dimensional *ordo*, must be held together in paradoxical tension: his goal is to hold together the first priority, God's work, and the second priority, the human person's response.[83] Here, we begin to see the integral role of the Christian life in salvation. As Colyer and Weborg rightly

---

of salvation, rather, "there is a chronology in both God's acts and man's responses, but God's time and man's time are not on the same level" (*Crisis of Piety*, 26). Bloesch states just a chapter later, "Salvation is not simply an event or act but a process or movement which has a beginning and an end" (35). In "Evangelical Spirituality" found in *Spirituality East & West*, Bloesch argues that justification, sanctification, and glorification mirror the progressive threefold stages in Catholicism, purgation, illumination, and union, for evangelicals: "Justification, sanctification, and glorification might be said to be the three stages of evangelical spirituality. It is interesting to compare these with the three stages of Catholic mystical spirituality—purgation, illumination, and union" (*Spirituality East & West*, 176).

81. Bloesch, *Crisis of Piety*, 27. This is a rare occasion in which Bloesch moves to appeal to the doctrine of the Trinity as a framing reality for articulating doctrine. While his doctrine of the Trinity holds a primarily epistemological thrust throughout his corpus, here we find appeal to its ontological force in governing a proper understanding of the *ordo salutis*.

82. Bloesch, *Crisis of Piety*, 28.

83. Bloesch, *Crisis of Piety*, 28.

note, "By holding the divine and human in paradoxical tension Bloesch argues that the Christian life is not simply a pointer to a salvation already accomplished."[84] Colyer and Weborg are correct in their assessment, but more can be said here regarding Bloesch's use of the language of "paradox."

Bloesch's "paradox" of divine and human action in salvation is not by necessity a conceptual paradox.[85] Bloesch states, "A paradox in the context of biblical faith is not a logical contradiction but a confrontation with the mystery of God's revealing action in human history—a mystery that defies human imagination even while throwing light on the human condition."[86]

---

84. Colyer and Weborg, "Bloesch's Doctrine of the Christian Life," 155.

85. Hasel makes a reasonable argument that Bloesch's understanding of paradox is inherited from Kierkegaard: "Kierkegaard's emphasis on the paradoxical nature of truth is repeatedly reflected in Bloesch's theology" (Hasel, "Scripture in the Theologies," 277). Hasel is correct that Bloesch is influenced by Kierkagaard. Bloesch states, "My ancestral tree from a theological perspective includes . . . Kierkegaard" (*Essentials of Evangelical Theology*, 1:4). Hasel, goes on to argue that Bloesch not only uses Kierkegaard's notion of paradox, but follows Kierkegaard in his companion "doctrine that the truth is subjectivity" (Hasel, "Scripture in the Theologies," 277). I disagree with Hasel on this point. Bloesch is at pains to avoid a subjectivist account. Specific to Kierkegaard, Bloesch states:

> It was Kierkegaard who through the use of an existential dialectic and the language of paradox helped to safeguard the reality of mystery and transcendence in Christian faith in a time when rationalism and immanentism practically reigned supreme in both philosophy and theology. Yet by focusing so much on the infinite distance between God and humanity, he failed to do justice to the indwelling Christ and the sanctifying and illuminating work of the Holy Spirit, which leads one into a deeper appreciation of the truth of the Christian message. . . . The theology of paradox needs to be superseded by a theology of Word and Spirit in which the light of God's truth breaks through our present darkness, so that paradox does not simply mark the limitations of reason but facilitates the appropriation of the wisdom and power of Christ by the company of the committed. (*Theology of Word & Spirit*, 65–66)

86. Bloesch, *Theological Notebook*, 5:8. This particular definition offered by Bloesch reflects an influence from Kierkegaard. Bloesch's particular interest in Kierkegaard's understanding of paradox appears to be focused on Kierkegaard's famous work *Fear and Trembling* (Bloesch, *Theology of Word & Spirit*, 286). In particular, Kierkegaard's section entitled, "Is There an Absolute Duty to God?," where he discusses what he calls the "paradox of faith" seems to be in view for Bloesch (Kierkegaard, *Fear and Trembling*, 68–81). I believe Sylvia Walsh's outline of Kierkegaard's view of paradox will help to highlight some of the commonalities between Bloesch and Kierkegaard:

> According to Kierkegaard, paradox is a limit concept that constitutes the passion of thought in its drive to discover that which thought cannot think. When the understanding (*Forstanden*) comes up against that which it cannot comprehend, it must either will its own downfall in recognition of

Applying this account of paradox to soteriology, Bloesch states, "The paradox of salvation must not be pressed in a direction that either compromises divine sovereignty or subverts human responsibility."[87] Bloesch uses the language of paradox to achieve a particular end. Rather than striving for conceptual comprehension of the mysterious relation of divine and human action in salvation, Bloesch instead appeals to the notion of paradox to uphold the apparent tension between divine and human agency.[88] For Bloesch, the language of paradox points to the divine-human encounter that defines the Christian life. It is a paradox of experience in the dynamic divine-human encounter.[89] The Christian life is a personal experience of the paradoxical relation of God's action and human action.

> an absolute difference that cannot be grasped (resulting in the happy passion of faith) or else take affront at its offense, declaring the paradox to be foolishness. In either case, Kierkegaard claims, the Absolute Paradox is not something discovered by the understanding, but it announces itself as a paradox to the understanding. In itself, the Absolute Paradox is not absurd, nor is it absurd to the Christian believer; only from the standpoint of the understanding does the Absolute Paradox appear as the absurd so that the understanding may grasp the fact that it cannot be understood. The most that the understanding can do is to acknowledge that the Absolute Paradox is. In Kierkegaard's view, however, the Absolute Paradox does not constitute a logical contradiction but rather a qualitative contradiction based on the infinite difference between God and being an individual human person. (Walsh, "Paradox," 347)

87. Bloesch, *Theological Notebook*, 5:68–69.

88. Bloesch states, "Our task as theologians is not to penetrate or resolve the central paradox of faith but to highlight it, to show that reason remains confounded by it" (Bloesch, *Theological Notebook*, 5:70). Bloesch also states, "I heartily endorse this admirable definition of 'paradox' by Willis Elliott: 'In a paradox, two incommensurables are put "side by side," perhaps both true, one counterintuitive to the other, the along "side" ness contrary to expectation, the tension not logically resolvable' *Elliot Thinksheets* (Cragville, MA, Jan. 2003) 3142" (5:163).

89. My argument here is supported by Bloesch's use of paradox language elsewhere:

> Holiness is a paradox that transcends reason rather than a proposition that reinforces reason. In this context a paradox is an affirmation that appears to be contradictory but makes some sense when it is more thoroughly examined. Even when we discern the nuances of meaning that paradox embraces, there is still residue of mystery that can never be rationally assimilated. In the themes that I am probing in this book there always remains a tension between the two sides of the polarity in question—one that is never fully resolved. Holiness is paradoxical because it is both God's work and our work. It is God's work in and through and sometimes over against our effort and labors. Holiness is God coming down to our level and at the same time humanity being raised to God's level. Moreover, the way of ascent is also the

Bloesch not only shapes the *ordo salutis* "paradoxically" but also argues that these paradoxical components of the *ordo salutis* are correlative.[90] As the diagram above demonstrates, each component of the temporal order correlates to a component in the eternal order. For example, "seeking for help" corresponds to "predestination," and "obedience in faith" corresponds to "sanctification." There is a particular human response in the temporal order that is ordinarily and fittingly connected to particular components of divine action in the eternal order of salvation. However, this correlative feature of his two-order schema is not rigid. Bloesch views the components of the *ordo* as "interacting" realities. By "interacting," Bloesch seeks to articulate that these are not hermetically sealed realities. By way of illustration, Bloesch states, "Seeking for help is included in repentance, obedience, and even perfect love. Predestination is included and realized in justification, sanctification, and glorification."[91]

Bloesch's correlative account of the *ordo* is designed to ward off an error he has already named: separating the Christian life and salvation. This is demonstrated in his unwavering commitment to the role of human activity in the eternal-temporal *ordo*. While God's action is given priority in the *ordo*, human participation remains necessary. Predestination, justification, sanctification, and glorification are all gifts of God, and yet their blessing cannot be fully realized apart from human reception and retention. Once again, the material force of the Christian life shows up in Bloesch's principle of correlation in the *ordo*. Faith and obedience are indispensable to justification and sanctification.

Along with the correlative feature of Bloesch's account of the *ordo salutis*, Bloesch holds that each part of the *ordo* is transhistorical. Bloesch argues that there are three tenses in salvation—past, present, and future. Bloesch holds that all four dimensions of the eternal order can properly be understood in all three tenses. We read, "Not only salvation itself, but every facet of salvation participates in all three dimensions of time. Election, justification, sanctification, and perfection are all to be found in the

---

way of descent. We find God not by aiming for the highest, but by descending to the lowest. (*Paradox of Holiness*, 3)

Notice here that Bloesch appeals to the paradox of divine and human action once again, but this time directly points it to the Christian life. The paradox of holiness is the domain in which the paradox of divine and human action is played out, precisely because it is the domain of the divine-human encounter.

90. See Bloesch, *Christian Life and Salvation*, 27.
91. Bloesch, *Christian Life and Salvation*, 26.

past, present, and future."[92] Bloesch's construal of the *ordo* in this manner demonstrates the material pressure of the Christian life on his doctrine of salvation. How it is that a component of the order, such as justification, can "participate" in the past and the present is of particular interest.[93]

According to Bloesch, the *past tense* of salvation places an emphasis on the historically objective reality of God's saving activity. Here, the focus is on the person and work of Jesus Christ within the broader biblical narrative of salvation history. As a result, the *ordo salutis* rests upon the *historia salutis*. For Bloesch the *present tense* of salvation places an emphasis on the appropriation of the work of Christ in our lives now by the Holy Spirit. As Bloesch states, "It is not only the perfected life of Christ in the past but the faithful life of the believer in the present that makes salvation effectual."[94] It is noteworthy that Bloesch uses the language of making "salvation effectual" to articulate what a faithful life entails. In this sense the Christian life is the arena of every part of the *ordo salutis*. Components of the *ordo*, traditionally understood as past, objective events, become present ongoing events brought to their completion in the Christian's life of obedience. The Christian life is the location in which the whole of salvation is fought for and maintained. Bloesch's construal of all the components of the *ordo* as both past and present realities means that the life of obedience is a life of participatory appropriation of the accomplished work of Christ.

Bloesch's paradoxical, correlative, transhistorical account of soteriology demonstrates the material influence of the Christian life in salvation. These unique features of his account emphasize the importance of human agency, tie specific features of the Christian life to the eternal components of the *ordo*, and position the present life of the Christian as the arena of salvation. In closing, I briefly demonstrate how this material influence impacts Bloesch's account of one noteworthy component of the *ordo salutis*—justification.

The doctrine of justification traditionally viewed as a divine act of determination and declaration is integrally bound to the human acts of repentance and faith. Bloesch does not deny that justification is an objective "event in which God declares us righteous because of the perfect sacrifice of

---

92. Bloesch, *Christian Life and Salvation*, 43–44.

93. While I do not explore the future tense of salvation here, it is worth briefly noting what it means for Bloesch. The future tense grounds a properly eschatological orientation applied to salvation, such that a hope remains of "final justification and eternal life with the saints in glory" (Bloesch, *Christian Life and Salvation*, 43).

94. Bloesch, *Christian Life and Salvation*, 43.

Jesus Christ on the cross and his glorious resurrection."[95] In fact, he strikes a decidedly traditional Reformed note in arguing that justification is not, "simply an event that initiates a process of salvation: it is the event on which our salvation is forever based."[96] And yet, for Bloesch it is the enduring nature of this event that provides space for the temporal or human side, of justification. While affirming a Reformed emphasis on the nature of justification, as divine determination and declaration, Bloesch's view of the *ordo* embraces subjective experience, pushing against a Reformed propensity to assert objectivity at the expense of a lived reality.[97]

For Bloesch the event of justification, accomplished in the eternal *ordo*, must be experienced in the temporal *ordo*. In other words, justification is ultimately realized in the Christian life. As Bloesch states, "we need to make experiential contact with this redemptive work if it is to be effective in our lives."[98] This experiential contact is not merely an assent to belief nor a moment of reception, but rather an ongoing reality of the Christian life. It is precisely because the Christian remains a sinner, even though the Christian has been declared righteous, that he or she must continue to experience his/her justification as he/she lives a life of repentance, faith, and obedience. By faith, the Christian continues to embrace God's declaration of righteousness. By repentance, the Christian receives with gratitude the justifying work of Christ in his/her life. By obedience, the Christian grows in holiness, and as such, appropriates his/her justification. In the Christian life the call to seek for help, to obey God, to keep the faith, and to repent of sin are all interactively part of the Christian's devotion to protect and preserve his/her salvation.[99]

---

95. Bloesch, *Jesus Christ*, 180.

96. Bloesch, *Jesus Christ*, 180.

97. "Against that kind of Reformed theology that speaks only of extrinsic justification, I maintain that salvation is realized in both the work of God and the decision of man. Its locus is both the cross of Christ and the Christian life. Indeed, salvation cannot be said to have occurred apart from the obedience of faith" (Bloesch, *Crisis of Piety*, 114). In a later work Bloesch balances this line of argumentation. He states, "We are not co-redeemers in procuring the light of salvation, but we are co-workers in manifesting this light. Christian practice is the proof and consequence of authentic discipleship (John 15:8)" (*Essentials of Evangelical Theology*, 1:32).

98. Bloesch, *Jesus Christ*, 178.

99. Bloesch, *Essentials of Evangelical Theology*, 1:30–31. Bloesch maintains a belief that salvation can be lost, and it is a turn he makes throughout his corpus: "Our obedience is not salvific, but our disobedience threatens our salvific status. Our salvation is a free gift of God, but our salvation can be imperiled through arrogance and sloth" (*Holy Spirit*, 324).

The Paradox of Salvation

In my exploration of the material pressure the Christian life has on Bloesch's doctrine of salvation, a repeated theme of paradox surfaced. The distinctiveness of this feature of Bloesch's soteriology demands further consideration. Bloesch refers to this as the "paradox of salvation" which "expresses the coincidence of divine and human freedom."[100] I noted that Bloesch's language of paradox was a pointer to the critical role of the Christian life in salvation. The goal of salvation is the divine-human encounter of the Christian life, and a genuine encounter requires the integrity of both divine and human agency to be upheld. Bloesch seeks to bring the divine and human together as much as possible. To this end, Bloesch employs Emil Brunner's theological concept of "theoanthropocentric" to fully articulate the integrated relationship of divine and human agency.[101] Here, we see Bloesch's pietistic emphasis on the human person's responsibility to "work out one's salvation" (Phil 2:12), and his commitment to a Reformed emphasis on the primacy of divine action in salvation.[102]

---

100. Bloesch, *Christian Life and Salvation*, 127. We find this repeated emphasis on the paradox of salvation in *Essentials of Evangelical Theology*: "The paradox of salvation might be expressed in this way: only the person who is transformed by divine grace can make a positive response to God's gracious invitation, but only the one who does make such a response is indeed transformed by grace" (*Essentials of Evangelical Theology*, 1:202).

101. Bloesch, *Spirituality Old & New*, 98. Bloesch states, "We must be careful not to reduce the self to nothingness. We should steer clear of a theocentric objectivism that severs the glory of God from any human happiness and well-being. We should neither elevate the self unduly nor demean it unnecessarily but see it in its proper perspective" (98). In *The Crisis of Piety* we find Bloesch employing Brunner's term with constructive force: "Biblical piety will be centered upon the cross of Christ, for it is there that our salvation was procured. But such piety will also concern itself with the bearing of the cross by believers. It will be at the same time fully theocentric and radically anthropocentric, since it is related to both the glory of God and the restoration and well-being of humanity" (*Crisis of Piety*, 6). In *The Holy Spirit* Bloesch repeats this paradoxical embrace of theoanthropocentrism: "Christianity is not exclusively theocentric but theoanthropocentric. It seeks not only the exaltation of God but also the restoration and transfiguration of humanity" (*Holy Spirit*, 332).

102. Bloesch outlines this distinctively Reformed emphasis in the introduction to *The Christian Life and Salvation*:

> In this ecumenical era there is a need to re-examine the role of the Christian life in our salvation. Whereas Catholic and evangelical theologians agree that the Christian life is the response of the Christian to the salvation won for us by Christ, they tend to differ on how such a life is related to the appropriation and fulfillment of this salvation. The Reformation concern has

In his mature theological writing Bloesch refers to the divine and human side of this paradox via the language of "objective" and "subjective," language I have briefly employed in my analysis of the influence of the doctrine of the Christian life on the doctrine of salvation. Bloesch states, salvation is "to be understood as objective-subjective rather than fundamentally objective ... or predominately subjective."[103] As Fred Sanders observes, for Bloesch, "Salvation ... has to be described in a way that rejects false dichotomies, and does so even at the cost of resorting to the language of paradox; it is simultaneously objective and subjective, or, as Bloesch often prefers, one single complex hyphenated reality: objective-subjective."[104] Sanders rightly asserts that Bloesch's paradox of salvation can be described as an objective-subjective account of salvation. What does this mean? Sanders continues,

> Salvation is a complex unified reality that pulls in two directions at once: the theologian wants to say that it is a finished work then and there, but also that it is a present reality here and now. Salvation "then and there" means objectively for us in Christ; but salvation "here and now" means subjectively in us by the Spirit.[105]

Bloesch wishes to retain the "then and there" salvific accomplishment of Christ, and at the same time hold onto the "here and now," working out of that salvation by the Spirit in the Christian life. As I have argued, Bloesch wants to uphold both past and present tenses of salvation. This is in evidence throughout Bloesch's theological project.

For example, in the second volume of Bloesch's *Essentials of Evangelical Theology* we encounter a more developed expression of this paradoxical understanding of divine and human agency coupled with a commitment to the unbinding relation of the Christian life and salvation. There we read, "only the person who is transformed by divine grace can make a positive

---

been to preserve the divine initiative in the whole process of salvation; the Catholic concern has been the pursuit of holiness. Whereas the Reformers held that glory belongs to God alone (*soli Deo Gloria*) and that salvation is only by His grace, Catholic theologians have emphasized the need for a holy life. In Reformation theology the justification of God is the guiding motif; in Catholic thought the accent is placed on the transformation and sanctification of man. (*Christian Life and Salvation*, 13)

103. Bloesch, *Theology of Word & Spirit*, 14–15.
104. Sanders, "Saved by Word and Spirit," 83.
105. Sanders, "Saved by Word and Spirit," 84.

DEFINING THE CHRISTIAN LIFE

response to God's gracious invitation, but only the one who does make such a response is indeed transformed by grace."[106] Bloesch uses the language of "grace" to discuss divine agency and "response" to discuss human agency. Upholding the paradox of salvation is critical in order to elude two errors threatening the doctrine of salvation: monergism and synergism.[107] These two errors of agency relatedness correspond to the two errors discussed earlier regarding the relation of the Christian life and salvation: grounding salvation in the Christian life and separating the Christian life from salvation. Bloesch defines these two errors, putting them in contrast with his paradoxical approach:

> The first heresy makes God alone the actor and reduces man to an automaton. The synergistic heresy affirms that man works alongside of God in the gaining of his salvation. The paradox asserts that it is not Christ in and of Himself but Christ in man who accomplishes our salvation; it is effectuated not by the independent or autonomous man who works with Christ but by the Spirit-empowered man, the man in Christ.[108]

According to Bloesch, monergism privileges divine agency in salvation to such a degree that human agency is rendered irrelevant.[109] In short, it is

---

106. Bloesch, *Essentials of Evangelical Theology*, 2:202.

107. Bloesch, *Essentials of Evangelical Theology*, 2:128.

108. Bloesch, *Essentials of Evangelical Theology*, 2:129. Echoing this distinction, Bloesch uses the language of "grace" and "faith" to make the same point:

> Our position is that we must affirm both the sovereignty of grace and the responsibility of believers. The two errors to be avoided are the following: that one is saved exclusively by the work of grace upon him thereby not including or allowing for personal faith and decision in the salvific process; and that one is saved by grace and free will together so that salvation depends partly on grace and partly on free will. (2:201)

109. Bloesch provides an example of an account of salvation that has monergistic leanings and expresses in more detail his criticism of such a position. In a brief closing appendix in *The Holy Spirit*, Bloesch demonstrates what an overly objective account of salvation looks like. The appendix is titled "Theology of the Cross." It is a brief but critical engagement with theologian Michael Horton's early work *In the Face of God*. After succinctly articulating the primary arguments of Horton's project, Bloesch articulates Horton's central concern as he understands it. Bloesch states, "In place of a theology of religious experience Horton champions a theology of the cross—centered not in signs and wonders that confound the imagination but in historical events that remain true even when the message they carry is rejected. In a theology of the cross the Christian is both a sinner and righteous at the same time" (*Holy Spirit*, 336). According to Bloesch, Horton's concern is a pietistic faith in which experience is a primary vehicle of revelation,

an all-too objectivist account of agency. Conversely, synergism privileges human agency in such a manner that the sufficiency of divine agency is neutered. In short, it is an all-too subjectivist account of salvation.[110] In

and the Spirit's work is unmoored from the objective, historical work of Christ's incarnation and ministry. In response to Horton's position, Bloesch communicates where he stands on such matters. Bloesch's response is instructive:

> The reader will not be surprised that I stand with Horton in his trenchant warnings against Gnosticism and his impassioned call for worship that is done in spirit and in truth. At the same time the book leaves me with a profound sense of uneasiness: in correcting one grave imbalance he seems to create another. Horton is to be commended for his indictment of egocentric piety, but does he see the danger on the other side: a religion that disparagers the biblical call to holiness, the cheap grace that subverts human responsibility in working out the implications of salvation in fear and trembling? He defines the gospel as "the announcement of our free justification in Christ." While the declaration of justification belongs to the essence of the gospel, it is not the whole of the gospel, for the gospel includes not only the good news of God's free grace but also the power unto salvation that enables us to live lives of victory over sin (cf. Rom 1:16; 1 Cor 1:18). In Horton's view the reborn Christian must settle for a "partial victory" over sin, and while it is true that sin continues in every Christian, surely the gospel holds out the possibility of total victory over any particular sin, even though this possibility is not always realized in daily life. (*Holy Spirit*, 337)

For Bloesch, Horton's error is not his critique of subjective piety but his overly reactive objective confessionalism. In short, Bloesch is concerned that Horton's appeal to re-center things on the Word has neglected the Spirit. His extrinsic account of the gospel tends toward a rationalistic and propositional faith absent a meaningful account of life in the Spirit. As Bloesch states, "The answer to subjectivism is not objectivism but a theology of divine-human encounter in which truth is both declared from the outside and appropriated from the inside. The answer to experientialism is not creedalism or confessionalism but a theology of Word and Spirit in which truth does not remain external and historical but becomes by the action of the Spirit internal and existential" (338). For Bloesch, Horton's assertion of Reformed roots for his position, and in particular his appeal to Calvin and Luther, fails to recognize the "mystical dimension" that remains in the magisterial Reformers. Horton's "objective revelation," absent an account of subjective existential appropriation of such revelation by the Spirit in individual human hearts by grace through faith, is a failure to recognize the experience of faith which both Calvin and Luther speak of as they discuss the Christian life and sanctification. As Bloesch will go on to say, "a faith without a small dose of mysticism can only grow cold and formalistic" (339).

110. Bloesch is weary of the synergistic approach in which human effort is overly emphasized. Interestingly, the very same word used to provoke a sense of what Bloesch feels is missing in Horton's account, "mysticism," will now be used by Bloesch in a derisive manner as he critiques the synergistic error. We find the criticism of this error within the same volume of his seven-volume dogmatic theology:

> It is fair to say that the predominant stance in Christian mysticism is synergism: God does his part and we do our part in procuring our salvation.

contrast to monergism and synergism, Bloesch positions his paradoxical account as the solution to maintain the properly integrated relation of divine and human agency. On Bloesch's account the *objective* accomplishment of salvation by divine agency was expressed with human agency in the incarnation. Likewise, the *subjective* effectuation of salvation by human beings is possible only by the power of the Holy Spirit.[111]

Bloesch's paradox of salvation is designed for integration, and as it integrates it also serves to maintain order. As we saw in his constructive account of the *ordo*, divine agency always precedes human agency, both

> Before we are illumined, we must undergo self-purification, which makes us receptive to the Spirit. This implies that Christians are co-redeemers with Christ, since we attain eternal blessedness with the aid of the Spirit. (Bloesch, *Holy Spirit*, 96)

This assessment is a culminating argument furnished by Bloesch on the heels of a brief survey of the synergistic propensity found in several mystical writers, such as Meister Eckhart, John Chrysostom, and the author of *The Cloud of Unknowing*. Interestingly, if we look elsewhere in Bloesch's *The Holy Spirit* volume for a critique of synergism we discover that it is levied against his own household: "A more serious problem with Pietism was its synergistic theology in which we cooperate with prevenient or preparatory grace in coming to a saving knowledge of God in Christ" (Bloesch, *Holy Spirit*, 32). Bloesch's response to this Pietistic error is quite clear: "In my theology we are moved by prevenient grace to seek for salvation, but we are not drawn into the kingdom of God except through the transforming work of the Spirit of God within us. We do not cooperate with grace in facilitating the new birth, but we respond to grace in bearing witness to the new birth" (32). Always cautious of a slide into subjectivism and anthropocentrism, Bloesch warns that his own tribe has often fallen prey to this fatal error. We find this concern all throughout his corpus. Indeed, earlier in Bloesch's writing career we read:

> If there has been a shift in my perspective, I believe more strongly than before that a theology of Christian commitment must be united with a theology of the Word of God if it is not to lapse into subjectivism and anthropocentrism. The focus on personal piety must never supplant the more basic focus on the life, death, and resurrection of Jesus Christ. The bane of classical Pietism was that it sought to cultivate the Christian life without a corresponding emphasis on the decision of God for humanity in Jesus Christ. (*Crisis of Piety*, xii)

Notice, the basic focus must be on the objective work of Christ Jesus. If the emphasis on the experience of God in the Christian life is to have any value, it must be grounded in this. The subjective and objective must be held together, but this does not mean that the objective does not hold proper priority as we have seen earlier. Divine action governs but does not void human action.

111. These two dangers of objectivism and subjectivism, and Bloesch's solution of an objective-subjective account of salvation and agency, will be revisited in more thorough investigation in chapter 3 by exploring the implications of these two errors in regard to the doctrine of revelation.

historically and theologically. This paradoxical ordering, divine then human agency, is maintained by Bloesch throughout his theological career.[112] The language Bloesch employs to solidify this proper ordering of agency is striking:

> What I am upholding is a monergy that embraces synergy. God's grace brings about the desired effect-faith and obedience, but it does this by animating and motivating the human subject to believe and obey. Synergism as such means that we contribute to our salvation through our own power, that God does some and we do some. We need to avoid both monergism and synergism by maintaining that God does all-but in and through human action. We believe and overcome through the power of grace, not through our own power-even in part.[113]

In familiar rejection of the two errors, monergism and synergism, Bloesch labels his integrative ordering as "monergy that embraces synergy." Divine agency is given primacy, but the effect of divine action is expressed in and through human faith and obedience. Or, to use the language of Bloesch's account of the *ordo*, in accomplishing salvation, God's action in the eternal ordo is necessarily tied to the Christian's action in the temporal ordo.

Bloesch's paradox of salvation seeks to maintain an integrated yet ordered account of divine and human agency in salvation. As Elmer Colyer states, "Bloesch wants to keep divine agency and human agency in balance in Christian life and salvation."[114] The language of paradox is employed specifically to communicate this "balance." While balance is maintained, Bloesch's goal is clear. He wishes to maintain the indispensability of the

---

112. For example, "Synergism is of course a real danger, but we must also recognize the complementary danger of monergism in which God is portrayed as the sole actor in our salvation. God is the sole source and mainspring of all redemptive action, but he is not the sole actor. He is the sole efficient cause of salvation but not the only causal factor in salvation. There are also secondary and instrumental causes that have to be taken into account" (Bloesch, *Essentials of Evangelical Theology*, 1:201).

113. Bloesch, *Church*, 62. We hear a very similar note in Bloesch's earlier personal theological reflections. In the opening reflection of Bloesch's second *Theological Notebook* he states, "Against orthodox Calvinism I maintain that we are saved not only *through* faith but also *by* faith. This is to say, we are not only passive recipients of the grace of God but also active participants in this grace. Faith involves not only God's gift but our decision as well. Nevertheless, our decision is made possible by God's Spirit; our cooperation with God is grounded not in our free will but solely in free grace" (Bloesch, *Theological Notebook*, 2:1). There is a consistency of thought demonstrated in these early theological reflections and later formal theological statements.

114. Colyer, *Evangelical Theology in Transition*, 153.

Christian life in salvation. Bloesch is concerned that human agency will be consumed by talk of divine action. As Bloesch will go on to argue, "The Holy Spirit himself is indeed the sanctifier, the one who works sanctity within us. But we too have a role—not in the creation of sanctity but in its manifestation and proclamation. Theologians often err by overemphasizing divine sovereignty and minimizing human responsibility in salvation."[115] Bloesch's interest is not in human agency as such, but rather the life of the Christian as directed and empowered by the Holy Spirit.[116] All to say, his abiding emphasis on the Spirit empowered role of human agency in salvation reflects a determination to maintain the Christian life as the appropriating arena of salvation. As Bloesch firmly asserts, "The fact that the free gift of salvation demands not simply an outward intellectual assent or a voluntary submission to the Gospel but total commitment and lifelong discipleship under the cross was lost sight of in the mainstream of Protestantism."[117] For Bloesch the salvation achieved in Christ must be "appropriated" in a life of discipleship. "It is not enough," says Bloesch, "to accept Jesus Christ as Savior. We must also acknowledge him as Lord and follow him as our Example and Pattern for living."[118] An account of the gospel, according to Bloesch, that diminishes the critical role of the Christian life in salvation is a gospel of cheap grace.

The Threat Mysticism

Throughout Bloesch's constructive theological work he repeatedly clarifies his doctrinal positions by surveying and analyzing competing options. While often surveying a variety of positions, he consistently chooses one view with which to engage in greater detail. Bloesch applies this methodological approach to the doctrine of the Christian life. As he engages the doctrine of the Christian life throughout his dogmatic project, one particular competing view is repeatedly engaged—mysticism. Bloesch's engagement with mysticism is primarily one of pastoral concern for the church.[119] In Bloesch's mind, mysticism is a dangerous, competing account of the Christian life.

---

115. Bloesch, *Holy Spirit*, 329.
116. Bloesch, *Christian Life and Salvation*, 129.
117. Bloesch, *Essentials of Evangelical Theology*, 2:207.
118. Bloesch, *Essentials of Evangelical Theology*, 2:208.
119. At times this is because another view poses a threat, and so he polemically

I offer a detailed analysis of Bloesch's account of mysticism for three reasons. First, for Bloesch, mysticism represents an anti-evangelical account of the Christian life. Therefore, as a contrastive account of spirituality, analyzing mysticism can provide clarity regarding Bloesch's explicitly evangelical account. Second, I repeatedly appeal to his divergence from mysticism throughout this project. By offering a detailed analysis of his account of mysticism here, I hope to inform later discussion of the subject with proper meaning and significance. Third, as a historical phenomenon, mysticism is "exceedingly difficult to define, like the word 'religion.'"[120] As such, accurately articulating Bloesch's definition of mysticism is critically important. Bloesch's account of mysticism is distinctive. According

---

identifies its key errors with a pastoral concern of protecting the church. Sometimes it is because another view, while different, has been a source of formative influence in his own constructive development. At other times it is because a view is similar enough to his own that he believes providing clear lines of demarcation is important in order to clarify the distinctiveness of his own view. Of course, in some cases it is for multiple reasons.

120. Jones, "Mysticism, Human and Divine," 18. One source that provides a particularly helpful grid for mapping the different approaches to mysticism is *Christian Mysticism: An Introduction to Contemporary Theoretical Approaches*. There, the authors provide a list of four contemporary "theoretical approaches" to Christian mysticism (Magill et al., *Christian Mysticism*, 2). In short, they present four hermeneutical methods of engaging the texts of mysticism. They define these four approaches as "feminist, perennialist, performative and contextualist" (2–3). According to Magill et al., the *feminist* approach argues the vast majority of contemporary methods of interpreting mystical texts have been detrimentally masculine. Therefore, the feminist reading has sought to correct an overly masculine prioritization of mystical texts and to place emphasis on female mystical writers. It has also endeavored to communicate a distinctively female reading of mystical texts that highlights common blind spots in contemporary interpretation dominated by men (18). The *perennialist* approach views mysticism through the lens of shared mystical experience which has forged a written tradition of expression (10). Texts are engaged with an eye for the experience they articulate. The *contextualist* approach, on the other hand, views mysticism not so much through the "post-experiential reports of mystics," but instead through the "pre-experiential mediating condition" (12). In other words, contextualists are not primarily interested in the communicated consequence of mystical experience but instead the context in which such experiences have occurred, and mystical texts have been written. Lastly, the *performative* mode of analysis rejects the notion that experience is the driving force shaping mystical texts. Ultimately, this mode of interpretation argues that the language of mystical texts is not merely the raw reflections of ineffable experience with the divine but rather performative in function, designed to "communicate an epistemological message (that is, knowledge about God)" (15). In light of Magill et al.'s four theoretical approaches, Bloesch's approach might be identified as a combination of perennialist and contextualist. Bloesch believes mystical texts ought to be read as expressions of spiritual experience, but likewise he is keen to identify the philosophical and/or theological context which undergirds these texts.

to Bloesch, there are two species of mysticism—classical and new. In what follows I analyze Bloesch's definition of both classical mysticism and new mysticism, and I investigate the danger, Bloesch believes, these deviant accounts of the Christian life pose to the church.

Classical Mysticism

Classical mysticism is the primary form of mysticism that Bloesch constructively engages and critiques. For Bloesch, it represents the greatest historical threat to an evangelical account of the Christian life marked by personal divine-human encounter. For all this, Bloesch's analysis of classical mysticism is nuanced. Classical mysticism can refer to either a direct experience of God's presence, or it can refer to a "system of thought, a philosophy of life, a type of religion."[121]

While this distinction between experiential and philosophical mysticism may seem both historically and textually arbitrary, it serves his constructive needs well; a text may articulate a particular experience but also give expression to a certain philosophical commitment at the same time. The distinction allows him to reject parts of the mystical tradition without losing the entirety as a resource in developing an evangelical spirituality.[122]

---

121. Bloesch, *Ground of Certainty*, 141.

122. Bloesch's proposed two modes of mysticism has potential shortcomings. As Bernard McGinn rightly argues, "Although it may be possible to make theoretical distinctions between mysticism and mystical theology, I believe that it is dangerous to separate the two in the history of Christianity" (McGinn, *Foundations of Mysticism*, xiii–xiv). McGinn's concern here is fundamentally historical. He goes on to argue, "The fact that the term 'mystical theology' antedated the coining of the term 'mysticism' by over a millennium points us in the right direction for appreciating the complex and unbreakable bonds between mysticism conceived of as a religious way of life and mystical theology" (McGinn, *Foundations of Mysticism*, xiv). Buttressing this point, Magill et al. state, "It is a surprising but significant fact that, while medieval Christian mystics talk about both 'mystical' theology and a 'mystical' sense of scripture, they never talk about 'mysticism' or refer to each other as 'mystics'" (Magill et al., *Christian Mysticism*, 1). Mark McIntosh adds to this argument but focuses attention on the earliest categories of description regarding "mysticism": "Today we often use the term 'mysticism' though this is really something of an academic invention; earlier eras referred to the most intimate and transforming encounter with God as 'contemplation.' It is a term that holds together two elements we often see contrasted as though they were mutually exclusive, namely the affective or loving impulse and the intellectual or knowing impulse" (McIntosh, *Mystical Theology*, 11). And yet, despite this critique, McGinn himself leaves the door open for use of distinctions "theoretically": "Three headings: mysticism as a part or element of religion; mysticism as a process or way of life; and mysticism as an attempt to express a direct consciousness

An Evangelical Spiritual Theology

Bloesch is open to experiential mysticism but is highly critical of mysticism as a philosophical (or theological) system. Ultimately, this distinction leaves open the possibility of a kind of mystical experience within evangelical spirituality, while at the same time it eschews dangerous philosophical underpinnings of classical mysticism that lead to a religious system in opposition to sound Christian doctrine.

This subtle, yet significant, distinction in Bloesch's engagement with classical mysticism is at times lost to readers. Consequently, his rejection of philosophical mysticism can often be seen as a rejection of the tradition outright. More specifically it can be viewed as a rejection of experiential forms of spirituality. For example, in his monograph *Soul Recreation*, Tom Schwanda argues that as a student of Karl Barth, Bloesch follows Barth's "trajectory of resistance to mystical experiences."[123] Schwanda recognizes that Bloesch has a positive account of mysticism in some form but does not follow this trail to see where it leads. Instead, he views it as a hiccup in an otherwise full-throated and clear rejection of mystical spirituality. Schwanda rightly identifies Bloesch's concern with mysticism, as specifically expressed in *Spirituality Old & New*, but he fails to recognize what specific form of mysticism Bloesch critiques.

Bloesch, the pietistic evangelical, is not in principle critical of spiritual experience. In fact, as I demonstrate in the next chapter, he explicitly parts ways with Barth's resistance to a subjective, experiential component to divine revelation. What Bloesch does reject is *classical* mysticism as a resource for evangelical spirituality.[124] In principle, this is not a rejection

---

of the presence of God" (McGinn, *Foundations of Mysticism*, xv–xvi). Such a threefold distinction appears not all that different from Bloesch's twofold distinction.

123. Schwanda, *Soul Recreation*, 216.

124. Bloesch is confident that his rejection of mysticism is in step with the evangelical theological tradition:

> Evangelical theologians have always sought to distinguish faith from mystical religion. Even where the mystical element in Christian spirituality is acknowledged, they have taken pains to point out that Christianity is not mysticism. John Wesley wrote that "all the other enemies of Christianity are triflers: The Mystics are the most dangerous of its enemies. They stab it in the vitals." In the words of Benjamin Warfield: "We may be mystics, or we may be Christians. We cannot be both. And the pretension of being both usually merely veils defection from Christianity." Among other evangelically oriented scholars who have taken a forthright stand against mysticism are Karl Barth, Anders Nygren, Reinhold Niebuhr, Emil Brunner and Friedrich Heiler. (*Ground of Certainty*, 140)

of the spiritual experiences recorded within the mystical tradition but is a rejection of the philosophical system often presupposed by—and therefore expressed through—this tradition. Bloesch specifies his concerns with the philosophy of classical mysticism by identifying four key features which together form a system of thought he believes is in opposition to authentic Christian faith.

First, Bloesch believes mysticism holds to a notion of unmediated encounter with God, referring to it as "an immediate or direct experience of God that may well bypass the ordinary channels of redemption, such as the Word and the sacraments."[125] This direct contact with God is "shrouded in mystery."[126] This unmediated encounter with God underwrites another alarming feature of classical mysticism, namely that "this experience is an encounter with mystery" and is consequently "ineffable."[127] The ineffable quality of spiritual experience, casts knowledge of God as a kind of "participatory knowledge" rather than a kind of rational or intellectual knowledge.[128] For Bloesch, a key aspect of this mode of knowledge is the apophatic grammar of negation when speaking of the divine-human encounter.[129]

---

125. Bloesch, *Spirituality Old & New*, 35. Bloesch states elsewhere, "The hallmark of mystical religion is a direct experience of God apart from external mediation" (*Struggle of Prayer*, 101). Bloesch continues by highlighting a few exemplars of this approach: "In the words of Ruysbroeck: 'The inward man performs his introspection simply . . . above all activity and . . . all virtues, through a simple inward gazing in the fruition of love. And here he meets God without intermediary.' 'God', Eckhart declares, 'acts without instrumentality and without ideas.' Schleirmacher views the mystical experience as 'immediate self-consciousness'" (101). In his seven-volume dogmatics Bloesch addresses this concern about mysticism within his *The Holy Spirit* volume: "Mysticism involves a direct experience of God, which means that the mediation of the church can be bypassed. Moreover, mysticism calls us to trust in a God beyond the reach of the sense, and this implies beyond outward signs and rites" (*Holy Spirit*, 92).

126. Bloesch, *Spirituality Old & New*, 51.

127. Bloesch, *Crisis of Piety*, 84. Bloesch echoes this line elsewhere: "Mysticism connotes a direct experience of the divine presence, one that is ineffable and ecstatic" (*Holy Spirit*, 91).

128. Bloesch, *Spirituality Old & New*, 35.

129. Bloesch summarizes the ineffable feature of classical mysticism: "We can have negative knowledge of God, but not positive knowledge or univocal knowledge. We can say what God is not, but we cannot comprehend his majesty. God is beyond reason, but he is not irrational. We can have an immediate awareness of God but not a rational grasp of his being and his attributes" (*Spirituality Old & New*, 51). Bloesch expresses his concerns regarding the Neoplatonic influence in classical mysticism and its positing a God that can be spoken of only in the form of negation. He states, "We must, of course, avoid the temptation of the neo-Platonic type of mysticism where God is so far beyond

Second, classical mysticism, according to Bloesch, presents a "God above God—the ground of being beyond all particular beings. Showing the influence of Neoplatonism, mystics posit a God beyond all thought, beyond growth, decay and death."[130] The mystical tradition here has sought to establish a doctrine of God unencumbered by unbecoming anthropomorphisms.[131] For Bloesch, the Neo-Platonic propensity of classical mysticism stands in opposition to creaturely titles and categories.[132] He goes on to state, "This is the immutable, impassible God of Greek philosophy, and this God was identified by both Christian mystics and scholastics with the living God of Christian faith."[133] For Bloesch, such notions of God run contrary to classical orthodoxy and its firm commitment to the doctrine of the Trinity.

---

the categories of the understanding that he can be described only in terms of negation" (*Essentials of Evangelical Theology*, 2:281).

130. Bloesch, *Spirituality Old & New*, 51. Bloesch strikes a repeated note in the introductory volume of his dogmatic set: "Among the Christian mystics we discern a similar attempt to rise to the 'God above God,' the undifferentiated unity beyond personality, temporality and individuality" (*Theology of Word & Spirit*, 87). This idea of God being beyond and above devalues creation in Bloesch's mind. As a result, Bloesch believes classical mysticism is given over to a view of spirituality that requires a transcending of the created order to a spiritual realm unencumbered by creaturely realities: "A common understanding in these circles is that the goal in life is to transcend the material and to escape into the spiritual" (*Future of Evangelical Christianity*, 132).

131. Bloesch, *Crisis of Piety*, 84.

132. Bloesch, *Spirituality Old & New*, 51. Bloesch echoes this analysis in greater detail in *The Crisis of Piety*:

> The Neo-Platonic philosopher Plotinus identified god with "the One" that transcends all existence. In mystical literature God is often depicted as being above and beyond being (Gregory of Nyssa, Origen, Eckhart). He is the source and ground of all existence. He is both the world Soul and the core and center of the human soul. He is frequently spoken of as "the undifferentiated unity." He is "above love and affection" (Meister Eckhart). We "cannot even say . . . that he is an objective reality" (Berdyaev). (*Crisis of Piety*, 84)

Bloesch says elsewhere,

> The whole mystical tradition of the church has a neo-Platonic tinge which stresses the immanence of God over his transcendence and thereby frequently ends up in a type of pantheism or panentheism. This is not true of those mystics who sought to preserve the personalistic element in religion, such as Bernard of Clairvaux and Augustine, though it is true of the more radical mystics, such as Angelus Silesius, who envisioned God as the sum total of existence. In this perspective one cannot see God and all things in God until one has himself "become the All." (*Essentials of Evangelical Theology*, 2:243)

133. Bloesch, *Spirituality Old & New*, 51.

DEFINING THE CHRISTIAN LIFE

Bloesch acknowledges that some Christian mystics advance a spirituality that seeks to maintain personal contact with God, and yet their misguided commitment to Neo-Platonic principles ultimately results in positing a mysterious and ineffable deity behind the revealed Triune God.[134] In the end, this mystical account commends a "God beyond the personal and therefore one that contradicts the original vision of Christian faith."[135]

The third feature of classical mysticism that concerns Bloesch is anthropological divination.[136] Mysticism posits a "divine spark implanted in the human heart."[137] As Bloesch states, "In mystical religion and philosophy man is understood as being in basic continuity with God."[138] This collapsing of the divine into the human person, not only generates a distorted anthropology, but likewise also a distorted doctrine of creation. Bloesch states, "When the world is seen as an emanation of God rather than a creation out of nothing (*creation ex nihilo*), the reality of a world distinctly other than God is called into question."[139] In summary, for Bloesch, classical Christian mysticism's insipid pantheism undermines the integrity of the Godhead; by blurring the Creator-creature distinction, it strikes at the heart of what is essential to orthodox Christian faith.

The final feature of classical mysticism is ascension.[140] The mystical account of ascension is tethered to the mystical account of divination just mentioned. Bloesch summarizes this feature,

---

134. "In a mystical monotheism everything concrete disappears in the infinite abyss. God becomes the impersonal Absolute, an undifferentiated substratum, beyond plurality" (Bloesch, *Essentials of Evangelical Theology*, 1:36).

135. Bloesch, *Spirituality Old & New*, 52.

136. Andrew Louth offers a helpful, brief definition of divination: "Deification (or divinization, in Greek: *theosis*): the doctrine that the destiny of humankind, or indeed of the cosmos as a whole, is to share in the divine life, and actually to become God, though by grace rather than by nature. The doctrine, that has become particularly characteristic of Eastern Orthodox theology, developed out of a host of suggestions in the Bible that human engagement with God involves a profound intimacy" (Louth, "Deification," 229).

137. Bloesch, *Crisis of Piety*, 85.

138. Bloesch, *Crisis of Piety*, 85.

139. Bloesch, *Spirituality East & West*, 53.

140. Regarding the concept of ascent in the tradition of mysticism, Greg Peters states, "Another common theme in the history of spirituality is that of spiritual ascent. Making use of images such as Jacob's Ladder and Moses' ascent of Mt. Sinai, Christian spiritual theologians regularly structured their spiritual texts around the ideas of progression and ascent" (Peters, "Spiritual Theology," 85).

An Evangelical Spiritual Theology

> One of the fundamental motifs that runs through almost every kind of mysticism is the ascent to divinity. The hope of the restless spirit to become joined to divinity was already evident in Platonism and Neoplatonism. For Plato the aim of the person's action should be to gain freedom from the bonds of the flesh and to strive with virtue and wisdom "to become like God, even in this life."[141]

The quest to become like God is an ascent of the soul to the divine. The climb of the mystical ladder was often framed in classical mysticism as a three-stage process—purgation, illumination, and union.[142] At the stage of union, which was the final stage, there was an ultimate arrival point envisioned by classical mysticism.[143] Bloesch describes it this way:

> The highest stage within union is called by some mystical writers "spiritual marriage," in which the soul is completely transfigured and upon death goes directly into heaven (without the intermediate state of purgatory). Such a soul is pictured as being totally sanctified or perfected. The final goal is the beatific vision of God, which is generally believed to occur only after death.[144]

The mystical vision of prayer followed a similar logic. Alongside the stages of ascension was an understanding of prayer that was progressive in nature, moving from the more introductory to the meaningful, beginning with petition and moving toward contemplation. Ultimately, the highest form of prayer was "beyond word in which we simply gaze upon the glory and majesty of the holy God."[145] Elsewhere, Bloesch refers to this kind of mystical prayer as "the phenomenon of jubilation—prayer without words or prayer with sighs too deep for words (Rom 8:26)."[146]

---

141. Bloesch, *Spirituality Old & New*, 54.
142. Bloesch, *Holy Spirit*, 93.
143. Bloesch, *Crisis of Piety*, 86.
144. Bloesch, *Crisis of Piety*, 86.
145. Bloesch, *Spirituality Old & New*, 56. Bloesch articulates the difference between biblical spirituality and mystical spirituality born out in their competing forms of prayer in *A Theology of Word & Spirit*: "The gulf between mystical and prophetic religion is similarly striking in the way they conceive of prayer. In mysticism prayer is rising above petition in order to gain an immediate apprehension of the beauty or goodness of God. It is not the pouring out of the soul before God (as in biblical spirituality) but contemplating the divine being" (*Theology of Word & Spirit*, 98).
146. Bloesch, *Holy Spirit*, 95. Bloesch goes on to state that jubilation "is not an actual spoken language but wordless, vocalized prayer. It consists basically of wordless sounds, the utterance of cries and exclamations of joy" (95).

The Threat of Classical Mysticism

Bloesch believes classical mysticism has infected not only the church catholic but also, more specifically, the evangelical church. As a theologian seeking to renew evangelicalism for the sake of renewing the church catholic, this is cause for deep concern. In Bloesch's mind, classical mysticism is an active threat to authentic evangelical spirituality. As Bloesch turns his attention to the evangelical church, he identifies a fusing of "biblical" principles with those of classical mysticism. He repeatedly refers to this blending as the "Biblical-Classical Synthesis."[147] This synthesis of classical mysticism and biblical spirituality has produced an account of spirituality not proper to the Christian faith and especially the evangelical church.

The biblical-classical synthesis produces a version of spirituality directly opposed to Bloesch's account of the Christian life. While Bloesch's vision of encounter with God is informed by the biblical notion of fellowship, biblical-classical spirituality tends to move away from the idea of fellowship and toward notions of divination and comingling. It collapses the two sides of the divine-human encounter into one another such that the personal nature of the encounter is blurred. Yet still, while Bloesch's biblical-personal account is built on God's personal availability by way of his economic operations, biblical-classical spirituality proposes "a God beyond and outside the personal."[148] Instead of focusing on the central themes of redemption and reconciliation, which was critical to Bloesch's evangelical vision of the divine-human encounter, the biblical-classical synthesis tends to reject a traditional account of sin, rendering God's redemptive and reconciling work unmeaningful and unnecessary. While Bloesch's evangelical account of the Christian life is marked by both personal and social obedience, the biblical-classical synthesis mode of spirituality emphasizes the human person's internal spiritual experience to such a degree that the fundamental command to love one's neighbor is marginalized.[149] Finally, in

---

147. Bloesch, *Spirituality Old & New*, 60. I have chosen to follow Bloesch's own terminology here. Admittedly, Bloesch's chosen language of "classical mysticism" and "biblical-classical synthesis" can be difficult to follow given the overlapping language. While the overlapping of language can lead to some confusion for readers, Bloesch is committed to its use for the sake of articulating the concern of comingling between classical mysticism and biblical Christianity. I follow Bloesch's language as I believe it is critical to the nature of his argument. Any location in which I use the language "biblical-classical" refers to the deviant form of spirituality that Bloesch calls "the biblical-classical synthesis."

148. Bloesch, *Crisis of Piety*, 106.

149. Bloesch states, "In mysticism, on the other hand, the service of our neighbor is

opposition to Bloesch's evangelically shaped account of the life of devotion, the biblical-classical account of the Christian life strikes a note of "works righteousness" in which one's devotion and discipline can achieve holiness with the assistance of grace.[150]

As Bloesch examines the evangelical church, he sees this sort of expression of the Christian life operative. As a result, he is deeply concerned about the influence of classical mysticism on evangelical spirituality. According to Bloesch, an evangelical spirituality informed by classical mysticism tends to both depersonalize the divine-human encounter, and to privatize the Christian life to the neglect of social action. In chapter 4, I demonstrate how Bloesch's concerns in this regard specifically show up in the life of prayer. Once again, the concern has less to do with the influence of accounts of mystical experience but more with classical mystical philosophy. In what Bloesch refers to as the biblical-classical synthesis, he identifies a mode of spirituality expressed within the evangelical church that owes its heritage to philosophical mysticism rather than Scripture. While Bloesch acknowledges there are some in church history who have adopted classical mysticism and have maintained a strong enough commitment to biblical principles such that their account of spirituality remains genuinely Christian, he is nonetheless concerned that many have uncritically embraced principles of classical mysticism to the detriment of the Christian life. In the end, Bloesch concludes, "Despite the explicit Christian commitment of so many of the great mystics, it cannot be denied that there is a fundamental incongruity between mysticism and biblical Christianity."[151] For Bloesch then, classical mysticism as a *religious-philosophical system* is incongruent with an evangelical account of the Christian life.

---

considered less important than service to the supreme object or highest good. We serve God in humanity rather than humanity as such" (*Struggle of Prayer*, 102).

150. Bloesch, *Spirituality Old & New*, 60–66. In his *The Holy Spirit* volume Bloesch refers to this as a spirituality of "synergism" in which "God does his part and we do our part in procuring our salvation. Before we are illumined, we must undergo self-purification, which makes us receptive to the Spirit. This implies that Christians are co-redeemers with Christ, since we attain eternal blessedness with the aid of the Spirit" (*Holy Spirit*, 96).

151. Bloesch, *Spirituality Old & New*, 68.

New Mysticism

Along with classical mysticism, Bloesch is concerned with what he calls new mysticism. However, it is important to note that Bloesch spends more time engaging and critiquing classical mysticism in his corpus. Classical mysticism is clearly of greater concern to Bloesch. Consequently, my treatment of new mysticism is briefer. That being said, Bloesch remains concerned with this form of mysticism and similarly its influence on the evangelical church. This form of mysticism poses a threat to an authentically evangelical account of spirituality and must therefore be critically engaged. Perhaps it is the case that, had Bloesch's theological career extended further than it did, he would have engaged new mysticism more. As it stands, at the time of his writing he only viewed it as an emerging threat to evangelicalism.[152]

Bloesch draws a distinction between what he views as classical mysticism and what he identifies as new mysticism.[153] It is easy to miss this distinction, but surrounding context and synonymous terms such as "new age" and "new spirituality" ought to tip us off to this particular mode of mysticism. While "new spirituality" is distinct from classical mysticism, it is nonetheless fitting to refer to it as a form of mysticism itself given its prevailing philosophical principles. Bloesch states, "It can be legitimately described as a secular mysticism."[154]

---

152. In reference to "new mysticism," Bloesch states, "It is incontrovertible that we are witnessing the dawning of a new spirituality" (*Spirituality Old & New*, 101). We read elsewhere, "The New Age is the tip of an iceberg that I choose to call 'the new spirituality,' which connotes the dawning of a mysticism of the earth that sharply challenges both classical Christian mysticism and biblical, prophetic religion" (Bloesch, *Holy Spirit*, 166–67). While "new spirituality" is identified by Bloesch as seemingly synonymously with "new age," there is a tradition of thought here that Bloesch does believe lies behind much of its spiritual/philosophical system. In short, while the movement is new and in many ways populist in its cultural influence, it does have a series of luminaries tied to its thought. Bloesch identifies a few of these thought leaders, "proponents of the new spirituality like Teilhard de Chardin, Kazantzakis, Ralph Waldo Emerson, Schelling, Hegel, Whitehead and Matthew Fox" (*Theology of Word & Spirit*, 159).

153. We read in *God the Almighty*, "New mysticism, a mysticism of the earth and history, which is to be carefully distinguished from the otherworldly mysticism fostered by Platonism and Neoplatonism" (Bloesch, *God the Almighty*, 15). We read elsewhere, "Besides Neoplatonic mystical spirituality, we must equally beware of modern, secular spirituality where the accent is on immersion in the world" (Bloesch, *Future of Evangelical Christianity*, 132).

154. Bloesch, *Spirituality Old & New*, 102.

As with classical mysticism, new mysticism has identifiable features that Bloesch finds evangelically problematic. First, new mysticism is grounded in what Bloesch calls "the new metaphysics, which subordinates being to becoming."[155] Second, unlike classical mysticism, new mysticism does not posit a God above or beyond creation but rather bound up within creation as an energy and life which is itself "evolving and changing."[156] In this sense, God is "not one who stands outside of nature but one who is the creative principle within nature."[157] In short, new mysticism advances a form of pantheism ripe for the celebration and exploration of the divine within the world itself.[158] Third, new mysticism places an emphasis on evolution and the future. All things are evolving, even God himself, orienting human persons toward a destiny. As Bloesch warns, "Even God has a future that he looks forward to and strives to bring into actuality."[159] Finally, in connection to this panentheistic and evolutionary emphases, new mysticism holds to a vision of God as finite or limited. "God" operates in a limited, infused and dispersed manner within creation. As Bloesch states,

> This god represents not supernaturalism but neo-naturalism. In this perspective God is in process, luring the world onward toward eternal ideals that have yet to be fully realized. In place of classical theism we have a process panentheism. Instead of a closed universe in which everything has been preordained, we have an

---

155. Bloesch, *Spirituality Old & New*, 105.

156. Bloesch, *Spirituality Old & New*, 105. Bloesch highlights a few emblematic ways of positing God that are ingredients to this form of spirituality in his *The Holy Spirit* volume: "God in this new perspective is 'the total energy field of the universe' (Alan Watts), 'the flowing river of Nature' (Emerson), 'the Life-Force' (Bergson) or the 'infinite abyss' (Tillich)" (*Holy Spirit*, 167). We read elsewhere, "The spiritual is seen as an aspect of the material, just as the supernatural is regarded as a dimension of the natural" (Bloesch, *Future of Evangelical Christianity*, 132).

157. Bloesch, *Spirituality Old & New*, 106. As Bloesch states elsewhere, "The New Age teaches neither creation by the will or decree of God nor emanation from the overflowing being of God but progression or evolution toward unity with God. It basically sees God and the world as inseparable. Its metaphysics can be called pantheistic, or better panentheistic, rather than theistic" (*Holy Spirit*, 169).

158. Bloesch's concern here seems to more accurately be described as "pantheism" than "panentheism." Bloesch opts for "panentheism" as the right descriptor, but he does seem to vacillate on the right terminology: "Classical theism has been supplanted by a this-worldly pantheism. Or better we should designate this new metaphysical stance as panentheism—God in the world and the world in God" (*Spirituality Old & New*, 106).

159. Bloesch, *Spirituality Old & New*, 106.

open universe where new possibilities are being realized through evolution.[160]

Unlike classical mysticism, new mysticism is not so much concerned with going beyond creation to a transcendent being but rather plunging into the divine within creation itself. The goal is to discover the divine within and to hitch oneself to the energy moving forward toward an evolving future.

The Threat of New Mysticism

Bloesch is concerned with new mysticism's impact within the evangelical church in much the same way he is with classical mysticism. He is concerned about the detrimental impact an embrace of new mysticism has on a properly evangelical account of spirituality. In contrast to Bloesch's vision of the Christian life being a pilgrimage of holiness, new spirituality endorses a "quest for heroic freedom."[161] The individual person is neither dependent upon a sovereign creator God, nor are they impacted by the human condition of sin. Human beings are free moral agents which may choose to rise above the travails of the world and consequently succeed in carving out a significant destiny. In total opposition to Bloesch's emphasis on obedience in the Christian life, the new spirituality places an undo emphasis on personal growth. Unlike classical mysticism, which is focused on asceticism and self-denial, new mysticism is focused on self-improvement. Bloesch states, "Growth entails human planning, but it has its basis in evolution. In the view of Schleiermacher, the human person is itself a product of the evolutionary advance."[162] As noted earlier, God himself is viewed as existing within this realm of evolutionary advancement.[163] Those who are spiritual, therefore, are participating in this evolutionary development which holds onto the belief in a greater and more actualized future. Therefore, unlike Bloesch's account of evangelical spirituality which stresses the call to love one's neighbor, in new spirituality a human being's calling toward others is

---

160. Bloesch, *Spirituality Old & New*, 106.
161. Bloesch, *Spirituality Old & New*, 107.
162. Bloesch, *Spirituality Old & New*, 108.
163. "The reconception of God is a sign of the crisis in spirituality today. God is no longer the personal-infinite God but the finite god who struggles as we do for self-fulfillment. He is not the creator of nature but the creative power or organizing force in nature. He does not transcend nature but is himself the divinization of nature. This is a god who meets us in the depths rather than a God who addresses us from the heights" (Bloesch, *Church*, 130–31).

to inspire them in their individual journey of growth. In total opposition to Bloesch's account of divine-human encounter, which is built upon God's objective economic operations, new spirituality emphasizes the divine within. Ultimately, the encounter is not between a transcendent, creator God and His human creatures but instead between creature and creation.[164] Where classical mysticism seeks to ascend to the God beyond, new mysticism seeks to find the divine already pragmatically accessible in nature.[165] The result in all of this is an account of prayer that is about actualizing the divine potential within, and an account of worship that is about an existential experience.[166] Prayer is not so much about transcending the material world as in classical mysticism, but rather "penetrating through the world to God."[167]

Mystical Spirituality versus Evangelical Spirituality

According to Bloesch, both classical and new mysticism fail to provide a form of spirituality in keeping with orthodox Christian doctrine. More specifically, they offer a mode of spirituality opposed to Bloesch's evangelical biblical-personalism. While their quests are different, they share in the same failed point of departure—humanity. As Bloesch states,

> Spirituality in the biblical panorama signifies not the ascent to divinity (as in the old mysticism) nor the ascent to a superhumanity (as in the new mysticism) but the descent of divinity to a sinful humanity. Through faith in Christ we are lifted into the presence of God, but this is an undeserved blessing from God rather than a mystical work of self-purification.[168]

Both classical and new mysticism begin with humanity's ascent, whether to the "divine" or "superhuman," rather than with God's descent to humanity. Both accounts of mysticism neglect the "crisis" of conversion necessary for

---

164. "In contrast to the theocentric or Christocentric perspective of biblical religion, New Age spirituality is biocentric (life-centered) and holocentric (centered in the whole of reality)" (Bloesch, *Holy Spirit*, 168).

165. Bloesch, *Spirituality Old & New*, 113.

166. "In reaction to the reduction of worship to prescribed formulas, the new spirituality seeks to cultivate an experience with God that bypasses the forms and rituals of the church tradition. Ecstasy rather than doctrinal purity or biblical fidelity is the primary concern in contemporary worship" (Bloesch, *Church*, 130).

167. Bloesch, *Future of Evangelical Christianity*, 132.

168. Bloesch, *Church*, 132.

encounter with the divine.[169] On Bloesch's account, faith is the vehicle of "ascension," but only in so far as Christ, who has brought God to us in the incarnation, brings us into God's presence.[170] No "mystical work" can achieve this end, but only the grace of God. This is because "the natural person does not even seek for God because sin has irrevocably bent the human will. The person who is corrupted by sin is not in search of God but in flight from God (Rom 3:9–18)." Consequently, "We need to be completely turned around if we are to know God and see God."[171]

Bloesch's evangelical account of the Christian life stresses God's search for humanity rather than humanity's search for the divine. In opposition to both forms of mysticism, Bloesch stresses the importance of divine revelation and condescension. Knowledge of God is central to Bloesch's evangelical spirituality, but such knowledge can be gained only by a God who makes Himself known by grace. As a result, this knowledge is *personal*. As Bloesch summarizes:

> The leitmotif of biblical spirituality is not a descent into the depths of the self where we make contact with the all-pervasive World Spirit but a confrontation with the living Christ, who answers the

---

169. Bloesch, *Spirituality Old & New*, 79.

170. It is worth noting that recent scholarship has shown the mystical notion of ascent is not as foreign from the Reformed tradition as Bloesch intimates throughout his writing. One monograph that has demonstrated an account of spiritual ascent within the Reformed tradition is Julie Canlis's *Calvin's Ladder*:

> Just as the fathers democratized mysticism, so did Calvin. While a rather elitist "intellectual mysticism" had been gathering force through the High Middle Ages, Calvin presented an "urban mysticism" centered on the triune God's desire for us, and particularly the Spirit's role in uniting us to Christ. For the average guildsman, who had no time to spend in intellectual contemplation and the uniting of the mind to God, this was indeed good news. But in bringing it down to earth, Calvin did not negate the heights of *unio cum Christo*. Even his famed emphasis on depravity (which prevents many from appreciating his mystical thrust) cannot repress the decided "upward" momentum in his theology. He simply restructured the "ladder to heaven" on quite another foundation. For Calvin, the ladder is Christ—not in the facile explanation that "Christ is the way," but that our ascent is profoundly bound up in Christ's ascension, by our *participation in his ascent*. In one deft move, Calvin has relocated "participation" from between impersonals (the soul in the divine nature) to personal (the human being in Christ, by the Spirit). Thus, a mystical encounter is not the goal (Calvin would hardly endorse an ascent to an ecstatic state); rather, the process itself is the mystical encounter. (Canlis, *Calvin's Ladder*, 50)

171. Bloesch, *Spirituality Old & New*, 79.

> longings of the human heart. What occurs is not a divine-human fusion but a divine-human encounter, which we see first in Jesus himself and then in the members of his mystical body. The subject-object antithesis is not overcome, as in mysticism, but is transfigured. God is no longer an object but now a living Subject who relates to us by his Spirit, empowering us from within.[172]

The goal of God's self-disclosure is a "divine-human encounter." Such an encounter is the heartbeat of what Bloesch has in mind when he thinks of evangelical spirituality as personal. As Bloesch fleshes out "biblical personalism," he presents a dialectical framework by which the divine-human encounter is achieved. As Bloesch argues,

> The divine-human encounter happened in past history—when God became man in Jesus Christ. But it happens ever again when mortals are confronted by the Spirit of Christ in the moment of decision. This is not simply an external meeting but an internal one as well. God not only speaks to us from the outside, but he also comes to dwell within us.[173]

On one side of the dialectic is the *objective* historical self-revelation of God in the person and work of Jesus Christ, and on the other side is the *subjective* experience of all that Christ has done internal to the human person by the work of the Spirit. Bloesch presents a divine movement of self-revelation for the sake of genuine, personal encounter with the living God. This account of divine-human encounter, which is both objective and subjective, points us to the doctrine of revelation. In the next chapter, I attend to the nature of the divine-human encounter as it is shaped by Bloesch's doctrine of revelation. In so doing, I explore Bloesch's objective-subjective account and note his critique of mysticism as a species of subjectivism.

As I demonstrate in the next chapter, an account of revelation significantly shapes the distinctions Bloesch seeks to draw between evangelical spirituality and the spiritualities of mysticism. Both classical and new mysticism have produced deviant forms of spirituality threatening the church. Bloesch is deeply concerned with the powerful impact of both biblical-classical spirituality and new spirituality in the evangelical church. Both streams of spirituality are sourced from unchristian tributaries. Bloesch states,

---

172. Bloesch, *Spirituality Old & New*, 80.
173. Bloesch, *Spirituality Old & New*, 82.

> A second form of old spirituality is what I have chosen to call biblical personalism. This stream of spiritual life has its source not in ancient philosophy but in the prophets and apostles of biblical faith. Other names for this pattern of spiritual consciousness are prophetic religion, evangelical piety, revelational religion and Puritan spirituality.[174]

Biblical personalism looks not to "ancient philosophy" but instead to the "prophets and apostles of biblical faith." Ultimately, biblical personalism "focuses upon the self-revealing God who calls people to fellowship with himself."[175] Biblical personalism looks to the self-revealing God of Scripture to define the nature of Christian life.

Conclusion

According to Bloesch the Christian life is a divine-human encounter. This encounter is known in personal obedience (piety) and expressed in social obedience (action). Through a life of faithful obedience, the Christian fights for and retains his/her salvation. As such, the Christian life is the arena of salvation. As the Christian presently strives for holiness through a life of faith, obedience, and repentance, he or she is subjectively appropriating God's objective saving action. This working out of salvation, subjectively in the life of the Christian, is true of all facets of the *ordo salutis*. In summary, while the Christian life is not the cause of salvation, it is integral to salvation. The Christian life genuinely contributes to the work of salvation initiated by God.

With Bloesch's definition of the doctrine of the Christian life in hand, I now focus attention on the theological presupposition rife throughout this chapter—the nature of divine and human agency. In particular, I investigate the nature of the divine and human relationship and its transhistorical encounter via past and present events. In order to accomplish this, I turn our

---

174. Bloesch, *Spirituality Old & New*, 77. Here, we collect a few more terms in Bloesch's vocabulary of the Christian life than we identified in the last chapter—"prophetic religion," "evangelical piety," "revelational religion," and "Puritan spirituality." As I noted in chapter 1, Bloesch employs a wide spectrum of terminology to discuss the Christian life. Here we get other terms than those focused on in chapter 1. It is important to note that Bloesch will move in and out of these terms, often exchanging them for each other or using them with a certain degree of redundancy to make his point. For example, "What is needed today is a piety grounded not in religious enthusiasm but in biblical personalism" (*Theological Notebook*, 2:90).

175. Bloesch, *Spirituality Old & New*, 77.

attention to the doctrine of revelation in the next chapter. This is of little surprise since Bloesch's doctrine of revelation is *the* formally distributive doctrine of his theological system. As attention is turned to the doctrine of revelation, the primary concern must be the role of the doctrine of the Christian life.

3

Distributing the Christian Life

IN CHAPTER 2, *DEFINING the Christian Life*, I provided an initial definition of the Christian life according to Bloesch's theology, looking throughout his corpus as he articulates, from beginning to end, a fundamental role for the Christian life in his work. After surveying his primary vocabulary of the Christian life—piety, devotion, spirituality, and biblical personalism, I analyzed Bloesch's primary constructive account of the Christian life in relation to the doctrine of salvation. According to Bloesch, the Christian life is the arena of salvation. It is the location of salvific appropriation through a pneumatically charged active obedience. Building on that previous analysis, I now thoroughly examine and explicate the distributive role of the Christian life in Bloesch's dogmatic project. Here, in particular, I focus on the doctrinal territory of revelation. The goal in this section is not to provide a robust re-articulation of Bloesch's doctrine of revelation. Rather, the goal is to pay attention to the influence of the doctrine of the Christian life on the doctrine of revelation.

The choice to turn to the doctrine of revelation to demonstrate the material distribution of the Christian life is not arbitrary. The doctrine of revelation is the *formal* doctrine of distribution for Bloesch's entire system. Therefore, I prioritize the doctrine of revelation here precisely because Bloesch does so. Recalling a point noted earlier, Bloesch's theology follows the contours of the way of knowing and not the way of being. This is clearly demonstrated by how Bloesch orders his systematic work of theology, *Christian Foundations*, prioritizing his doctrine of revelation in his first two volumes: (1) *A Theology of Word & Spirit: Authority and Method in Theology* and (2) *Holy Scripture: Revelation, Inspiration & Interpretation*, and following those two volumes with three volumes on the persons of God: (3) *God the Almighty: Power, Wisdom, Holiness, Love*; (4) *Jesus Christ: Savior & Lord*; and (5) *The Holy Spirit: Works & Gifts*.[1] What drives this prioritization is not merely a preference for the way of knowing but the instinct that this is necessary for a truly *evangelical* theology. To begin with revelation is to begin with the gospel, and the gospel is the "very heart and soul of evangelical theology."[2] As expected, this evangelical impulse is informed by a Reformed commitment to God's revealing self-disclosure.[3]

1. Bloesch explicitly signals this in a short section of *A Theology of Word & Spirit* entitled "Theology Defined":

> From this perspective, theology is the systematic reflection within a particular culture on the self-revelation of God in Jesus Christ as attested in Holy Scripture and witnessed to in the tradition of the catholic church. Theology in this sense is both biblical and contextual. Its norm is Scripture, but its field or arena of action is the cultural context in which we find ourselves. It is engaged in reflection not on abstract divinity or on concrete humanity but on the Word made flesh, the divine in the human. (*Theology of Word & Spirit*, 114)

The divine-human encounter, discussed shortly, is a shorthand definition for Bloesch's doctrine of revelation and is to be the abiding material of theological contemplation for Bloesch.

2. Bloesch, *Essentials of Evangelical Theology*, 1:4. Bloesch provides further description of the gospel in *A Theology of Word & Spirit*:

> The gospel is the surprising movement of God into the human history recorded in the Bible culminating in the life, death and resurrection of Jesus Christ and the corresponding movement of God in the personal history of those who believe. The gospel is the divinely given interpretation of the eternal significance of the teaching and work of Jesus Christ, an interpretation that must be given anew to every one of us as we struggle for a fuller understanding of the New Testament accounts of God's act of redemption in Jesus Christ. (*Theology of Word & Spirit*, 12–13)

The gospel is defined as a movement of God, but a movement in two parts. First, it is a movement of God in human history, centering on the person and work of Christ. Second, it is a movement of God in the personal history of believers. Thus, while the gospel is a "revelation from God," it is a revelation brought forth not only in the objective work of Christ, but also in the subjective experience of the believer (by the Spirit). The language of "arena" which Bloesch employed in the previous chapter to discuss locating the Christian life with salvation can be applied here as well. The Christian life ultimately is the "arena" of revelation in the secondary mode of God's movement in the gospel. Bloesch states, "I see the gospel as irreversible revelation from God that transcends every human formulation but is nonetheless inseparable from the New Testament kerygma or evangelical proclamation" (12). This point is further supported by a distinction Bloesch seeks to make between the gospel itself and the human articulation of this good news. He states, "A distinction I wish to make between the gospel and the kerygma brings out the qualitative difference between revelation and its human articulation" (136).

3. As Bloesch articulates regarding his method, "My method is to begin with God,

In what follows, I show that the Christian life is materially *presupposed* within the doctrine of revelation by way of Bloesch's definition of revelation—divine-human encounter. Revelation is a divine-human encounter in which the human person comes to know the person of the Son by the person of the Spirit. Likewise, I show that concern for the Christian life is materially *pervasive* throughout his doctrine of revelation by way of his governing taxonomy of revelation—Word (objective) & Spirit (subjective). Revelation is a transhistorical event of encounter initiated by the objective work of the Word and consummated by the subjective work of the Spirit. The arena of the Spirit's subjective work is the Christian life. Consequently, everywhere Bloesch speaks of the subjective work of the Spirit, he speaks of the Christian's life of personal and social obedience.

The doctrine of revelation is the fountainhead of Bloesch's systematic theology, and therefore the material distribution of the Christian life in revelation will flow throughout Bloesch's entire system. Bloesch's complete theological system is to be understood in light of the divine-human encounter of revelation. The revelational dialectic of Word (objective) and Spirit (subjective) shapes the contours of every doctrine within the whole of his system. By demonstrating the material distribution of the Christian life within the Spirit pole of revelation, I am demonstrating its material distribution throughout Bloesch's entire dogmatic arrangement. The doctrine of revelation is the engine driving the train of Bloesch's theology, and it is powered by the fuel of the Christian life.

Revelation as Divine-Human Encounter

In Bloesch's first constructive account of the doctrine of revelation *The Ground of Certainty*, he provides a rudimentary definition of revelation. When Bloesch later develops this in his mature account of revelation in *Christian Foundations*, he builds from and develops this early definition. In *The Ground of Certainty*, Bloesch states,

---

with his self-disclosure in Jesus Christ, and then proceed to humanity, with its search for God, which paradoxically takes the form of a flight from God. In this theological perspective revelation is prior to reason, grace is prior to faith, faith is prior to work, dogmatics is prior to apologetics" (*Theological Notebook*, 3:1). In his essay "Fideistic Revelationism" found in *Evangelical Theology in Transition*, Stanley Grenz says this about Bloesch's doctrine of revelation: "Like his rationalist colleagues, Bloesch believes that the starting point for theology lies in revelation understood as the divine self-disclosure" (Grenz, "Fideistic Revelationism," 39).

> Revelation is a divine-human encounter, an encounter that took place once for all between God and Jesus and also one that takes place ever again between Jesus Christ and the believer. When revelation happens, the Christ-event of the past and the encounter of faith in the present are brought together in an indissoluble unity.[4]

Revelation is a "divine-human encounter," and it is a transhistorical event that *has* taken place and *continues* to take place. For Bloesch, key redemptive events are open-ended. There is a completeness to them, but this completeness is always held dialectically with their incompleteness. The open-ended nature of redemption, for Bloesch, leads him to address the various tenses inherent in these doctrines—past, present, and future—as noted in the previous chapter in his doctrine of justification. There is a completeness to revelation, it *has happened* in the incarnation, but there is an openness and an incompleteness present as well, something that is fulfilled through the believer's communion with Christ, waiting ultimate fulfillment in eternity. Bloesch goes on to claim in his characteristic idiom of objective and subjective: "Revelation has both an objective and a subjective pole. The former signifies the disclosure of meaning in the historical events mirrored in the Bible and also in the biblical testimony itself. The subjective pole refers to the mystical or inward illumination of the Holy Spirit."[5] We observed Bloesch turning to the language of *objective* and *subjective* already at several key points, perhaps most clearly in the paradox of salvation. Likewise, he employs it here to articulate another kind of paradox in his doctrine of revelation. Revelation is an objective-subjective dialectic, in that it is a divine-human encounter that paradoxically occurs as both complete in the objective work of Christ in the past made known through Scripture, and at the same time as incomplete in that the subjective work of the Spirit must fulfill this encounter with the believer in the present.

The dialectical relationship of the objective and subjective does not negate the need for an order of priority regarding revelation. According to Bloesch, "The foundation of revelation is objective, but its realization is subjective."[6] For Bloesch, the event of revelation begins in the objective-

---

4. Bloesch, *Ground of Certainty*, 70.

5. Bloesch, *Ground of Certainty*, 70. As Bloesch talks about the "historical events mirrored in the Bible," he is primarily thinking of the event associated with the incarnation of Christ. This is evidenced by the paragraph preceding this quotation which is focused on the person and work of Christ. This is made clearer as Bloesch proceeds to discuss the "Christ-event of the past."

6. Bloesch, *Ground of Certainty*, 73. This very much echoes Brunner. We read in *The*

historical context but is completed in the subjective-experiential context. In this sense, the divine side of the divine-human encounter takes priority over the human. Bloesch never leaves these initial inclinations behind but builds upon and advances this rudimentary definition of revelation in his mature work. The core ingredients of Bloesch's constructive account of revelation endure. These core ingredients are twofold—that revelation is a "divine-human encounter" and that this encounter has both an objective and subjective pole. A brief analysis of Bloesch's introduction of these core ingredients, begins to draw our attention to the materially distributive role of the Christian life. The material distribution of the Christian life within the doctrine of revelation supports my thesis that the Christian life is a doctrine of definitive interest and influence in Bloesch's theological project. In this initial survey of Bloesch's early development of the doctrine of revelation, the presuppositional and pervasive material influence of the Christian life is on display.

First, the Christian life is materially presupposed in his primal definition of the doctrine as a "divine-human encounter." Bloesch is not content to talk about revelation as strictly divine-disclosure but rather as fundamentally a "divine-human encounter." This is significant. I have already

Christian Doctrine of God:

> In all these forms revelation is understood as something objective, as something which confronts us, something outside ourselves. But this is a very improper and inexact way of speaking; for revelation is certainly not a "Something," a "thing"; but it is a process, an event, and indeed an event which happens to us and in us. Neither the prophetic Word of the Old Testament, nor Jesus Christ, nor the witness of the Apostles, nor of the preachers of the Church who proclaim Him, "is" the revelation; the reality of the revelation culminates in the "subject" who receives it. Indeed, it is quite possible that none of these forms of revelation may become revelation to *us*. If there is no faith, then the revelation has not been consummated: it has not actually happened, so to speak, but it is only at the first stage. All objective forms of revelation need the "subject" in whom they become revelation. (Brunner, *Christian Doctrine of God*, 19)

Brunner strikes a similar note a few pages later:

> The revelation in Christ is not completed with the Life, Death, and Resurrection of Jesus: it only attains its goal when it becomes actually manifest; that is, when a man or woman *knows* Jesus to be the Christ. Revelation is not a starkly objective process, but a transitive one: God makes himself known to someone. This revealing action of God is a twofold stooping to man: historically objective, in the Incarnation of the Son, and inwardly subjective, in the witness borne to the Son through the Spirit in the heart of man—first of all, in that of the Apostles. (29)

noted that Bloesch holds the "divine-human encounter" as the "leitmotif of biblical spirituality."[7] Bloesch uses the phrase "divine-human encounter" as a description of the spiritual encounter at the heart of his biblical-personalism, and therefore it is central to his description of the Christian life. That Bloesch leverages this term once again in his doctrine of revelation is perhaps a glimpse into the impact of one of his theological mentors, Emil Brunner. Like Brunner, Bloesch believes that revelation is ultimately about "a life-giving and a life-renewing communion."[8] Therefore, as evidenced in his most primal definition of revelation, Bloesch's enduring commitment to

---

7. Bloesch, *Spirituality Old & New*, 80.

8. Brunner, *Christian Doctrine of God*, 20. Brunner states a few pages later in the same volume that "Revelation and faith now mean personal encounter, personal communion" (26). I quote Brunner here because Bloesch tells us in his *Theological Notebook* that Brunner has had a significant impact on him, in particular Brunner's *The Christian Doctrine of God* and *The Divine-Human Encounter* (Bloesch, *Theological Notebook*, 5:191, 214). Throughout the footnotes in this chapter I reference points in which the influence of Brunner's thought on Bloesch's doctrine of revelation can be found. Bloesch has clearly followed some of Brunner's conceptual framing of the doctrine including his language (for example, "divine-human encounter"). Bloesch, himself, argues that for Brunner "revelation is interpreted in terms of a divine-human encounter, an encounter which became decisive in the incarnation of God in Jesus Christ. The divine-human encounter occurs anew whenever men meet the risen Christ through the power of the Holy Spirit" (Bloesch, *Christian Witness in a Secular Age*, 46). The influence on Bloesch is undeniable. One wonders if Bloesch, the evangelical theologian, stands more in the company of Brunner and other neo-Reformers than he does with conservative evangelical theologians like Carl Henry regarding this doctrine. Peter Jensen helpfully narrates the response of Brunner and the neo-orthodox to the likes of a Carl Henry on the issue of revelation, Scripture, and authority. Jensen states, "However, there has been an overwhelming decision to move the chief locus of revelation away from the Bible. Emil Brunner, for example, referred to the 'fatal equation of revelation with the inspiration of the Scriptures,' and inspiration is now typically understood either in an attenuated way, or as the illumination of the receiving agent" (Jensen, *Revelation of God*, 18–19). Regarding Brunner and his company of neo-orthodox, Jensen continues, "Thus they frequently reject propositional revelation as being intellectualist and emphasize the experience of divine-human encounter. They often favour a dynamic revelation focusing on God's historical deeds rather than on a static set of words" (19). While Bloesch is perhaps more inclined toward Brunner's construal of revelation than he is Henry's, he is nevertheless concerned with Brunner's muting of the propositional component of revelation. Bloesch states, "Brunner acknowledges that the message of faith is not only address and claim but also the communication of meaning. Yet by divorcing faith and reflection he is unable to affirm that objective, rational truth is communicated in revelation" (*Christian Witness in a Secular Age*, 50). In the end, Bloesch's language and emphasis in the doctrine of revelation reflect the disposition of Brunner more than Henry. However, Bloesch ultimately seeks to strike a balance of the competing views, settling as a mediating theologian of the doctrine of revelation in this regard.

spiritual experience governs his account of revelation, driving it to embrace a reciprocity in the divine self-disclosure, such that it is, in a real sense, incomplete without it.

Second, while considering Bloesch's objective and subjective dialectic of revelation, a hint at the material pervasiveness of the Christian life arises. The fullness of revelation requires that the objective work of God in history be realized subjectively in the life of the believer. As Bloesch states, it is the "encounter of faith in the present," (i.e., the Christian life), that completes the event of revelation.[9] As Bloesch argues, the subjective pole of revelation occurring within the believer is marked by "mystical or inward illumination by the Spirit."[10] Here, it shows that the Christian life is not an alien force applying pressure from the outside upon Bloesch's doctrine of revelation but rather is a force applying pressure from within as it were. As the content of the subjective pole of revelation, the Christian life takes up permanent residence within the doctrine. The materially pervasive role of the Christian life in revelation is found in its embeddedness within the subjective pole. The remainder of this chapter demonstrates this material pervasiveness.

Bloesch's early definition of revelation as a divine-human encounter demonstrates the material presupposition of the Christian life. While this supports my argument that the Christian life is Bloesch's abiding doctrinal emphasis, the real force of the Christian life's influence on his constructive project is demonstrated by its material pervasiveness in the extended development of his doctrine of revelation. This initial definition of revelation as an objective and subjective event has provided an early window into the pervasive role of the Christian life in revelation, but the resilient influence of the Christian life in Bloesch's mature account of revelation requires further investigation.

The Divine-Human Encounter by Word & Spirit

Having noted Bloesch's early definition of revelation and how the Christian life asserts internal pressure on his account of revelation, I now explore Bloesch's mature account of the doctrine to see how this develops throughout his theological enterprise. As I demonstrate, Bloesch moves toward new language to articulate the objective and subjective dialectic of

9. Bloesch, *Ground of Certainty*, 70.
10. Bloesch, *Ground of Certainty*, 70.

An Evangelical Spiritual Theology

revelation and, in so doing, sharpens the distinctiveness of his constructive account. In his mature work, Bloesch privileges the categories of Word and Spirit when talking about the objective and subjective. In what follows, I investigate how Bloesch's mature articulation of the objective-subjective divine-human encounter, as a Word & Spirit event, further demonstrates the material distribution of the Christian life. A deep dive into Bloesch's mature constructive account of revelation could prove to be a rather daunting task in light of the breadth of doctrinal terrain revelation covers. Therefore, in order to address this feature of Bloesch's thought, I follow the lead of Avery Dulles.[11] Dulles's inquiry into the doctrine of revelation in *Models of Revelation* pays particular attention to modern theology which is valuable because Bloesch's project is a self-conscious engagement with the very same theological time period.[12] Furthermore, Dulles directly engages with Bloesch's doctrine of revelation in his contribution to the volume *Evangelical Theology in Transition*.

In *Models of Revelation*, Dulles provides a typological apparatus helpful for mapping various accounts of revelation. While his typology may not account for every nuance of an individual theologian's enunciation of the doctrine, it does provide a helpful vocabulary to pinpoint common or corresponding motifs across theological projects.[13] To this end, Dulles ar-

---

11. Dulles has established himself as a theologian of hermeneutical value for theologians seeking to examine the doctrine of revelation. His monograph, *Models of Revelation*, has been consistently engaged by contemporary theologians seeking to explore the doctrine of revelation both historically and constructively. Dulles's taxonomy is frequently engaged with and referenced by contemporary theologians: for example, see Jensen, *Revelation of God*, 19; Levering, *Engaging the Doctrine of Revelation*, 10–11; Treier, *Introducing Evangelical Theology*, 24.

12. At the outset of Bloesch's seven-volume dogmatic magnum opus, *Christian Foundations*, he identifies this nineteenth- and twentieth-century context as the soil from which his own project grew. In the foreword to his first volume, *A Theology of Word & Spirit*, Bloesch makes reference to Adolf von Harnack, Walter Raushenbusch, Hans Küng, Schleiermacher, Tillich, Brunner, and Barth. The references themselves implicitly locate Bloesch within this historical-theological milieu as he charts his initial engagement with the doctrine of revelation. However, more can be explicitly gleaned in Bloesch's invocation of these figures in his choice to identify them as primary dialogue partners for the entirety of his project. Bloesch aims to make clear that his dogmatic project seeks to claim its own occupancy in the doctrinal environment, well inhabited by theological luminaries of the nineteenth and twentieth centuries. He endeavors to overcome perceived failures and victories of modern theological consideration of the doctrine of revelation while establishing his own unique constructive account of the doctrine. See Bloesch, *Theology of Word & Spirit*, 11–15.

13. Dulles, *Models of Revelation*, 21.

gues that there are five major types (or models) of revelation to help locate the various iterations of this doctrine in modern theology. In order, these five models are—revelation as doctrine, as history, as inner experience, as dialectical presence, and as new awareness.[14] In his essay in *Evangelical Theology in Transition,* Dulles applies this five-model framework to Bloesch's account of revelation, locating Bloesch within the fourth model in his schema. Dulles argues the necessary and sufficient conditions of the fourth model can be identified with four key considerations—form, content, salvific value, and proper response. According to Dulles, the fourth model is one in which the form of revelation is the person of Christ, the content of revelation is God himself, revelation is intrinsically salvific, and the only proper response to revelation is faith.[15] Dulles recognizes in Bloesch these characteristic features. He also recognizes the characteristic dialectical tension of the fourth model, expressed primarily through Bloesch's Word & Spirit axiomatic idiom.[16] Dulles believes this idiom is *the* distinguishing feature of Bloesch's doctrine of revelation.[17] He argues,

14. A brief outline of Dulles's five types/models is worth noting here. The first model of revelation in Dulles's view is "revelation as doctrine." He states, "According to this view revelation is principally found in clear propositional statements attributed to God as authoritative teacher" (Dulles, *Models of Revelation,* 27). According to Dulles, in the Catholic tradition this is demonstrated by an account of revelation with a singular emphasis placed on tradition. In the Protestant tradition this singular emphasis is Scripture. The second model of revelation according to Dulles is "revelation as history." This position holds that God reveals himself primarily in a historical sense. Scripture and tradition are witnesses of these historical events of revelation in history. The third type in Dulles's taxonomy is "revelation as inner experience." This position emphasizes the experiential and personal. Revelation is an interior experience of God's presence. Fourth, Dulles argues is "revelation as dialectical presence." This position seeks to correct the overly objective account of the first two models and the overly subjective account of the third model (28). Dulles states, "God encounters the human subject when it pleases him by means of a word in which faith recognizes him to be present. The word of God simultaneously reveals and conceals the divine presence" (28). Dulles's fifth model is "revelation as new awareness." Under this account of the doctrine, divine revelation transcends the objective and subjective, leaning toward concreteness on one side and individualistic experience on the other. Instead, revelation is encountered as one makes contact with the "movement of secular history." God is mysteriously present in the human narrative in a transcendent manner.

15. Dulles, *Models of Revelation,* 92–93.

16. Dulles, "Donald Bloesch on Revelation," 62.

17. Of course, a theology of Word and Spirit is not unique to Bloesch. He himself recognizes this by consciously affirming the Reformational tree from which he has picked this fruit. As discussed in chapter 1, Bloesch is self-consciously appealing to the work of the magisterial Reformers in his theological endeavor. This is no more explicit than

> The event of revelation, for Bloesch, has two poles. He describes these sometimes as Word and Spirit, and sometimes as the historical and the experiential. Revelation is God speaking and the human being responding through the power of the Holy Spirit. Revelation consists in the conjunction between the divine act of self-disclosure and the human act of acceptance.[18]

Dulles identifies here the shift from Bloesch's early rudimentary definition of revelation to his later mature articulation when he employs the theological categories of Word and Spirit. According to Dulles, in Bloesch's mature work on revelation, one discovers the theological categories of Word and Spirit used to describe and explain the *historical-objective* and *experientially-subjective* poles of revelation. These two poles represent a conjunction of divine self-disclosure and human acceptance; or, perhaps better, the poles name the encounter between the divine and the human. As a divine-human encounter, revelation begins with the Word initiating divine-disclosure and is completed in the Spirit's enablement of human acceptance.

By moving to the language of Word & Spirit to articulate his early vision of the doctrine, Bloesch anchors revelation in the doctrine of God more explicitly. The second and third person of the Trinity are the shaping agents of the doctrine. Dulles secures this point as he goes on to tell us,

> Bloesch's doctrine of Word and Spirit does remarkable justice to both the objective and the subjective aspects of revelation. The Word represents that which comes from outside; the Spirit, that which emerges from within, enabling recipients to recognize and interpret the external Word. In revelation the Word never comes apart from the Spirit, nor is the Spirit given without the presence of the Word.[19]

Dulles is correct; Word & Spirit are dialectical companions in Bloesch's doctrine, and in fact, throughout the whole of his theology. One cannot consider Word apart from Spirit, nor Spirit apart from Word, which establishes the objective-subjective dialectic in the grounding instincts of his

---

in his *Theology of Word & Spirit*. See Bloesch, *Theology of Word & Spirit*, 14. We read in *The Holy Spirit*, "Where I fully concur with the Reformers is in their emphasis on the complementarity of Word and Spirit" (*Holy Spirit*, 15). However, in Bloesch's mind what is distinct is his retrieval of this tradition as "in later orthodoxy the paradoxical unity of Word and Spirit was sundered, being replaced by an objectivism of the Word" (*Theology of Word & Spirit*, 14).

18. Dulles, "Donald Bloesch on Revelation," 61.
19. Dulles, "Donald Bloesch on Revelation," 61.

systematics. Bloesch reveals, "What I am advocating is a biblical theology of Word and Spirit in which the sanctifying work of the Spirit is tied to the redeeming work of Jesus Christ on the cross."[20] The finished work of the Word is wedded to the ongoing work of the Spirit. This account consistently locates the work of the Word primarily in the past and the work of the Spirit in the present. Consequently, one finds in Bloesch a bloated account of the completed work of Christ and a thin account of the present work of Christ. The Spirit takes over the domain of the present, and the ongoing work of the Son is diminished. While the Word may be primarily tied to the past and the Spirit to the present, Bloesch is sure to maintain the essential role of both Word and Spirit in accomplishing revelation. According to Bloesch, what God has joined together in revelation, no one shall separate.[21]

The self-disclosing Triune God has revealed himself in the undivided economic operations of Word & Spirit. Revelation is an objective divine disclosure by the Word, external to the human person; in the objective sense, it is a revelatory disclosure that *has* happened. This revelation is, at the same time, a subjective internal human acceptance of this disclosure made possible by the Spirit. In the subjective sense, the divine-human encounter in revelation *is* happening and requires a subjective acceptance. As Bloesch states,

> The event of revelation has two poles: the historical and the experiential. Revelation is God speaking and the human being responding through the power of God's Spirit. God speaks not only in the Bible but also in the human heart. Revelation is the conjunction of divine revealing action and human response. The external knowledge of Scripture united with the internal knowledge given by the Holy Spirit.[22]

Here, Bloesch not only emphasizes the ontological ground of revelation as the missions of Son and Spirit, but he makes a point of emphasizing the importance of the Christian life as the participatory arena of these missions. The Christian life cannot be seen apart from the missions of Son and Spirit, but instead must be viewed as the culminating telos of their

---

20. Bloesch, *Holy Spirit*, 29.

21. Bloesch is concerned with the separation of Word and Spirit as individual theological categories within theological work contemporaneous to his own: "In the present theological milieu Word and Spirit are increasingly separated, and this cleavage runs through evangelicalism as well" (*Holy Spirit*, 21).

22. Bloesch, *Holy Scripture*, 50.

united missions. The objective work of the Son remains incomplete apart from the subjective work of the Spirit, a work known in the experience of the believer. The human response to this knowing plays a meaningful role in bringing to completion the goal of divine self-disclosure. In this sense, revelation is an already-but-not-yet divine-human encounter. It initially comes from without but must come to be grasped from within if the encounter is a true *encounter*.

Bloesch's use of a Word & Spirit taxonomy in his mature construction of the doctrine of revelation accomplishes several things. First, by defining revelation as a Word & Spirit event, Bloesch ensures a fitting priority and authority is given to the doctrine of God in his account. Consequently, in his own way, Bloesch renders the doctrine of revelation as a "derivative" doctrine.[23] As a derivative doctrine, revelation ultimately seeks to articulate the act of God. For Bloesch, that act includes within it, necessarily, a reciprocal act of humankind in the Spirit. Nevertheless, in speaking of the human response to revelation, we are still speaking of God's action by the Spirit. Second, by holding Word & Spirit together, Bloesch guards against bifurcating or truncating the objective and subjective poles of revelation because the result would be a breakdown of the divine-human encounter that is the telos of revelation.[24] If Word & Spirit are separated, the encounter would lose its distinctively *personal* characteristics—it would be an encounter of, so to speak, *deity*, rather than the Father in the Son by the Spirit. If one is collapsed into the other, losing the viability of the mission, the integrity and reciprocity of the encounter is threatened.

Grasping Bloesch's mature formulation of the doctrine of revelation confirms my hypothesis that the Christian life is presupposed in the doctrine. I have identified the retention of both "divine-human encounter" and

---

23. I am loosely applying John Webster's definition of a "derivative doctrine" here to Bloesch's work. For example, Webster states, "Soteriology is a derivative doctrine, and no derivative doctrine may occupy the material place which is properly reserved for the Christian doctrine of God, from which alone all other doctrines derive" (Webster, "It Was the Will of the Lord," 16).

24. Bloesch states:

> Some theologians have erred by subordinating the Spirit to the Word; others by elevating the Spirit over the Word. If we mean by the latter the living Word, Jesus Christ, then we must view him as equal to the Spirit, though he has a certain priority in the economy of salvation. If we are thinking of the written Word, however, the Spirit clearly has precedence, since the bible was produced by the inspiration of the Spirit, and the Spirit uses the bible to bring sinners to the knowledge of Jesus Christ. (*Holy Spirit*, 57)

"objective-subjective" notions of revelation within Bloesch's mature Word & Spirit revelational idiom. In particular, Bloesch's prioritization of "Spirit" language in describing the subjective pole of revelation specifies the trinitarian shape of the ongoing divine-human encounter. The infusion of the "Spirit" pole with the notion of "experience" also demonstrates Bloesch's pietistic impulse and driving doctrinal commitment to the Christian life. Therefore, the Christian life has clear abiding influence on Bloesch's doctrine of revelation. More than that, since the doctrine of revelation is a formally distributed doctrine of his entire system, Bloesch's commitment to the subjective-Spirit pole of revelation portends an enduring commitment to the Christian life throughout his entire system. In other words, the material distribution of the Christian life found within the doctrine of revelation leads to material distribution of this doctrine throughout his entire dogmatic arrangement. Bloesch's theology is one of Word & Spirit and therefore is a theology of encounter and experience.

The Meaning of Word & Spirit

Bloesch's doctrine of revelation is defined by his Word & Spirit idiom. Since the doctrine of revelation is *the* formally distributed doctrine in Bloesch's theological system, it follows that Word & Spirit is the defining category of his entire system.[25] Consequently, a deeper analysis of the meaning of "Word" and "Spirit" is demanded. In what follows, I investigate the meaning of Word & Spirit in their order of priority as specified by Bloesch, Word (objective) first and Spirit (subjective) second. In doing so, it is important to remember this mode of analysis is conceptually foreign to Bloesch's understanding, who always seeks to talk about Word & Spirit in dialectical relatedness. Nevertheless, I investigate them individually for the sake of clarity, keeping in mind the inextricable bond of Word & Spirit within Bloesch's theology. In preferencing Word & Spirit in this discussion, I am not taking focus off the Christian life as a materially distributed doctrine but seek to reveal how and why this is true in light of Bloesch's theology of Word & Spirit.

As presented earlier, Bloesch develops his doctrine of revelation as a personal encounter of the human person with the person of the Word by the person of the Spirit. Bloesch's language clearly grounds revelation in the

---

25. Bloesch makes it clear that this is the defining feature of his doctrine of revelation and indeed of his theology as a whole. See Bloesch, *Theology of Word & Spirit*, 13–14.

doctrine of the Trinity, but it becomes evident that Bloesch is not interested in the ontology of Word & Spirit. In Bloesch's system, Word & Spirit have their home in the doctrine of revelation such that they are primarily economic realities and epistemological categories referencing the objective and subjective sides of revelation. Unsurprisingly, in light of that, when Word & Spirit are invoked throughout his theology, the doctrine of revelation is inevitably found. Bloesch's description of the economy addresses Word & Spirit, not by developing the *personhood* of the Word & Spirit, but to address the objective and subjective dimension of revelation; he tells us who they are by telling us what they do, and he tells us what they do primarily in respect to the divine-human encounter. Unlike his theological mentor, Karl Barth, Bloesch does not put "the doctrine of the Trinity at the head of all dogmatics."[26] For Barth, "The first question that must be answered is: Who is it that reveals Himself here? Who is God here? and then we must ask what He does and thirdly what He effects, accomplishes, creates and gives in His revelation."[27] As we will see, in many respects Bloesch reverses the order proposed by Barth. Bloesch foregrounds what God "effects, accomplishes, creates, and gives in His revelation,"[28] and allows this to drive his dogmatic venture.

Bloesch's *Christian Foundations* includes three volumes that help articulate his meaning of Word & Spirit—*Jesus Christ: Savior & Lord* and *The Holy Spirit: Works & Gifts* and *Holy Scripture: Revelation, Inspiration & Interpretation*.[29] In *Jesus Christ* and *The Holy Spirit*, one might expect him to articulate *who* the Word & Spirit are, but close attention to the subtitles, *Savior & Lord* and *Works & Gifts*, signal a different emphasis. Bloesch is primarily concerned in these two volumes with telling us what Word & Spirit do. In *Jesus Christ*, Bloesch articulates the saving work and reigning power of Christ. Likewise, in *The Holy Spirit*, Bloesch develops the empowering and indwelling presence of the Holy Spirit in the church. This does not mean Bloesch avoids specifying who the Word & Spirit are, but he does so primarily by telling what they do. Bloesch seeks not to ground his theological reflection in God's life *in se*,

---

26. Barth, *Doctrine of the Word of God*, 300. In reference to Barth's *Church Dogmatics*, Bloesch specifies that it is one of a handful of books that "have most shaped my thought and life" (*Theological Notebook*, 5:191).

27. Barth, *Doctrine of the Word of God*, 297.

28. Barth, *Doctrine of the Word of God*, 297.

29. The three volumes *Jesus Christ, Holy Spirit,* and *Holy Scripture* are all written by Donald G. Bloesch.

but rather in God's acts in the economy of Word & Spirit.³⁰ Likewise, in his volume *Holy Scripture*, Bloesch articulates the means by which the saving Lord makes himself known. Rather than focusing on an ontology of the text, Bloesch focuses on Scripture as an epistemological means of revelation. He is not so much concerned with giving "an account of what Holy Scripture *is* in the saving economy of God's loving and regenerative self-communication," but instead is concerned to provide an account of what Scripture *does* in achieving the divine-human encounter.³¹

A Theology of the Word

I begin with Bloesch's definition of the Word as found in his volume *Jesus Christ* and further developed in *Holy Scripture*. In *Jesus Christ* Bloesch purposefully positions readers within the "historical Jesus" debates of biblical scholarship and the Christological debates instigated by liberationist, feminist, and process theologians. With a polemical tone setting the agenda of the volumes, the remainder invests most of its energy navigating issues like the virgin birth, the preexistence of Christ, and atonement theories. His method of engagement with these issues is consistent throughout the volume: he surveys the tradition and narrates contemporary voices on each doctrinal matter, he provides an irenic but critical assessment of this survey, and he concludes by providing his own answer to the questions and challenges presented. Often, his answer is developed through a dialectical consideration of commonly competing perspectives on a particular doctrinal matter. When Bloesch moves into his polemical mode, he almost always sees two major mistakes taking place on the doctrinal horizon before him, and, with equal consistency, he sees these as the Scylla and Charybdis between which his own view must navigate.

Noticeably, Bloesch invests but limited space to an exploration of the ontological identity of Jesus (the Word) within the Triune Godhead.³² For

---

30. This is made all the more evident by the manner in which Bloesch engages the doctrine of God proper in his seven-volume work. It appears in neither *Jesus Christ* nor *The Holy Spirit* in any robust sense, but rather in the volume immediately prior to these two, *God the Almighty*. There, Bloesch treats the doctrine of the Trinity not as a theologically formative doctrine which shapes the dogmatic decisions to follow, but instead as a discretely important loci which requires orthodox affirmation.

31. Webster, *Holy Scripture*, 2.

32. The only place we find meaningful discussion of Jesus in his immanent relation to Father and Spirit is in a short section titled "A Reaffirmation of Orthodox Christology,"

Bloesch, the Word that actually matters theologically is the Word made flesh that dwelt among us. In contradistinction with a Christology from below and Christology from above, Bloesch posits a "Christology from the center,"[33] stating,

> In my Christology I choose to begin neither with an abstract concept of God or Christ removed from history nor with the historical man Jesus. Instead my point of departure is the paradox of God himself entering world history at a particular place and time, in a particular historical figure—Jesus of Nazareth. I wish to begin with the Word made flesh rather than with the preexistent Logos or with the historical Jesus.[34]

Already, in his formal definition of the Word, Bloesch is signaling his central commitment to the two poles of the divine-human encounter. Bloesch is averse to a Christology from above, fearing it would give undue priority to the divine side, and averse to a Christology from below because it would give undue priority to the human side; instead, Bloesch seeks a *Christology from the center*, concentrating on the divine-human encounter objectively achieved in the person of Jesus Christ. Bloesch employs two pieces of Christological machinery to build his Christology from the center. First is the redemptive work of Christ: namely, his life, death, and resurrection. Bloesch grounds the objective nature of his Christology from the center on the historical events of Christ's redemptive work. Second, Bloesch turns to the hypostatic union, claiming, "Our faith is not in the Jesus of history or in the eternal Christ but in the historical Jesus Christ, who was both fully divine

---

which follows on the heels of Bloesch's summary of the major historic Christological heresies. In this section we find Bloesch affirming Chalcedon: "With the church fathers I affirm that Jesus was consubstantial with the Father, according to his divinity, and consubstantial with us mortals (except for sin) according to his humanity" (*Jesus Christ*, 69).

33. When Bloesch speaks of a Christology from the center this is what he is talking about, a divine act of self-communication the living Word as central to divine revelation, and as an objective reality, this is what he is referring to. It is appropriate to start with the incarnation of Christ in understanding the Word within Bloesch's thoughts, for he himself states, "There is a direct identity between the Word of God and the personhood of Jesus but only an indirect identity between the living Word of God and the Bible or the sermon" (Bloesch, *Jesus Christ*, 73). However, it is important to note that for Bloesch objective revelation of the living Word is made known only by the written Word. In order to fully do justice to Bloesch's account of the Word, it is time to explore his understanding of the written Word and its relation to the living Word.

34. Bloesch, *Jesus Christ*, 70.

and fully human at the same time."[35] In Jesus, the God-man who lived, died, and rose again, a divine-human encounter has objectively occurred.[36]

Bloesch's Christology from the center not only places an emphasis on the economic activity of the Word over his immanent life, but it also clearly places an emphasis on divine revelation. Bloesch acknowledges as much in stating that he "would define revelation as the movement of God into a particular human history, namely, the personal history of Jesus Christ, and the self-communication of God to his people through both the events surrounding Jesus Christ and the inspired witness to these events, which constitutes Holy Scripture."[37] In short, the incarnation of Jesus Christ *is* the objective pole of revelation. God has revealed himself in the person and work of Christ so that he might be known. In focusing on the incarnation as the objective pole of revelation, Bloesch understands the incarnation as a revelatory event which is both particular and universal.[38] This divine act of self-disclosure is exclusively available in Christ, but it includes all those who have faith in its historical-objective occurrence. As Bloesch himself argues,

> Whereas philosophy ponders the nature of God in the abstract, theology reflects on the divine-human encounter in history as we find this in Jesus Christ. The way to knowledge of God is through

---

35. Bloesch, *Jesus Christ*, 72.

36. On this point we find Bloesch echoing Brunner. Brunner states, "Jesus Christ Himself is more than all the words about Him; and the 'Word' of God, the decisive self-communication of God, is a Person, a human being, the man in whom God Himself meets us" (Brunner, *Christian Doctrine of God*, 15).

37. Bloesch, *Jesus Christ*, 239.

38. In the final chapter of his *Jesus Christ* volume, entitled "The Finality of Christ," Bloesch expresses concern regarding the impact of "the theology of religions" (*Jesus Christ*, 230). His concern here is that a "theology of religions" approach to revelation strips Christianity of its uniquely Christ-centered account of divine revelation. Ultimately, he believes the fruit of "theology of religions" is pluralism and relativity, both of which challenge the uniqueness and centrality of the person and work of Christ in revelation (231–33). He also highlights some alarming shifts within Christianity towards obscuring the uniqueness and centrality of the person and work of Christ (235–36). Consequently, he argues that Christology is the centerpiece of Christian theology, and that the uniqueness of his incarnation, death, resurrection, and ascension are critical. It is in light of this discussion that he argues for a kind of particularity regarding Christ's work. Picking up on the language of Brunner, Bloesch states, "God revealed himself once for all times in this particular event or series of events attested and mirrored in the Bible" (236). In regard to universality Bloesch states, "that this one revelation is intended for all, that Christ's salvation goes out to all, including the outsider and the sinner" (237).

knowledge of Christ, and the way to knowledge of Christ is by faith in his promises as revealed in the Bible.[39]

Bloesch is not interested in God in the abstract because for him, "To know the nature of God we must see his face in Jesus Christ. To know the plan of God for the world we must see this plan realized in the cross of Christ and fulfilled in his resurrection and second advent."[40] Saving knowledge of God is the goal, and it is achieved by the objective-historical, divine-human encounter of the life, death, and resurrection of Jesus Christ of Nazareth. The formal meaning of the "Word" is the mission of the Son, which is the objective pole of revelation. However, a question remains: How is it that creatures come to have knowledge of this objective divine-human encounter in the life, death, and resurrection of Jesus? Bloesch has already tipped his hand; it is only through a "knowledge of Christ . . . by faith in his promises revealed in the Bible."[41]

While the overarching contours of this are clear, Bloesch further develops his theology of the Word in his volume on *Holy Scripture*. Knowledge of the Word made flesh, as Bloesch develops it, is indirect rather than direct. In consonance with his criticism of the ineffable spirituality of mysticism, Bloesch argues, "We can know God because God truly reveals himself to us, though God does not communicate with us directly—face to face—but indirectly by means of his mighty deeds in biblical history culminating in Jesus Christ. Revelation as Kierkegaard saw so clearly, is fundamentally indirect communication."[42] Bloesch's affirmation of Kierkegaard stands in line with a common distinction within Reformed theology between archetypal knowledge and ectypal knowledge. God alone has archetypal, or direct, knowledge of himself, while human persons have ectypal, or indirect, knowledge of God.[43] Nevertheless, Bloesch seeks to maintain his emphasis

---

39. Bloesch, *Jesus Christ*, 16.
40. Bloesch, *Jesus Christ*, 15.
41. Bloesch, *Jesus Christ*, 16.
42. Bloesch, *God the Almighty*, 61. Bloesch will go on to state, "We know God indirectly through creaturely signs and works. We know God by faith, not by direct vision" (61).
43. Asselt argues "Reformed scholastics" used "distinctions between God as Creator and God as Redeemer, and between non-saving natural knowledge and saving revealed knowledge of God." He goes on to argue that "the Reformed orthodox theologians posited these distinctions within" the "categories of *theologia vera* and, subordinate to that, *theologia archetypa* and *theologia ectypa*" (Asselt, "Fundamental Meaning of Theology," 320). He then proceeds to define *theologia archetypa* and *theologia ectypa*. In following

on encounter, and as a result he posits the knowledge of revelation as "mediated immediacy."[44]

This notion of mediated immediacy is an important one for Bloesch's doctrine of revelation. True knowledge of God is from God Himself, and at the same time true knowledge of God is mediated through creaturely forms. Importantly, on this account, a real encounter is taking place, however much it is mediated. The "indirect communication" of revelation simply means that God uses creaturely means to achieve the divine-human encounter. Bloesch avers, "We hear and see but indirectly through external means: the Scriptures and the church proclamation of the scriptural message."[45] The two mediating means of revelation are Scripture and preaching. The "ultimate criterion" of revelation, "is neither religious experience nor the biblical record but God's self-revelation in Jesus Christ, which comes to us through various means, especially Scripture and the preaching of the gospel."[46] For Bloesch, Scripture and preaching are the two primary *objective instruments* of God's mediated immediacy. As one might expect, Bloesch argues for an order of priority regarding these means: "Scripture is one step removed from revelation, and the sermon two steps removed."[47]

Junius he states *theologia archetypa* is "God's knowledge of himself and his works" and *theologia ectypa* is "creaturely knowledge of God and his works" (321). In *Union with Christ* Billings notes that Bavinck appeals to the categories of archetypal and ectypal as well. With a direct quotation from Bavinck included, Billings argues, "A key way that Bavinck pulls together the language of accommodation and analogy is through the notion of archetype and ectype: 'God's self-consciousness is archetypal; our knowledge of God, drawn from his Word, is ectypal'" (Billings, *Union with Christ*, 78). Muller highlights the use of this distinction as well in stating, "In Cocceius' view, moreover, the theologia archetypa is an inward trinitarian knowing, the Father knowing the Son, the Son knowing the Father, and the Spirit searching out the deep things of God—a cognitive parallel with Cocceius' doctrine of the pactum salutis. Cocceius' definition of archetypal theology also coincides with his insistence that theology is a practical discipline oriented toward the goal of salvation" (Muller, *Prolegomena to Theology*, 234).

44. Bloesch, *God the Almighty*, 74. Bloesch echoes this sentiment in *The Ground of Certainty*. Here Bloesch argues that the Christian faith embraces a kind of mystical understanding of faith as self-authentication. Yet, in a transformative manner this self-authentication is an "experience . . . occasioned by the hearing of the Word of God" (*Ground of Certainty*, 135). Bloesch does believe we have a "direct experience of God in faith," and yet, "this experience is always tied to a knowledge of what God has done for us in Jesus Christ, witnessed to in the Bible and the sermon" (135).

45. Bloesch, *God the Almighty*, 74.

46. Bloesch, *Holy Spirit*, 46.

47. Bloesch, *Holy Scripture*, 68.

Nevertheless, both are given substantial authority in Bloesch's Word & Spirit account of revelation.

If God's people are one or two steps removed from revelation, one might wonder if Bloesch's doctrine has moved beyond revelation to be a kind of witness to God's revelation. How this is a mode of the Word is less than obvious at first glance. In thinking about the meaning of the "Word," Bloesch adopts Barth's threefold sense: "Karl Barth made a helpful distinction between three forms of the Word of God—the revealed Word or living Word (Christ), the written Word (Scripture) and the proclaimed Word (the church)."[48] The living Word, Jesus Christ, is the primal form of divine revelation, while Scripture and preaching are corresponding instruments of this revelation. All three are united by the objective-*Word*.[49] Bloesch's adoption of Barth's threefold Word upholds the instrumental integrity of the written and proclaimed Word, while expectedly driving toward the *personal* dimension of revelation. This Barthian schema services Bloesch's emphasis on the divine-human encounter, while establishing proper order and distinction in the movement of divine revelation. How Bloesch upholds the order and explains the relation of living, written, and proclaimed Word requires further investigation.

The Written Word

First, I turn our attention to the relationship between the living Word and the written Word. Here, Bloesch employs Barth's concept of "correspondence" as an inroad to understanding the nature of Scripture's indirect identity to the living Word.[50] While Bloesch finds Barth's language of corre-

---

48. Bloesch, *Theology of Word & Spirit*, 190. Bloesch underlines this point in his *Holy Scripture* volume when he states, "One can see that Barth's typology of the three forms of the Word of God—the living Word, the written Word, and the proclaimed Word—rests on solid Christian and evangelical tradition" (*Holy Scripture*, 62).

49. As stated in *Holy Scripture*, "Jesus participated in the Word of God directly and immediately. Jesus was completely transparent to God, though only to the eyes of faith. The Bible is transparent to God, though only to the eyes of faith. The Bible is translucent to God. Jesus was one with the Logos of God; the words of the Bible are one with the Word of God only indirectly. Jesus was and is the Word in and of himself" (Bloesch, *Holy Scripture*, 70). Here Bloesch makes the primal identity of the Word, Jesus Christ Himself. He employs familiar language of "direct" and "indirect" in helping to delineate the relation of Scripture and, as we shall see, proclamation to this living Word.

50. Bloesch, *Holy Scripture*, 58. Once again, Bloesch is clear that this correspondence is made possible only by the "interior illumination of the Spirit" in faith (26).

spondence helpful, he takes it a step further by using the language of "conjunction." The written Word exists in conjunction with the living Word. For Bloesch, conjunction means, "What we hear is not simply a reverberation of the Word of God but the very Word of God . . . not by necessity but by an act of free grace."[51] At face value, this shift in semantics may appear innocuous in material difference. Yet, the decision is clearly meaningful to Bloesch himself. This shift in terminology gives stronger emphasis to the immediacy within the mediation of Scripture, and more importantly, it retains the genuineness of the divine-human encounter.

Bloesch does not believe the words of Scripture possess revelation univocally, but he does wish to maintain an unbinding analogical relation between the words of the Bible and divine self-disclosure.[52] Scripture is a form of divine-human encounter as the human authors are inspired by the Spirit to communicate the Word.[53] Bloesch uses an image of light and a light bulb to explain the logic of his doctrine of Scripture as it relates to revelation:

> One might say that the Bible is the Word of God in a formal sense—as a light bulb is related to light. The light bulb is not itself the light but its medium. The light of God's truth is ordinarily shining in the Bible, but it is discerned only by the eyes of faith.[54]

51. Bloesch, *Holy Scripture*, 58.

52. In an article entitled "Evangelical Rationalism and Propositional Revelation" Bloesch highlights his rejection of "univocal" and "equivocal" language and his affirmation of "analogical" language in regard to Scripture:

> The theology of Word and Spirit I propose is not to be confused with either narrational or propositional theology, though it acknowledges that the Bible contains both realistic narrative and propositional truth. It seeks to transcend the cleavage between dogmatism and mysticism, logos and mythos. It perceives the unity of logos and mythos in the dramatic unfolding of the salvation history mirrored in the Bible. With both Thomas Aquinas and Karl Barth, it propounds a middle way between equivocity and univocity— the way of analogy. ("Evangelical Rationalism," 173)

Elsewhere Bloesch states, "The criterion for deciding what analogical language is most appropriate is the self-revelation of God in Jesus Christ given in the Bible. To begin from human nature and experience and then posit in God the perfection of the creature is to end in the impasse of natural theology" (*Is the Bible Sexist?*, 78).

53. Bloesch states, "Their witness points to revelation, but it also mediates revelation, since the Spirit acts through the persons and words that he inspires" (*Holy Scripture*, 56).

54. Bloesch, *Holy Scripture*, 59. Bloesch continues to provide a detailed account of the function of this revelatory lightbulb. He gives a fourfold description of the mechanical structure of this instrument of divine communication:

The true light, which is the living Word, shines through the light bulb, which is the written Word. Scripture is not the light itself but is the normative medium of the light.[55] The objective living Word has willed to make

> First, it brings us a message from God. Its words are the symbols and channels of the revelatory core of meaning that comes from God. Second, it is the inspired witness to revelation: it is the written Word of God. Third, it is the vehicle and carrier of revelation, the source of continuing revelation. Finally, it is the document of the final revelation and by the action of the Spirit participates in this revelation. Form and content penetrate each other in Scripture and cannot be separated (Herman Bavinck). The Bible can be held to embody revelation, for the truth of revelation resides in the Bible. (70)

The distinctions between these four aspects of Scripture's revelatory function are challenging to parse. There is an overlapping of commitments as one reads through the four descriptors. In summary, Bloesch argues that Scripture in its form and content is *the* faithful and true vehicle and witness of divine revelation. Scripture has a unique and powerful revelatory capacity assigned by God. According to Bloesch, there are two components to this revelatory capacity in Scripture—the original historical happenings recorded and the written witness of such events. Bloesch states, "We do not really know God until he speaks and acts, and he has done so decisively and definitely in the history mirrored in Holy Scripture, culminating in Jesus Christ—the center and goal of Scripture. But at the same time, he reveals himself through the historical witness to his incomparable act of incarnation and condescension" (*God the Almighty*, 74).

55. It is clear that Bloesch is not always consistent on this point. It is here that I quickly identify what appears to be a tension in Bloesch's own thought regarding Scripture's role in revelation. On the one hand Bloesch tells us, "The Bible is not in and of itself the revelation of God but the divinely appointed means and channel of this revelation" (*Holy Scripture*, 57). However, just a few pages later we encounter what appears to be a contradictory argument. Bloesch enumerates, "The Bible is both the revelation and the means and bearer of revelation. It is revelation cast in written form and the original witness to revelation. It is a component of revelation and a vehicle of revelation. It objectively contains revelation in the sense that its witness is based on revelation, but it becomes revelation for us only in the moment of decision, in the awakening of faith" (63). On the one hand Bloesch clearly identifies that Scripture is strictly a means of revelation, and on the other hand he argues it is revelation in itself. What lies at the heart of the apparent internal contradiction? Earlier in his *Holy Scripture* volume Bloesch wrestles with this same apparent contradiction identified here. It is perhaps the element of Bloesch's thought that is most vexing to clarify. Bloesch engages J. I. Packer's doctrine of Scripture, and in principle agrees with Packer that Scripture is both the Word of God instrumentally and intrinsically. The instrument role of Scripture is not surprising, but the intrinsic is perhaps. Again, the seeming contradiction of Scripture being the Word and not being the Word appears here. This engagement with Packer is helpful in this regard as Bloesch qualifies his agreement with Packer's view. In regard to the Word being intrinsic to Scripture, Bloesch eschews any sense in which this is a static reality in the text apart from the active work of the Holy Spirit. It is the Spirit "who fills the words with meaning and power" (Bloesch, *Holy Scripture*, 27). Bloesch provides an intriguing account of this work of the Spirit in stating, "One may also say that the Bible is intrinsically the Word of God

himself known through the objective written Word. Scripture is a conduit of the divine-human encounter.

While Bloesch argues for "conjunction," a line of demarcation must be drawn between the primal mode of revelation, the living Word, and Scripture's instrumental participation in this revelation. Bloesch argues, "The Word of God transcends the human witness, and yet it comes to us only in the servant form of the human word."[56] How does Bloesch establish this distinction between the transcendent Word and the human witness of Scripture? Bloesch asserts,

> There is an inseparable connection between the revealed Word of God or the "mind of Christ" and the Bible. We can even speak of a unity of identity of witness and revelation, but it is an indirect identity, not a property of the witness but a matter of divine grace. I hold that the Word of God or the truth of revelation is embedded in Scripture because Scripture is encompassed by the presence of the Spirit of Christ. It is possible to argue that there is a direct identity between the substance or matter of the Bible and the transcendent Word and an indirect identity between the letter (*grammar*) and the Word. There is an inseparable relation but not an absolute identity between God's Word and the scriptural witness (cf. Ex 4:14–16; Ps 139:6; 1 Pet 1:10; 1 Cor 7:12, 25). When the

---

in that it is encompassed by the 'Word presence,' the living reality of the Spirit of Christ" (27). Here Bloesch turns to the sacramental vocabulary of "sign" and "signification" to parse out the distinction between living Word and written Word. Thus, according to Bloesch, "the Bible is included in the redemptive act of Christ as his Spirit works in the community of faith" (27). In closing, Bloesch sounds a familiar note to the quotations initially recognized in the body of my monograph above. We read, "The Bible in and of itself is not the Word of God—divine revelation—but it is translucent to this revelation by virtue of the Spirit of God working within it and within the mind of the reader and hearer" (27). In short, the language reflects Bloesch's attempt to take Scripture's authority seriously, while refusing to behold Scripture as the ultimate authority of faith. As Stanley Grenz rightly observes, "If revelation is not simply the Bible but the dynamic of the divine encounter, then Scripture cannot be the ultimate norm for theology. Instead, this norm can only be revelation itself" (Grenz, *Evangelical Theology in Transition*, 45–46). The answer to Bloesch's apparent internal contradiction lies in his understanding of the distinction between the living Word and written Word stemming from Barth. Bloesch wants to uphold ultimate revelatory authority in the person of Christ Himself while not losing the primary instrumental authority of Scripture as a vehicle of revelation. Bloesch's inconsistency in articulating the role of Scripture as demonstrated by these two passages is due to his conviction that Scripture is first and foremost a means of grace.

56. Bloesch, *Holy Scripture*, 57.

letter is separated from the Spirit who brings us life and salvation, it becomes a written code that kills (2 Cor 3:6).[57]

The concept of indirect versus direct identity is a key feature anchoring Word & Spirit as authoritative in the act of revelation. Importantly, it is not only the "Word" that governs Scripture, but likewise the "Spirit." Here, we see the inseparability of the Word & Spirit, even within Bloesch's enunciation of the meaning of the Word. While epistemology is the focus, it is not void of ontology. In revelation the primary actors are Word & Spirit, accomplishing a work that only they can accomplish. Scripture is a tool in the hands of Word & Spirit, achieving the goal of divine self-disclosure leading to salvation. Authority rests ultimately not in Scripture as such, but in Word & Spirit.[58]

The Proclaimed Word

Having detailed the role of the written word as the primary means of revelation, I now briefly turn attention to the proclaimed word as a *secondary* primary means of revelation.[59] Bloesch summarizes the relatedness of living Word, written Word, and proclaimed Word in stating,

> One may speak of the Bible as the word and the church as the mouth. The church is the instrument of Christ, who reaffirms the word that he spoke in sacred Scripture. Scripture is the unique word of God, but we hear this word as it is proclaimed by its messengers and heralds.[60]

The proclaimed word of the church is under the authority of the written Word, which is ultimately directed by the living Word Himself, Christ. For Bloesch, the proclaimed Word is the totality of church proclamation. It includes both the historical datum of tradition and the ongoing heralding of the gospel in contemporary pulpits.[61]

In a brief appendix in *A Theology of Word & Spirit*, Bloesch explores the relationship between gospel and kerygma, and it is here that he clearly

---

57. Bloesch, *Holy Scripture*, 57–58.

58. Bloesch states, "Yet the final authority is not what the Bible says but what God says in the Bible" (*Holy Scripture*, 60).

59. Bloesch, *Holy Scripture*, 59.

60. Bloesch, *Holy Scripture*, 156.

61. Bloesch, *Holy Scripture*, 160–61.

develops his understanding of the role of proclamation in God's act of self-revelation. For Bloesch, "gospel" is simply another word for revelation. Bloesch states, "The gospel, therefore, is not a creation of the human mind but a message revealed by God."[62] Bloesch ties this together with his already established definition of revelation when he states that the content of the gospel is "the living Christ."[63] Conversely, "kerygma" is another word for proclamation/preaching.[64] While the kerygma is God's established means of communicating the gospel, it is not necessarily the case that it accomplishes this task. Rather, the preacher is caught up in the drama of divine revelation that is dependent upon the primary actors of Word & Spirit to achieve the necessary performance. Bloesch claims,

> It is possible to receive the message of salvation merely as a human word rather than the Word of God (1 Thess 2:13); this means that the gospel itself, Christ for us and in us, cannot be equated with the cultural and religious form in which it comes to us. Apart from the illumination of the Spirit, the gospel is nothing more than the kerygma, the preaching of the gospel. Ideally, the kerygma is the preaching of Christ plus its content, the risen Christ. Yet apart from the descent of the risen Christ into the words of the preacher, the kerygma remains simply an announcement or proclamation devoid of transforming power and existential meaning. When the proclamation is enlivened and illumined by the Spirit of Christ, it then becomes the gospel, the revivifying message of salvation.[65]

Here, Bloesch is primarily focused on the necessity of Word & Spirit operating in the act of proclamation. The preacher is dependent, not primarily on his or her own understanding or capacity to articulate the truth, but on the movement of God by Word & Spirit. According to Bloesch, the risen Christ, the living Word, must descend into the words of the preacher for the preacher's words to contain the power of the gospel. The language of descent signals the preacher's dependence on divine action and condescension. The preacher cannot ascend to the Word in his or her words, but by the work of the Holy Spirit the Word can be encountered in his or her

---

62. Bloesch, *Theology of Word & Spirit*, 136. Bloesch goes on to state, "Because the gospel is God's revelation, not a product of theological imagination (1 Cor 2:9; Gal 1:11), it is not an obvious truth for those whom the god of this world has blinded (2 Cor 4:3–4)" (136).

63. Bloesch, *Theology of Word & Spirit*, 138.

64. Bloesch, *Theology of Word & Spirit*, 136.

65. Bloesch, *Theology of Word & Spirit*, 136.

words. Bloesch reiterates this emphasis on the crucial role of the Spirit in the proclamation of the Word when he argues, "Church authority cannot hand out [the] Word, but it can serve [the] Word when it places itself at the disposal of the Spirit, who alone revives the weary and converts the lost."[66] The conjunction of the proclaimed Word with the living Word is a work of the Spirit of the Word.

The need for Word & Spirit is not only on stage with the preacher, but in the audience. The hearers of proclamation only hear it as the Word by a work of Word & Spirit.[67] While a unity may be found between proclaimed Word and living Word, the Spirit must make this clear to the listener. As Bloesch states, "The words of the kerygma are therefore not identical with the Word of God. But there is nevertheless a paradoxical unity between them, a unity hidden from natural reason until we are enlightened by the Holy Spirit."[68] Bloesch is assuming a particular Pauline trope here, namely, that the gospel is veiled to those who are outside Christ. Grasping the gospel requires eyes of faith which can be had only by the illuminating work of the Spirit in Christ; to truly see the living Christ in his revealed Word, the Spirit must be at work not only in the proclamation of the preacher but in the hearing of the listeners.[69] When this happens, both parts of revelation are operational, objective and subjective, and the divine-human encounter occurs.

A Theology of the Spirit

My investigation of Bloesch's use of "Word" in his work *Jesus Christ*, and its development through his book *Holy Scripture*, demonstrates how its epistemological focus has a formal impact on his doctrine of revelation which, in turn, grounds the objective-subjective dialectic at the heart of his system.

---

66. Bloesch, *Holy Scripture*, 160–61.

67. Bloesch assumes a doctrine of sin here. It reads elsewhere, "The problem of human conversion must be understood in the light of the biblical affirmation that fallen humanity is both unable and unwilling to come to God in faith and repentance" (Bloesch, *Theology of Word & Spirit*, 221). Bloesch goes on to state, "Scripture speaks in this context not of physical inability but of moral inability. Because the human will is in bondage to the power of sin, we of our own power could not turn from the way of destruction even if we were intellectually persuaded that this was the right thing to do" (221).

68. Bloesch, *Theology of Word & Spirit*, 138.

69. Bloesch states, "The gospel is a word that goes out from God and does not return to him empty (Is 55:11). It is a word that remains the property of God, but a word that we can hear and know through the action of the Spirit of God upon us" (*Theology of Word & Spirit*, 137).

This also demonstrates the enduring role of the Spirit in revelation—an impulse that reveals the formal and material impact of Bloesch's pietism. More than mere application, the Spirit's role in bringing the Word by means of Scripture and church proclamation is an essential aspect of revelation itself. Revelation *qua* encounter entails more than a moment in history; the event of revelation is left open in its objectivity only to be closed through a reciprocated subjectivity.

Turning to the Spirit's role specifically, Bloesch begins his volume *The Holy Spirit* by identifying it as "a book on spirituality" alongside of historical and systematic theology.[70] What does it mean to say that this is a book on spirituality? It focuses "on the work of the Spirit in renewing the church and shaping the Christian life rather than on his person."[71] Bloesch explicitly confirms the previously stated heuristic: Word & Spirit name revelation in an epistemic register. He is not concerned with articulating the Spirit ontologically but is focused on the role of the Spirit in the divine economy.[72] In this economic account the emphasis on ecclesial renewal and

70. Bloesch, *Holy Spirit*, 14.
71. Bloesch, *Holy Spirit*, 19.
72. Bloesch, *Holy Spirit*, 19. In an early chapter of *The Holy Spirit*, we find a short section titled "The Person of the Spirit." While Bloesch has stated his primary goal is not to develop an ontological account of the third person of the Trinity, one expects Bloesch to at minimum have something to say in this regard in this one-and-a-half-page section. Instead, in a striking display of his disinterest in doing so, the entirety of this brief section is dedicated strictly to a survey of challenges, questions, and issues in theology related to the personhood of the Holy Spirit with no constructive development of his own on the topic (50–52). The tenth chapter of the volume is titled "The Holy Spirit: Person & Mission." Here Bloesch does provide somewhat of a constructive account of the third person of the Trinity in relation to Father and Son within the immanent life of the Trinity. Particular focus is given on the debate over the *filioque clause,* of which Bloesch commits himself to an affirmation of its inclusion in the Creed. It is here that Bloesch puts forth the most developed articulation of the person of the Trinity ontologically:

> I do not see the Father as the only actor in the Trinity, nor is he the sole source of action (monopatrism). The Father presents a plan and the Son carries through the plan with the aid of the Spirit. But the Son and the Spirit also contribute to this plan. The Spirit not only receives from the Father and the Son but also responds creatively. The Spirit is not only acted upon by the Father and the Son but forges the bond of unity between Father and Son. He searches the depths of God and brings the intentions of God to fruition and realization (1 Cor 2:10–11). (*Holy Spirit*, 273)

Bloesch goes on to state,

> There exists within God an interdependency and a dependency. Son and Spirit are both dependent on the Father, but the Father is also dependent on

the Christian life comes to the fore, evidenced materially in the volume through an exploration of topics like the nature of faith, spiritual gifts, and holiness. Similar to his mode of writing in *Jesus Christ,* Bloesch narrates a theological survey, followed by a critical assessment, and only then turning to his own doctrinal construction. There is a clear emphasis in this volume on the missional work of the third person of the Trinity, and consequently, an emphasis on the subjective-experiential pole of revelation.

To clarify his distinct account of the Spirit's role in revelation, Bloesch appeals to George Lindbeck's *The Nature of Doctrine.*[73] Bloesch outlines Lindbeck's typological grid for identifying different approaches to the theological task. First, the cognitive-propositional, "which reduces the message of faith to propositional declarations accessible to human reason."[74] Second, the experiential-expressive, "which finds the ground of theology in a universal human experience."[75] Third, the cultural-linguistic, "which sees the task of theology as transmitting the language and symbols of the faith from one generation to another."[76] While Bloesch's affirmation of Lindbeck is interesting, it is more helpful to identify what he thinks Lindbeck misses. He notes, "The problem with his typology is that it does not adequately cover a major strand in contemporary theology, including Karl Barth, Thomas Torrance, Kenneth Hamilton, Arthur Cochrane and Donald Bloesch."[77] Bloesch focuses his constructive response to this perceived gap in Lindbeck's typology on the doctrine of revelation. According to Bloesch, his account of revelation, however distinct from Barth, is akin to a school of thought that is foreign to Lindbeck's types. It is here that Bloesch provides the clearest window into the Spirit component of his Word-Spirit theology. Intentionally contrasting his language with Lindbeck's, Bloesch states,

> I propose another option in theology, which I prefer to call *revelational-pneumatic*. Here the appeal is not to a mystical experience or a universal human experience but to a divine revelation

---

the other two for the implementation of his will. The Spirit is dependent on the Son, but the Son also needs the Spirit for the perfecting of his work. The Spirit is both person and force. He is both life-giving energy and one who speaks and prays. He utters prayers within us and helps us in our prayers (Rom 8:26–27). (273–74)

73. Bloesch, *Holy Spirit*, 22n1.
74. Bloesch, *Holy Spirit*, 22.
75. Bloesch, *Holy Spirit*, 22.
76. Bloesch, *Holy Spirit*, 22.
77. Bloesch, *Holy Spirit*, 23.

in a particular history, a revelation recorded and enshrined in the Bible. The focal point of attention is not stories and shared experiences of people of faith but the intervention of God in human history, particularly in the person of Jesus Christ. Priority is given neither to experience nor to language but to the divine-human encounter in the Jesus Christ of biblical history.[78]

What stands out in Bloesch's "revelational-pneumatic" theology is the resilience of the objective-Word. Bloesch claims, "Priority is given . . . to the divine-human encounter in the Jesus Christ of biblical history."[79] As we have already seen in Bloesch's Word & Spirit taxonomy, order matters. The objective-historical comes before the subjective-experiential, or to state it along the contours of redemption history, Word proceeds Spirit. Having identified the proper starting place, Bloesch is now free to focus on the Spirit's role in this "revelational-pneumatic" model, which he identifies as "moving the will to accept the Word" and "making known the Word."[80] The Spirit illuminates the objective revelation of Christ and gives the human being eyes to see. Revelation entails a reception on the part of human persons, but such a reception is instigated by the internal work of the Holy Spirit.[81]

78. Bloesch, *Holy Spirit*, 23.
79. Bloesch, *Holy Spirit*, 23.
80. Bloesch, *Holy Spirit*, 23–24.
81. This ordered relation of Word & Spirit is the source of a debate between Bloesch and Frank Macchia in a series of articles in the *Journal of Pentecostal Theology*. Macchia initiates the debate in a review of Bloesch's *The Holy Spirit*. In his review, Macchia's fundamental critique of Bloesch is that the Spirit is subordinated to the Word:

> Bloesch's focus on God's self-disclosure in Christ as the foundation of revelation, though praiseworthy, lacks Trinitarian fullness because it lacks an adequate pneumatology. Bloesch is definitely aware of the challenge of Spirit Christology, even granting token acknowledgements of its presence in the Synoptic gospels in one place. He seems to want a complementary relationship between Word and Spirit so as to avoid the rationalism of a logos Christology, but not at the cost of the subordination of the Spirit to the Word. (Macchia, "Toward a Theology of the Third Article," 8)

Macchia proposes "Spirit Christology" as a solution to this perceived weakness in Bloesch's account (9). Bloesch responds to Macchia's critique by rejecting Spirit Christology and clarifying the balance of his Word & Spirit account:

> Our main area of difference seems to be the legitimacy of a Spirit Christology, of which Macchia is a vigorous proponent. In opposition to a logos Christology, a Spirit Christology makes the work of the Holy Spirit central in the explication of the faith. I would be very reluctant to say, as does Macchia, that the Holy Spirit is "the foundation of the Christ event." ("Response to Frank Macchia," 19)

While Bloesch wants to anchor this subjective revelation in the objective Word, he does not shy away from the importance of human experience. He goes on to assert, "A revelational-pneumatic theology assigns an important place to Christian experience—not as the source of faith but as the medium of faith, the catalyst that deepens faith."[82] Spiritual experience is not the engine of revelation but the vehicle of revelation. It is not the starter of faith, but it is the catalyst of deepening faith. Through the vehicle of experience, the Spirit enables human beings to subjectively know the divine-human encounter that was objectively accomplished in the person of Christ. For Bloesch, this spiritual experience is always a personal experience in that it is an encounter through the person of the Spirit with the person of the Son.[83]

What becomes clear through his development in his volume *The Holy Spirit* is that Bloesch is consistent in his articulation of the Word & Spirit dialectic as a feature of revelation that establishes the objective-subjective dialectic. This is Bloesch's mature construction. The Word-Spirit construct is articulated, in contrast to alternative accounts, using the term "revelational-pneumatic" precisely to maintain the union between these two and the reciprocating encounter they presuppose. As with the Word, the language used to articulate this Spirit-empowered encounter is the language of the Christian life—faith and experience. The divine enterprise of self-disclosure entails a human knowing by way of the third person of the Trinity.

In both *Jesus Christ* and *The Holy Spirit*, Bloesch is concerned with identifying Word & Spirit in their economic operations rather than their immanent life. Bloesch's emphasis is not on the divine persons themselves but rather on the divine-human encounter they enable.[84] This is

---

Bloesch goes on to state:

> In place of both a Spirit Christology and a logos Christology I propose a Trinitarian Christology in which the Spirit voluntarily subordinates himself to the Father and the Son, and the Son in turn allows himself to be led by the Spirit as well as by the Father. The relationship between the members of the Trinity is reciprocal; nonetheless there is a pattern of voluntary subordination in which the Son and the Spirit are dependent on the Father, and the Spirit is dependent on the Son. (19)

In conclusion, Bloesch argues, "A Spirit Christology of the type advocated by Macchia seems to assume that the Spirit can lead one directly to the Father apart from the mediation of the Word" (20).

82. Bloesch, *Holy Spirit*, 24.
83. Bloesch, *Holy Spirit*, 24.
84. While Bloesch's theology of Word & Spirit is a governing doctrine for the totality of his project, it is such in an epistemological mode rather than an ontological mode. In

true throughout Bloesch's entire seven-volume *Christian Foundations*. As Bloesch conclusively states at the end of his seventh volume, "In these

other words, it is not Word & Spirit ontologically which serve as organizing principles, but rather Word & Spirit as categories of knowledge that serve as an organizing principle for Bloesch. Bloesch does not directly address the doctrine of the Trinity proper until the third volume of his *Christian Foundations*. One might be surprised by this given that his first volume is *A Theology of Word & Spirit*, but the doctrine of God is not directly engaged until his fifth volume *God the Almighty*, and even here Bloesch does not develop Word & Spirit as more powerful ontological actors in his project. It is this missing ontological ingredient of Word & Spirit which for Thomas F. Torrance is a disappointing feature of Bloesch's theology. Specific to the *God the Almighty* volume Torrance states:

> Hence I could have wished that at this point Bloesch had given us his chapter 7 on "The Mystery of the Trinity" and that in it he had given an account of the doctrine of the Holy Trinity not just "as the apex and goal of theology" but as the ultimate ground and all determining structure of Christian theology. This would take Bloesch's account of God's attributes and perfections down to a deeper level, where their evangelical import would be more effectively apparent. (Torrance, "Bloesch's Doctrine of God," 140)

Torrance is perhaps correct in his critique. If Bloesch put forth a more robust doctrine of God functioning as a grounding principle in his theology of Word and Spirit, it may very well have supported the "evangelical" objectives of Bloesch. Bloesch's stress on personal encounter with God may very well have been enriched by the move Torrance suggests. Helpfully, Bloesch responds to Torrance's critique within the same volume. In short, Bloesch states that he is "reluctant to identify the church's dogmatic articulation of the Trinity with the self-revelation of God as triune" (Bloesch, "Response to Thomas Torrance," in Colyer, *Evangelical Theology in Transition*, 198). Bloesch believes the doctrine of the Trinity is an implication of the gospel rather than the essence of the original revelatory gospel unveiling itself. What seems to perhaps be lost in this debate between Torrance and Bloesch is a clear distinction between the immanent and economic poles of the doctrine of the Trinity. Interestingly, Bloesch states, "there may be a convergence if a clear differentiation is made between the reality of the Trinity and the conceptualization of this reality" (199). What Bloesch seems to allude to here is a more economic account of Trinitarian theology that may indeed be acceptable. It is here that Torrance seems to believe Bloesch has a doctrinal "blind spot." Torrance critiques Bloesch's argument that the doctrine of the Trinity is both an "analytical development of the central act of divine revelation (as Barth maintained) and a synthetic construction drawn from the church's reflection upon this revelation" (Torrance, "Bloesch's Doctrine of God," 144). Torrance argues that the doctrine of the Trinity is not fundamentally a "synthetic" construction of church history's reflection of the gospel, but indeed is an organic component of the gospel itself. It is the Triune God that has revealed Himself; thus, revelation at the start and at the core is Triune in shape. Torrance states, "Does he not here lean too much to the notion that the doctrine of the Trinity is the product of theological reasoning? Rather, we must think of the triune God as himself the immediate content of his self-revelation" (145). Ultimately, Torrance is suspicious that the "blind spot" here is in fact based on a failed distinction between the immanent and economic Trinity. He concludes, "Bloesch is misled into an unclear notion of the relation between the economic Trinity and the immanent Trinity" (146).

volumes I have proposed a theology of Word and Spirit that strives to unite the objective and subjective poles of divine revelation."[85] "Word & Spirit," as a singular and inseparable construct, names the unified action of the second and third persons of the triune God. This instinct is the formal impulse that gives shape to Bloesch's theology which explains, materially, why space normally reserved for discussion of the triune *persons* shifts to the experience of the Christian. This does not signal a move away from creedal (or even confessional) Christianity—Bloesch does not lack in Nicaean or Chalcedonian credibility—but has determined the theologian's engagement with God is best articulated through naming the encounter that God initiates in the revelatory missions of Word & Spirit. As a result, Word & Spirit are chiefly used by Bloesch, materially, to talk about revelation by way of the economy of redemption. In Bloesch's words, "God reveals himself through himself: through his Word, who became incarnate in human flesh, and through his Spirit."[86] Bloesch tells us who Word & Spirit are by showing us what they do which is to establish the divine-human encounter.

The objective, external self-disclosure of God, cannot be fully articulated apart from the subjective, internal human experience of knowing God. "To affirm a theology of Word and Spirit," Bloesch notes, "is to affirm that the experience of faith is correlative with God's self-revelation in Jesus Christ."[87] This reveals the reasoning behind his fundamental commitment to the Christian life, and how the Christian life is, on this account, necessarily materially distributive. Bloesch's theology of revelation is a theology of the Christian life, and because revelation is the formally distributed doctrine for Bloesch's whole theological enterprise, concentrated concern for the Christian life shapes every doctrinal locus in the system. In Bloesch's account of revelation, the initiatory objective work of the Word is consummated by the subjective work of the Spirit in the life of the believer. As he explicitly claims, "A theology of Word and Spirit will be at the same time a theology of the Christian life, since the truth revealed in the Bible must be appropriated through the power of the Spirit in a life of obedience and

---

85. Bloesch, *Last Things*, 261.

86. Bloesch, *God the Almighty*, 74. Bloesch strikes a similar note in *The Holy Spirit* when he states, "It is my earnest conviction that the Spirit must not be separated from the Word, nor should the Word ever be divorced from the Spirit. There is no pathway to God that is direct and unmediated. We come to God through his revelation in Christ, which is communicated by the Spirit" (*Holy Spirit*, 30–31).

87. Bloesch, *Theology of Word & Spirit*, 15.

piety."[88] While the living Word has objectively initiated revelation in the written Word, this work must be consummated by the Spirit's subjective appropriation of that Word in the life of the Christian. Significantly, the appropriating work of the Spirit in this regard is not passively received by the believer, but rather is fought for and retained by active obedience and piety.

Objectivism & Subjectivism

Having articulated Bloesch's Word & Spirit account of revelation, it is worth pausing to note potentially competing approaches to revelation that Bloesch himself seeks to guard against. As I noted in the introduction, one stylistic feature of Bloesch's theological writing is his mapping of competing viewpoints. Seeking to chart the middle way, Bloesch frequently warns against two opposing temptations when constructing a doctrine of revelation—objectivism and subjectivism.[89] Analyzing these temptations brings further clarity to the distinctiveness of Bloesch's position.

Objectivism holds that "the human mind is called to submit to a purely external authority."[90] Subjectivism holds that "autonomous human reason or experience" are "determinant for Christian thinking and practice."[91] In a

88. Bloesch, *Holy Spirit*, 31.
89. Here, another example of Bloesch following the thought of Brunner is given:

> For the God-given power of the Reformation lies in the fact that through it the Church was enabled to escape from this fatal antithesis, Objectivism-Subjectivism, and to find the secret of moving both between and beyond these extremes. Its "epistemological" principle was a dialectic; that is, its form of expression was never the use of one concept, but always two logically contradictory ones: the Word of God in the Bible and the witness of the Holy Spirit, but these understood and experienced, not as a duality, but as a unity. (Brunner, *Divine-Human Encounter*, 20)

Brunner goes on to state, "This paradoxical unity of Word and Spirit, of historical revelation and God's contemporary presence, of 'Christ for us' and 'Christ in us'—that is the secret of the Reformation, of its power to renew Biblical faith and shake off the fetters of a century-long foreign rule, both theological and ecclesiastical" (20).

90. Bloesch, *Theology of Word & Spirit*, 131.
91. Bloesch, *Theology of Word & Spirit*, 130. Bloesch identifies these two errors in *The Ground of Certainty* as he discusses the nature of human certainty in relation to divine self-revelation. Bloesch is clear to establish the kind of certainty he is speaking of at the outset of the chapter. He states, "The theological understanding of certainty differs considerably from that of philosophy. What philosophers generally envision is a rational or demonstrable certainty. Theology speaks of the certainty of faith, the certainty of the heart which is more existential than rational" (*Ground of Certainty*, 68).

discussion of the nature of certainty, Bloesch identifies the objectivist error as *rationalism* and the subjectivist error as *mysticism*. Rationalism holds to a kind of certainty grounded in the human person's intellect and capacity for comprehending "conceptual truth" external to the self.[92] The mystic, by way of contrast, is one whose "perception or intuition rather than intellectual clarity is regarded as the ground of certainty."[93] For Bloesch, these two errors of rationalism and mysticism threaten a properly paradoxical Word & Spirit account of revelation.[94]

As Bloesch identifies these two errors in the doctrine of revelation, he frequently identifies Carl Henry as an exemplar of rationalism and Fredrich Schleiermacher as an exemplar of mysticism.[95] On the side of rationalism,

92. Bloesch, *Theology of Word & Spirit*, 69.

93. Bloesch, *Theology of Word & Spirit*, 69.

94. Stanley Grenz helpfully maps some of Bloesch's primary concerns with rationalism in *Evangelical Theology in Transition*. He highlights Bloesch's commitment to a robust account of the "fall" which includes the noetic effects of sin. This, according to Grenz, is Bloesch's primary sticking point with rationalism and in particular Protestant Scholasticism. Grenz gives us a window into Bloesch on this issue in stating, "The extent of our fallenness, he argues, leaves us devoid of any innate point of contact for the gospel. Even our reason is affected" (Grenz, "Fideistic Revelationalism," 40). Bloesch argues that the rationalists fail not only in their overly optimistic view of man's understanding, but also in their account of God's nature as well, "namely that he is primarily 'mind'" (40). Bloesch argues that God is not primarily mind, but rather "will." Grenz summarizes the consequence of such a position in stating, "Because God is will, Bloesch concludes, revelation is not chiefly concerned with transferring cognitive information from one rational mind (God's) to another (ours). More importantly it is an encounter of a sinful person with God through Jesus Christ that transforms the human will and thereby issues forth in obedience" (40). Bloesch consistently balances this concern with rationalism by guarding against the danger of mysticism on the other side. If rationalism is overly optimistic about the human persons mental capacity to understand what God communicates, then mysticism is overly optimistic about the human persons existential capacity for grasping the divine within. Bloesch argues, "Whereas Christian theology views the knowledge of God as something given in revelation, mysticism tends to see truth hidden in the depths of the soul and waiting only to be discovered" (*Ground of Certainty*, 135).

95. In his *Holy Scripture* volume, in a chapter titled "The Meaning of Revelation," Bloesch explores several accounts of divine revelation by looking for both the objectivist-rationalist and subjectivist-mystical errors to which they may have fallen prey. In doing so, Bloesch is critical of "much of the older Christian tradition," which gives an account of the nature of revelation that is rationalistic in its orientation (*Holy Scripture*, 46). Bloesch often identifies Carl Henry as a representative of the objectivist/rationalist approach, but of course Henry is not alone. Bloesch groups him in the rationalist camp with Hodge, Warfield, Erickson, Nash, and Sproul (40). Bloesch states, "In this perspective, which dominated both Catholic and Protestant scholasticism, revelation is the divine disclosure of information concerning the nature of God and his will and purpose for the world. It

Bloesch summarizes Henry's view as "an assent of the will to what reason has already shown to be true."[96] According to Bloesch, Henry views revelation as equivalent with "the propositional content of the Bible."[97] The rationalist construal of faith represented by Henry stresses a "univocal knowledge of God."[98] On the side of mysticism, Bloesch critiques Schleiermacher's theology. According to Bloesch, Schleiermacher posits revelation as fundamentally "affective rather than cognitive."[99] In contrast with Henry's equating of revelation and Scripture, Schleiermacher holds that the meaning to be found in reading Scripture is that of "religious experience."[100] Contra the univocal predication of Henry, Schleiermacher holds that "theological statements are possible only as statements of Christian self-awareness."[101]

While rationalism and mysticism are divergent streams, Bloesch believes that they flow from the same polluted headwaters. Rather than beginning with God, they begin with the human person. For rationalism, the

---

is both rational and propositional and thereby stands in direct continuity with ordinary knowledge" (46–47). On the opposite side of his concern, in *Holy Scripture* Bloesch is critical of the subjectivist neo-Protestant and neo-Catholic responses to this rationalist account of revelation. He is particularly concerned with their emphasis on the experiential and the existential to the neglect of the rational and propositional (47). Bloesch refers to this position as both "mystical" and "experiential" and points to Schleiermacher as a luminary. Bloesch frequently identifies Schleiermacher as a representative of the subjectivist/mystic approach. To be sure, he lists others such as Paul Tillich and Simone Weil. Regarding these figures he states, "This mystical-idealist tradition in the Christian faith stresses the continuity between God and humanity even while placing God beyond the compass of discursive reason. We find God by entering into ourselves and discovering the spark of divinity that links us to the eternal" (Bloesch, *God the Almighty*, 177). Specific to the mysticism of Tillich, Bloesch states elsewhere, "When he [Tillich] affirms that self-discovery is tantamount to God-discovery it would seem that he is much closer to Hinduism than to classical Christianity" (*Christian Witness in a Secular Age*, 79).

96. Bloesch, *Theology of Word & Spirit*, 58. Bloesch states, "The rationalism that Torrance warns against is exemplified in Carl Henry, who finds the unity of Scripture in a 'logical system of shared beliefs'" (*Holy Spirit*, 37).

97. Bloesch, *Theology of Word & Spirit*, 254. Bloesch argues that on Henry's account, "divine revelation become identical with the 'logical interconnected content' of Scripture" (Bloesch, *Holy Spirit*, 38). According to Bloesch, engaging Scripture on Henry's account is an attempt to "deduce true propositions" from the text (Bloesch, *Theology of Word & Spirit*, 118).

98. Bloesch, *Theology of Word & Spirit*, 68. In *The Holy Spirit*, Bloesch refers to Henry's position as "univocal predication" (*Holy Spirit*, 36–37).

99. Bloesch, *Theology of Word & Spirit*, 108.

100. Bloesch, *Theology of Word & Spirit*, 73.

101. Bloesch, *Theology of Word & Spirit*, 109.

An Evangelical Spiritual Theology

human person's cognitive capacity is the source of grasping revelation. For mysticism, the human person's existential capacity is the source of grasping revelation. According to Bloesch, both rationalism and mysticism are accounts of the human person ascending to God.[102] Bloesch summarizes helpfully, "Against both mystical and scholastic theology I maintain that we cannot reach God by the way of virtue or of thought, but God can come to us and enable us to think what was previously unthinkable."[103] Objectivist-rationalism is overly confident in *reason's* ability to grasp conceptual data made known by God and, in so doing, to comprehend God himself. Subjectivist-mysticism is overly confident in human virtue and the internal, existential exploration of the divine.

On Bloesch's account, God remains hidden apart from the divine-human encounter of revelation. This is why Bloesch's doctrinal work remains somewhat materially apophatic in regard to God himself. Bloesch is cautious about theological speculation. However, he is optimistic regarding knowing God, not because of human ascent by intellect or existential experience, but because God reveals himself in the economy of Word & Spirit. As Bloesch succinctly states, "The God of the Bible is both the *Deus revelatus* ('the revealed God') and the *Deus absconditus* ('the hidden God')."[104]

---

102. "For Christian faith and theology divine revelation, not human reason, is the basis for certainty. It is not what man can conceive or discover or accomplish but rather what God has done for man in Jesus Christ that gives the Christian his assurance. It is not the idea of God in the soul or His design in nature but the encounter with God in His Word that induces belief in Him" (Bloesch, *Theology of Word & Spirit*, 70).

103. Bloesch, *God the Almighty*, 61. Thomas F. Torrance identifies this in Bloesch's thought when he states, "Bloesch maintains against both mystical and scholastic theology that while we cannot reach God by ourselves, God himself comes to us, addressing us in his Word, and enables us to think what was previously unthinkable. That is what happens in and through the Lord Jesus Christ, in whom the mystery and wisdom of God have become incarnate in human flesh" (Torrance, "Bloesch's Doctrine of God," 137). Bloesch stresses that both rationalism and mysticism share an improper focus on the human person's capacity for ascending to God. In regard to mysticism he states, "The mystics, Meister Eckhart, Henry Suso, and Johann Tauler among others, also held that divine truth transcends reason, and that the way to truth lies in divesting oneself of all mental images. Yet the mystics returned not so much to the biblical sources of faith as to Neo-Platonic philosophy, which in the name of reason posited truth beyond reason" (Bloesch, *Ground of Certainty*, 34). In speaking of rationalism Bloesch states, "The predilection of philosophy is to overcome the polarities and ambiguities of life by arriving at a synthesis that perfects and crowns human reasoning. It cannot tolerate anything that defies rational comprehension, for this to acknowledge a surd in human existence" (*Theology of Word & Spirit*, 80).

104. Bloesch, *God the Almighty*, 49.

The arena in which the human person comes to know this hidden, yet revealed God is the Christian life.

Bloesch most often uses the terms rationalism and mysticism as synonyms for objectivism and subjectivism, respectively.[105] Both words capture the two deviant forms of the divine-human encounter with which Bloesch is concerned.[106] For my purposes, these descriptive categories are

---

105. Bloesch develops further the dialectical nature of his doctrine of revelation while furnishing many of the working categories in his *The Holy Spirit* volume. He clearly is seeking to maintain the wedded relation of Word & Spirit, objective & subjective, and it is here that we find the language of rationalism and mysticism:

> The contemporary scene is marked by a continuing tension between revelational theology and experiential theology. Do we gain knowledge of God through past revelation in Jesus Christ as found in the Bible, or does our knowledge of God derive from an experience of the Spirit who dwells within us? We should recognize that revelation itself contains an experiential or mystical dimension. Otherwise, revelation would be reduced to the communication of concepts that affect the mind but not the whole human being. (*Holy Spirit*, 223)

Bloesch goes on to state:

> A closely related polarity in contemporary theology is that between Logos Christology and Spirit Christology. Theologians who espouse the former tilt toward rationalism, whereas those who defend the latter lean toward mysticism or spiritualism. The challenge today seems to be to rediscover the complementarity of Logos and Spirit while still maintaining the subordination of Spirit to Logos (which is the biblical pattern). A Logos Christology does not necessarily preserve the transcendence of God, for the emphasis could be on the continuity rather than the discontinuity between the divine Logos and human reason (as in evangelical rationalism). A Spirit Christology is always in danger of forfeiting transcendence by its stress on the immanence of God in history and nature. (223)

Interestingly, this shows the dialectical balance, instead of the proper ordering of Word and Spirit, objective and subjective here, which has already been discussed. Bloesch then concludes by locating his own position as informed by expected interlocutors Barth and Brunner. It reads, "The dialectical theology associated with Karl Barth and Emil Brunner—and continuing with some modifications in John Thompson, Thomas Torrance, and Donald Bloesch—signifies a reaffirmation of Logos Christology but without denying the experiential element" (*Holy Spirit*, 223–24).

106. On the side of objectivism, Bloesch will use not only rationalism, but corresponding terms such as philosophy, reason, scholasticism. The actual history of rationalism is pointed toward in a couple of places in Bloesch's theological project. In *God the Almighty* Bloesch states, "Whereas the biblical-classical synthesis was endemic to a significant part of Christian theology in the past, since the dawning of the Renaissance theologians have been tempted to accommodate the faith to modernity" (*God the Almighty*, 241). In *A Theology of & Spirit* we read, "The incontrovertible triumph of the Enlightenment over both the Reformation and the Counter-Reformation has sapped the spiritual vitality of

An Evangelical Spiritual Theology

particularly intriguing. Bloesch's use of mysticism and rationalism shows the interconnection between a theological account of revelation and the lived response of that account; one's description of God's self-revelation asserts pressure across the doctrinal system to shape what it means to know and to follow him. Therefore, as these accounts are deviant forms of revelation, they embrace deviancy in the Christian life. By enlisting these categories, Bloesch quickly moves from errors in the doctrine of revelation to corresponding errors in the Christian life. Furthermore, Bloesch's Word & Spirit serves as a heuristic to name these errors that refuse to hold together the dialectic. Either, one fails to uphold the dialectic by losing the Spirit and therefore has an objective account without its subjective counterpart (rationalism), or it loses the Word, bolstering a merely subjective account (mysticism). Bloesch shows how his heuristic needs constant rehearsing, "Word and Spirit go together, and whenever we lose sight of their inseparable unity, we lapse into either moralism and rationalism on the one hand, or mysticism and spiritualism on the other."[107]

---

modern Western civilization. Since the eighteenth century, humanity rather than God has become the focal point of theology and philosophy. Trust in human reason has slowly but surely displaced trust in divine revelation as the infallible guide for life and thought" (Bloesch, *Theology of Word & Spirit*, 25). With this historical backdrop in mind Bloesch will state in *The Holy Spirit*, "Rationalism takes the form of either the logic of deduced conclusions (as in most idealistic philosophy) or the logic of evidential confirmations (as in empiricist philosophy). By contrast, the focus of biblical Christianity is on particular events in salvation history whose meaning is drawn out by faithful exposition under the illumination of the Spirit" (*Holy Spirit*, 35). Reformed scholar Richard Muller calls into question the historical conflation of rationalism and scholasticism: "'Scholasticism' identifies primarily a method whereas 'rationalism' identifies a particular philosophical stance concerning the foundation of knowing: the one does not entail the other—from a purely historical perspective, few of the scholastics can be classed as rationalists and most of the rationalists have not been scholastics. Of course, the question of the relationship of developing Protestant thought to the rise of rationalism remains" (Muller, *Prolegomena to Theology*, 132). On the side of subjectivism primarily marked by mysticism, Bloesch will use corresponding terms like existentialism, spiritualism, and experientialism. In *The Ground of Certainty* Bloesch identifies two forms of mysticism: "The first refers to an immediate experience of the presence of God"; the second is "a system of thought, a philosophy of life, a type of religion" (*Ground of Certainty*, 141). Bloesch continues, "As a type of religion mysticism is oriented about the mystic way, the stages that lead to the vision of God—purgation, illumination, union and ecstasy. Mysticism here is seen as a pathway to salvation; in this connection it entails asceticism, spiritual exercises that enable one to mount the ladder to perfection" (141). Bloesch argues that mysticism's influences include Platonism and Neo-Platonism, along with Eastern religions. As a result, he argues, "Christian mysticism is a result of the fusion of evangelical biblical faith with Platonic and Neo-Platonic (and perhaps also Oriental) philosophy" (142).

107. Bloesch, *Essentials of Evangelical Theology*, 2:259.

Bloesch's Objective-Subjective Doctrine of Revelation

Bloesch's commitment to maintain the unity of objective-Word and subjective-Spirit is designed to safeguard against the two errors of objectivity and subjectivity. Ultimately, Bloesch believes that avoiding these two errors is critical to maintain the integrity of the divine-human encounter; it is not that one must lose the rational and mystical, rather, the divine-human encounter is both rational *and* mystical.[108] Bloesch calls this objective-subjective position "fideistic revelationalism."[109] As he articulates clearly in his volume *A Theology of Word &Spirit*,

> Since faith is a work of the Spirit in the interiority of our being, the truth of the gospel is not only announced from without but also confirmed from within. In the theology presented here both revelation and salvation have to be understood as objective-subjective rather than fundamentally objective (as in evangelical rationalism) or predominantly subjective (as in existentialism and mysticism).[110]

Bloesch is determined to hold together the external revelation of God by the Word and the internal revelation of God by the Spirit in the life of the believer. Bloesch is wary of an objectivist account of revelation that neuters the power of the present action of God in the interior life of the Christian. Likewise, he is wary of a subjectivist account of revelation that collapses the scope of God's action into the interior of the Christian. Knowledge of God is objective-subjective; revelation is an encounter, one that calls the human before God as God reveals himself to them. In this vein Avery Dulles is clearly correct, generally speaking, when he argues that Bloesch's Word &

---

108. "The content of what is revealed is both a person and a message. Revelation is personal as well as rational, existential as well as propositional" (Bloesch, *Ground of Certainty*, 70).

109. Bloesch, *Theology of Word & Spirit*, 21. Brand rightly notes that "Bloesch insists that both rationalism and fideism, left alone, are off center" (Brand, "Donald George Bloesch's Contribution," 155). Brand recognizes that for Bloesch the only way forward in avoiding these two errors is a theology of Word & Spirit that seeks to uphold the rational and experiential components of the divine-human encounter. Brand goes on to argue that Bloesch's "fideistic revelationalism" is not "fideistic" in the usual sense of the word because "the ground and starting point is not the act of faith itself, but rather God's action through the Word and Spirit" (156–57). Earlier, Brand defines the "fideist" as one who "sees faith as an act of the will in which reason is suspended, an act which incorporates risk as a key component of its commitment" (123).

110. Bloesch, *Theology of Word &Spirit*, 15.

Spirit dialectic is the key feature which draws him into typological association with neo-orthodox luminaries like Barth, Brunner, and Bultmann.[111] As Dulles notes, "The same dialectical principles found in Barth, which seeks to retain the freedom of God in self-revelation and hold to a paradoxical relationship between our communication about God and God's self-communication in the person of Jesus Christ by the Holy Spirit, is found in the work of Donald Bloesch."[112] Nonetheless, while there is credibility to

---

111. Dulles argues that for these neo-Reformers "the content of revelation is not God in his abstract essence, but God who turns toward his creatures in judgment and forgiveness—that is to say, in Jesus Christ" (Dulles, "Models of Revelation," 86). The doctrine of revelation is ordered Christologically with an emphasis placed on the incarnation and an accent mark over the cross and resurrection. This amounts to "a rejection of the revelatory capacities of nature, of religious experience, and of non-Christian religious traditions" (87). Revelation is found in the self-communication of God in the person and work of Jesus Christ, and as a result revelation is necessarily salvific in nature. Consequently, this position holds that Scripture and preaching are the media of divine revelation. They bear witness to divine revelation by the grace of God, but they are not revelation in and of themselves (88). God's authority and action are constantly guarded in this account of revelation. With a particular focus on Barth, Dulles tells the reader, "The truth of revelation, Barth insists, is not what the preacher or the theologian conceptually asserts, but rather the very truth of God who asserts himself. God's word is only paradoxically or dialectically identified with the word of man" (88). Divine revelation does indeed occur now, but only by a work of the Spirit through these means. The content of divine revelation is nothing other than God himself. Dulles's association of Bloesch with these figures is well founded. Bloesch repeatedly appeals to neo-orthodox theologians in his constructive account of revelation. The two that he appeals to the most are Barth and Brunner. In particular, if we look to Bloesch, *Theology of Word & Spirit*, 11–13, we find his engagement with Brunner and Barth. While Bloesch looks to both theologians repeatedly throughout his work he clearly believes that he is doing something different, indeed, corrective in relation to these neo-orthodox theologians in regard to this doctrine. More follows in regard to this, particularly as it relates to the work of Karl Barth. I address in more detail Bloesch's relation to these theologians later in this chapter. For now, I attend to Dulles's work of locating Bloesch within a neo-Reformed account of the doctrine of revelation and seek to clarify the validity of this claim.

112. Dulles is reading Bloesch well here. Bloesch's opening volume to his seven-volume dogmatic work includes a discussion of dialectical theology. Here, Bloesch provides a grounding definition of dialectic, but quickly moves to a discussion of "modern dialectical theology" in which he highlights the work of Barth and Brunner. He states, "Modern dialectical theology (Barth, Brunner) is based on the view that there is neither an identity between thought and being (as in Platonic idealism), nor a direct correspondence (as in realism), but instead a cleavage, which is the result not of finitude per se but of sin. This cleavage is overcome in the paradoxical entry of eternity into time, that is, in the Incarnation of the infinite God in Jesus of Nazareth. All contradictions in human thinking concerning God and his relationship to us have their center in this absolute paradox (Kierkegaard), which is incomprehensible to human reason" (Bloesch, *Theology*

Dulles's association of Bloesch with neo-orthodox theologians, in particular Karl Barth, there are limits to the validity of this association. Putting these thinkers together creates significant reduction in their views forcing them into a grouping they might not recognize, often under the unhelpful banner of "Barthian."[113] As Dulles himself acknowledges, "So numerous are the schools and movements, and so subtle the shades of difference among them, that it is difficult to make general statements."[114] By focusing on commonalities, one often misses what is idiosyncratic, and with Bloesch, this is often exactly what happens.

Since my goal is to move beyond the general to the more particular and nuanced, I draw out Bloesch's idiosyncrasies. In particular, I pay attention to the ways in which Bloesch breaks rank with theologians he often affirms as well as those with whom he is often associated. What becomes clear is that the distinguishing characteristic of his theology of revelation separates him from his neo-Reformed compatriots, and that this bears itself out most explicitly in his doctrine of the Christian life. Bloesch's pietistic impulse drives him to advance a more robust emphasis on the Spirit, the subjective, and the experiential. This is perhaps most clear when Bloesch is put in conversation with Karl Barth.

While Bloesch finds much more to agree with in Barth's "theology of the Word of God" than he does in Schleiermacher's "experientialism," he remains wary of a theology of the Word at the expense of the Spirit.[115] Bloesch writes,

---

of Word & Spirit, 76). As Bloesch continues in this section he provides brief overviews of Brunner and Barth's account of dialectical theology, even tracing the ways in which it matures in their own theological projects. Ultimately, this gives way to a personal affirmation of their dialectical methodology. Bloesch states, "I agree with Barth that dialectical reasoning is necessary in the theological enterprise because the paradox of the eternal God dramatically entering the stream of human history in Jesus Christ can be grasped only through holding together aspects of the truth about God and his plan of salvation that seem contradictory to human reason" (78).

113. In his monograph *Jesus is Victor!* Bloesch engages the soteriology of Karl Barth. This volume provides a helpful window into Bloesch's general disposition toward Barth's theological project. Bloesch notes in the introduction that "in some areas of theology Barth has been an invaluable ally and in other areas a useful foil" (*Jesus is Victor!*, 12). While he appreciates elements of Barth's theology Bloesch wishes to make clear that he "shall never be a bona fide Barthian" (12).

114. Dulles, *Models of Revelation*, 21.

115. Bloesch, *Theology of Word & Spirit*, 13.

> While standing much closer to Barth than to either Schleiermacher or Tillich, I suggest a theology of Word and Spirit, signifying the unity of truth and power evident in both the Incarnation of God in Jesus Christ and the biblical rendition of this event. The word that proceeds from the mouth of God is filled with the power of the Spirit, bringing life and renewal to those dead in sin. By the action of the Spirit it is communicated to us through the gospel proclamation—found first of all in the bible and then in the church commentary on the Scriptures.[116]

Here, Bloesch characteristically confirms Word & Spirit as his governing framework, not only regarding the doctrine of revelation, but ultimately as the charter of his entire theological venture. Bloesch worries that Barth has positioned himself in such opposition to the subjective or experiential that he has erred toward an overly objective, Word-centric account of revelation.[117] For Bloesch, the dialectical balance of Word & Spirit must always be maintained; it is imperative for the Christian theologian to protect against any loss of the objective-historical and the subjective-experiential. Both the rational and the mystical must be maintained or else one will bloat and the other will shrivel. In this sense, rather than being primarily aligned with neo-orthodox theologians, Bloesch views himself as most closely aligned with Calvin and Luther.[118]

Bloesch's concern with Barth's muting of the Spirit side of the Word & Spirit dialectic is not simply that it fails to establish a properly Christian doctrine of revelation, however much that might be Bloesch's view. Rather, Bloesch worries that this kind of account diminishes the priority given to

---

116. Bloesch, *Theology of Word & Spirit*, 13.

117. Bloesch is concerned that "Barth does not always succeed in holding in balance certain emphases, which therefore gives his theology an objective cast" (*Jesus is Victor!*, 17). Bloesch's fundamental critique of Barth's theology as objectivist is enumerated more fully in his chapter "The Objectivist Slant" in *Jesus is Victor!* According to Bloesch, Barth does not fall prey to an "exclusively or wholly objectivist" theology, but he does fail at "holding together the objective and subjective dimensions of salvation in true dialectical relation" (106). Bloesch echoes his concern that Barth's theology leans objectivist in his brief chapter on Barth in *The Christian Witness in a Secular Age*. See Bloesch, *Christian Witness in a Secular Age*, 40–41.

118. "It will become obvious that my theological approach is strikingly similar to that of the magisterial Reformers (especially Luther and Calvin), who always saw the Word and Spirit together, never one apart from the other. . . . The Reformers' understanding of the relationship of Word and Spirit continued in early Protestant orthodoxy, although in later orthodoxy the paradoxical unity of Word and Spirit was sundered, being replaced by an objectivism of the Word" (Bloesch, *Theology of Word & Spirit*, 14).

the Christian life in the theological task. Once again, Bloesch's core commitment to the Christian life surfaces here in his critique of Barth. Bloesch acknowledges Barth shifted in his later writing, placing greater emphasis on the Christian life, but because Barth did not retain the kind of dialectical balance of Word & Spirit that Bloesch vies for, it ultimately falls short of playing the robust role it ought in regard to salvation and revelation. As Bloesch states,

> Karl Barth, too, gave special attention to the Christian life, despite his emphasis on the objectivity and all-sufficiency of Christ's work of atonement. His point was not that the Christian life could merit or secure our salvation but that it could proclaim and demonstrate Christ's salvation to others. His theology was essentially a theology of the Word of God, whereas mine is a theology of Word and Spirit. Yet the Holy Spirit played an ever more significant role as his theology unfolded, so that there are points of convergence between our systems. The major difference in emphasis lies in Barth's contention that the decision of faith follows the event of redemption, whereas I am inclined to say that the moment of decision is the culmination rather than the after effect of the work of redemption.[119]

---

119. Bloesch, *Holy Spirit*, 32. Bloesch is primarily concerned that Barth emphasizes the Word over the Spirit, or to use categories developed later in the present chapter, that he has emphasized the objective over the subjective, the historical over the experiential. This concern regarding Barth appears elsewhere in Bloesch's seven-volume dogmatic work. Here, Bloesch acknowledges what he sees as Barth's development in this area over the course of his work, and yet once again signals his same concern related to different doctrinal loci. In an exploration of the doctrine of the atonement, Bloesch states,

> In his discussion of the Holy Spirit Barth made a real place for the subjective pole of salvation. Yet the Holy Spirit does not create a further salvation but brings to light what has already happened to us and all humankind in Jesus Christ. The Holy Spirit makes manifest the reconciliation and redemption in Christ. Faith, which is a gift of the Spirit, entails "not our new creation and regeneration as accomplished in the cross and resurrection of Jesus Christ, but its present manifestation." My principal criticism of Barth is that he depicted the subjective pole of the atonement as wholly subordinate to the objective pole. It therefore has only epistemological and not ontological or soteriological significance. Barth admitted that the logic of his theology leads to the assertion that the very body of Christ includes and unites all people. While Barth acknowledges that the world is not yet redeemed in the sense that all have come to a knowledge of their redemption in Christ, in another sense the world is already redeemed since the spiritual situation of the human race has been irrevocably altered through the condescension and incarnation of Jesus Christ in human history. In his later writings Barth

What Bloesch identifies in Barth is a concern that the Christian life will have undue influence on revelation, whereas Bloesch asserts the opposite worry, that the Christian life will not influence revelation, and therefore will be alien to it. For Bloesch, a theology of Word & Spirit is by necessity a theology of the Christian life. As Bloesch states,

> Whereas Karl Barth offered a theology of the Word of God, I seek to expound a theology of the Christian life, based not on general moral principles nor on the universal human awareness of God but on God's self-revelation in Jesus Christ as attested in holy Scripture. A theology of Word and Spirit is at the same time a theology of the Christian life, since the Spirit not only illumines the criterion of the Word but also empowers people of faith to follow the Word in costly discipleship.[120]

In Bloesch's first quotation engaging Barth, he draws a distinction between Barth's theology of the Word of God and his theology of Word & Spirit. It is noteworthy that while making the same material distinction in this second quotation, Bloesch replaces his "theology of Word and Spirit" with "theology of the Christian life." According to Bloesch, his theology of Word and Spirit *is* a theology of the Christian life. The goal of revelation is the Spirit's empowering of the Christian to embrace a life of "costly discipleship" to the Word.

For Bloesch, all that is objective must be brought home by the Spirit who initiates a subjective experience and encounter of the living Word, in and through the written and proclaimed Word. As Bloesch himself states, "Revelation does not consist of revealed truths that are objectively 'there' in the Bible but rather in God's special act of condescension and the opening of our eyes to the significance of this act. Revelation is not exclusively objective but objective-subjective."[121] How does Bloesch retain the subjective pole of revelation through the means of Scripture and ecclesial proclamation?

---

gave more prominence to the subjective dimension of salvation and to the pivotal role of the Holy Spirit, who makes the cross and resurrection of Christ effective in the world. (*Jesus Christ*, 166)

Kevin Vanhoozer, identifying this area of disagreement between Bloesch and Barth, correctly recognizes that Bloesch remains much more tightly partnered with Barth in his theological methodology: "Though he does not agree with all of Barth's conclusions, Bloesch believes that 'we need to take his way of doing theology' over that of liberals like Paul Tillich and conservatives like Carl Henry" (Vanhoozer, "On the Very Idea of a Theological System," 147–48).

120. Bloesch, *Theological Notebook*, 5:28.
121. Bloesch, *Holy Scripture*, 67.

He does so by adding to Barth's threefold account of the Word, which he has previously affirmed.

In Bloesch's definition of "Word," it reveals his affirmation of the threefold account of the Word, but Bloesch adds his own emphasis, stating, "In relation to Barth's typology, I would add a fourth form—the inner Word."[122] Bloesch employs other synonyms to explain this idea—"the awakening of faith," "the voice of conscience," and the "inner light" are a few examples.[123] The inner Word is the subjective pole of revelation wrought forth by the work of the Spirit. Bloesch clarifies, "The written Word and the proclaimed Word have no efficacy unless Christ makes his abode within us by his Spirit. It is not only the light that comes to us from the Bible and the church but also the light that shines within us by the indwelling Spirit that convinces us of the truth."[124] Thus, the instrumental means of divine revelation are governed by Word & Spirit and retain both an objective and subjective pole in their service to the Triune God. Their purpose is always to provide a means by which people can encounter and experience the living Word in their inner being.[125]

In his emphasis on experience, Bloesch wants to make clear there is one further distinction between his account of revelation and that of neo-orthodox thinkers. Bloesch's commitment to an objective-subjective account of revelation informs his understanding of the divine self-disclosure at the heart of the divine-human encounter. Bloesch explains,

> Although open to the insights of existentialist and neo-orthodox theologies, I have sought to retain the conceptual character of revelation even while subordinating it to personal self-disclosure. As I see it, revelation is God's self-communication through his selected instrumentality, especially the inspired witness of his

---

122. Bloesch, *Theology of Word & Spirit*, 191. Bloesch repeats this point in *Holy Scripture*: "As I have indicated in a previous volume, this typology should be extended to include the inner word, the voice of conscience, for this too when united with Jesus Christ becomes an infallible criterion for faith and practice" (*Holy Scripture*, 62).

123. Bloesch, *Theology of Word & Spirit*, 188.

124. Bloesch, *Theology of Word & Spirit*, 191. As Bloesch articulates differently elsewhere, "In our reading of the Bible and in our hearing of the biblical message, we become, through the miraculous action of the Holy Spirit, contemporaneous with the moment of revelation. We experience the power and impact of the gospel directly through the word that we hear. In another sense, however, our experience of Jesus Christ is indirect, since it is mediated through the outward means of preaching and hearing" (*Holy Scripture*, 56–57).

125. Bloesch, *Theology of Word & Spirit*, 191.

> prophets and apostles. This act of self-communication entails not only the unveiling of his gracious and at the same time awesome presence but also the imparting of the knowledge of his will and purpose for humankind. This knowledge is conceptual as well as existential and can be formulated but never possessed or mastered in propositions.[126]

While Bloesch wants to give priority to "personal self-disclosure," he does not want to do so at the expense of the "conceptual" content of revelation. Here, Bloesch demonstrates his commitment to hold together the rational and mystical components of revelation without denying the personal or propositional elements of revelation.[127] As Kevin Vanhoozer correctly notes, for Bloesch "'Word and Spirit' says it all: revelation is not simply propositional (textual) but existential (spiritual)."[128] According to Bloesch, revelation is a divine speech-act that entails both personal communication and propositional communication of God's person and purposes.[129] This divine speech-act is heard-encountered in a life of personal and social obedience.

Case Studies in Distribution

The goal of this chapter is to show the distributive role of the Christian life in Bloesch's dogmatic project. Thus far I have demonstrated the presupposed

---

126. Bloesch, *Holy Scripture*, 48.

127. "The Word of God is not to be reduced to objective rational statements: it is God in action, God speaking and humans hearing. But this is an inward hearing that itself belongs to the miracle of revelation" (Bloesch, *Holy Scripture*, 48).

128. Vanhoozer, "On the Very Idea of a Theological System," 150.

129. Bloesch, *Ground of Certainty*, 128. As Bloesch argues, God is revealing truth, which is both personal-ontological as well as propositional-epistemological, or to use his own language it is both "conceptual and existential." In *The Ground of Certainty* Bloesch discusses the two different approaches to truth, one being philosophical and the other theological. Bloesch expectantly stands against the "philosophical" view, which posits truth as primarily an idea rather than a person: "In biblical theology truth is a liberating word with power given in a divine-human encounter; it is not an idea or principle that can be discovered or conceived. Truth is God in action, God revealing His will and purpose to mankind" (126). He goes on to state that truth "entails personal proposition and surrender" (126). Bloesch's emphasis on experience rings out here once again. For Bloesch, an apprehension of the truth is primarily an existential reality, rather than theoretical. Reason is not vacated from the equation here for Bloesch, but rather housed within and subordinate to the experience and encounter of the human person with the triune God. Bloesch says all of this differently in *Holy Scripture*, stating, "In the Scriptures revelation is truth and event at the same time" (*Holy Scripture*, 49).

and pervasive material distribution of the Christian life in revelation. This focus on the doctrine of revelation is appropriate, given the formal priority of revelation in Bloesch's thought. As I have argued, the distributive influence of the Christian life in revelation results in a thoroughgoing distribution of revelation across Bloesch's entire system. While I cannot provide an exhaustive account of every instance of this distributive influence, it is important to highlight the ways in which this carries over into other doctrinal loci. In what follows I offer two examples that are particularly instructive in demonstrating the distributive role of the Christian life in Bloesch's theology. First, I demonstrate the material pressure the Christian life applies to Bloesch's doctrine of God. Second, I show the material influence the Christian life has on Bloesch's doctrine of the atonement.

The Doctrine of God

In his volume on the doctrine of God, *God the Almighty*, Bloesch devotes space to what is commonly expected in doctrinal consideration regarding God and the divine attributes. His account is organized around three couplets of divine attributes—transcendence and immanence, power and wisdom, and holiness and love. For the purposes of this inquiry, I focus attention on Bloesch's final couplet of divine attributes, holiness and love. Bloesch argues that

> God's love and holiness constitute the inner nature of the living God. These two perfections coalesce in such a way that we may speak of the holy love of God . . . and of his merciful holiness. In the depth of God's love is revealed the beauty of his holiness. In the glory of his holiness is revealed the breadth of his love.[130]

Within his treatment of holiness and love, which Bloesch identifies as the dual "quintessential attribute of God,"[131] Bloesch detours from the doctrine of God proper and advances a discussion of the Christian vocation regarding love and holiness. As noted throughout this chapter, Bloesch's God is a revealing God. Therefore, when Bloesch contemplates God in himself, his mind does not depart from a consideration of God's relation to humanity.

---

130. Bloesch, *God the Almighty*, 141.

131. Bloesch, *God the Almighty*, 139. Bloesch enlists the dual attributes of holiness and love as his primary categories when discussing God's action in the atonement. He concludes, "So we may therefore speak of a holy love that characterizes the inner nature of God" (*Jesus Christ*, 158).

The divine-human encounter is always the goal. It is of little surprise that talk of God in himself assumes an encounter with human persons that is transformative.

A brief look at Bloesch's account of God's love and holiness, and how quickly Bloesch moves to the Christian's call to love and holiness, demonstrates the material distribution of the Christian life across Bloesch's entire system and the pressure it applies to his thought. God's love according to Bloesch is "agape—an outgoing and other-regarding concern for a lost and distraught humanity."[132] As argued, Bloesch's emphasis is not on God's love *ad intra*, but *ad extra*. He is concerned with God's love *for us*. After Bloesch discusses God's love for us, he then moves quickly to a discussion of the Christian's call "to love others as God loved us."[133] Likewise, Bloesch defines God's holiness as signifying "his majesty and inviolability."[134] Once again, the emphasis is on God's holiness in relation to his creatures as Bloesch turns immediately in his discussion of God's holiness to discuss the "awe and dread" that comes from an "encounter with the Holy."[135] As with "love," so with "holiness." Bloesch moves seamlessly from a discussion of divine holiness to a discussion of the Christian vocation of personal and social holiness.[136] It is here within Bloesch's doctrine of God that Bloesch argues, "All people have a vocation to holiness. We are all created for the glory of God. All are called to fear God and to keep his commandments."[137] Bloesch cannot sustain attention on God's love and holiness, as such, but in both

---

132. Bloesch, *God the Almighty*, 145. Bloesch's account of God's love is developed through the Greek distinction between philia, epithymia, eros, and agape. See Bloesch, *God the Almighty*, 145–48. This is a common turn for Bloesch. He frequently appeals to this taxonomy of love to define love. For example, in *Spirituality Old & New* we read, "In the New Testament this higher form of love is called agape" (Bloesch, *Spirituality Old & New*, 89). In *The Ground of Certainty* we read, "The concept of love in medieval theology was essentially that of the Greek Eros, man raising himself up to God, rather than the biblical Agape, God descending to the level of man" (Bloesch, *Ground of Certainty*, 34). Likewise, in *Theological Notebook*, it reads, "The love that comes from God (*agape*) goes beyond both paternalistic altruism and the spirit of moral justice" (Bloesch, *Theological Notebook*, 3:127). In *Essentials of Evangelical Theology*, we find that Bloesch's source for this taxonomy is Anders Nygren (Bloesch, *Essentials of Evangelical Theology*, 1:42).

133. Bloesch, *God the Almighty*, 152.

134. Bloesch, *God the Almighty*, 137.

135. Bloesch, *God the Almighty*, 137.

136. Bloesch, *God the Almighty*, 156.

137. Bloesch, *God the Almighty*, 158–59.

cases moves to a discussion of the Christian's vocation of love and holiness in a life of obedience.

In a typical systematic exposition of Christian doctrine, one would not expect to find an emphasis on the Christian life within a discussion of the divine attributes, but in Bloesch's theology that is exactly what one finds. The distributive nature of the doctrine of the Christian life is evident. Bloesch is not content to develop the doctrine of God proper as such, but as he ponders God's love and holiness, the primary issue he has in mind is always the divine-human encounter and its lived consequences. Consequently, he is comfortable moving quickly to considerations of the Christian life. For Bloesch, a discussion of divine love and holiness demands a discussion of the Christian's love and holiness. Bloesch believes, "Holiness and love comprise the essence of God and also the core of the Christian life."[138] Therefore, Bloesch is perfectly comfortable moving from a discussion of God's holy-love to a discussion of the Christian call to holy-love. He is comfortable, so comfortable in fact, that he concludes his discussion of love and holiness within a volume on the doctrine of God by discussing deeds of piety and prayer in the Christian life.[139]

The Doctrine of Atonement

Having explored the material distribution of the Christian life in Bloesch's doctrine of God through an emphasis on the divine-human encounter, I now briefly highlight the Christian life's influence on Bloesch's constructive account of the atonement. In a chapter titled "Christ's Atoning Sacrifice" found within the *Jesus Christ* volume, Bloesch provides an account of the doctrine of the atonement with a surprising emphasis on the Christian life. He begins his chapter, as expected, by tracing the contours of the doctrine of the atonement.[140] From there Bloesch moves into a constructive account of the doctrine, stressing the Scriptural basis and the consequential value of each theory of the atonement and placing particular emphasis on substitutionary atonement as central to a properly *evangelical* account of the doctrine.[141] Following his constructive argument for substitution, Bloesch

---

138. Bloesch, *Paradox of Holiness*, 2.

139. Bloesch, *God the Almighty*, 161.

140. Bloesch surveys the various theories of the atonement with an appeal to Gustaf Aulen's definitive work on the doctrine.

141. Bloesch, *Jesus Christ*, 158.

includes a section titled "The Two Poles of the Atonement," stating, "The atonement is an objective sacrifice that reverberates throughout history in the lives of those who trust in this sacrifice for their redemption. It includes both God's atoning work for us in the life history of Jesus Christ and the faith of the human subject in this work."[142] Here lies the familiar framing of the objective and subjective poles—the *objective* work upon the cross and the *subjective* appropriation of this work in individual lives.[143] Colyer and Weborg note, "In framing the doctrine of the atoning work of Christ, Bloesch strives for balance between these objective and subjective dimensions by eliminating the conjunction *and* putting a hyphen in its place so that expression now reads objective-subjective."[144] An emphasis on the objective character of the atonement is not terribly surprising or interesting, but its inclusion of the subjective dimension of the atonement ought to raise attention. Bloesch's definition of the subjective pole is particularly instructive. First, he argues the subjective pole is found in the objective sacrifice of Christ upon the cross. So, Bloesch can say, "In one sense Jesus Christ himself is the subjective side. Jesus as our representative appropriates the salvation of God on our behalf."[145] And yet, the subjective pole of the atonement has two parts: "Yet salvation remains incomplete until we ourselves participate in Christ's appropriation."[146] Bloesch continues this line of reasoning, arguing,

> The experience of faith constitutes the subjective side of salvation. The Christian life can also be said to comprise the subjective pole of the atonement. Jesus' life and obedience are the ground of our salvation, but our lives and obedience are the fruit and culmination of Christ's work of salvation.[147]

142. Bloesch, *Jesus Christ*, 162.

143. Bloesch, *Jesus Christ*, 162–67. Bloesch states,

> In articulating anew the atoning work of Christ on the cross we would do well to acknowledge both the objective and subjective dimensions of our salvation. Salvation has occurred outside of us in the atoning work of Christ on the cross. Through the shedding of his blood our sins are forgiven, and a new righteousness wells up within us. Yet this redemptive work does little good if it lies entirely outside our experience. We as forgiven sinners need to appropriate this salvation. ("Justification and Atonement," 231)

144. Colyer and Weborg, "Bloesch's Doctrine of the Christian Life," 161.

145. Colyer and Weborg, "Bloesch's Doctrine of the Christian Life," 163.

146. Bloesch, *Jesus Christ*, 163.

147. Bloesch, *Jesus Christ*, 163. Bloesch goes on to state, "The biblical-evangelical view takes into consideration both God's gracious initiative and the need for human

The Christian's subjective appropriation of the atonement is dependent upon Jesus Christ's subjective appropriation of God's salvation as "our representative."[148] There is a first order subjectivity accomplished by Christ himself in the initial divine-human encounter, but there is likewise a second order subjectivity in the divine-human encounter of the Christian life. The distributive force of the Christian life is powerfully on display here in Bloesch's subjective understanding of the atonement.

The embedded nature of Bloesch's doctrine of the Christian life is evident here in his constructive account of the doctrine of the atonement. This time it materializes in and through the language of "objective" and "subjective." Bloesch's language of subjectivity pertaining to the cross is designed to push toward the call to obedience in the Christian life. This does not mean that the Christian life somehow achieves the atonement, but it does mean that the Christian life is the location in which the achieved atoning work of Christ is fought for and retained. For Bloesch, a proper account of the atonement is ever in service of an evangelical account of the Christian life. As he argues,

> The atoning work of Christ is the basis of a biblical, evangelical spirituality. Here Christ is seen not simply as the representative of fallen humanity nor as the model of the new humanity but as Mediator, Expiator and Sin Bearer. Before he can be our example, he must be acknowledged as our Savior and Lord. True spirituality views the Christian life as primarily a sign and witness to the atoning work of Christ. The imitation of Christ is a token of our gratitude for his incomparable work of reconciliation and redemption on Calvary.[149]

The Christian life is at once a sharing in the accomplished work of Christ upon the cross and a bearing witness to that work. To speak properly of the atonement, one must speak not only of the objective historical event of Christ's death upon the cross but likewise of the ongoing call for believers to take up their cross and follow Him.

---

decision and obedience. Salvation involves both the objective work of Christ on the cross and the response of faith in a Christian life, made possible by the outpouring of the Holy Spirit. Salvation is a past accomplishment, a present experience and a future hope" (167).

148. Bloesch, *Jesus Christ*, 163.
149. Bloesch, *Future of Evangelical Christianity*, 133.

Conclusion

Bloesch's account of revelation demonstrates the material distribution of the Christian life. For Bloesch, revelation is an event in which God "confronts the whole person."[150] Bloesch notes, "Revelation is a 'meeting' between God and the believer whereby God speaks and we hear."[151] Emphasis is placed on the subjective—the experience of divine revelation as one listening to the Word—which is a signal to Bloesch's enduring commitment to the Christian life. What is clear is that the Christian life is not only the arena of salvation, but likewise of revelation. As Bloesch boldly states, "Revelation happened in a final and definitive form in the apostolic encounter with Jesus Christ. But revelation happens again and again in the experience of the Spirit of Christ."[152] Bloesch is willing to hold onto a continuation of divine revelation in a meaningful sense in the Christian life. This talk of the objective historical event and ongoing "events" of revelation by the Spirit could sound disjointed, but for Bloesch such is not the case. In all of this Bloesch is speaking of one event, an event that is open-ended throughout history until the conclusion of the age. It is an event climactically occurring in the incarnation of Christ but correspondingly happening beyond that moment in the lives of Christ's followers. It is the encounter between God and humankind.

To put this in a different light, the telos of divine revelation, the end of which God instantiates the divine-human encounter, is to lead a people "into a personal relationship with the living Christ."[153] This encounter for relationship "motivates the will to demonstrate the truth of the gospel in daily obedience."[154] To use the language of Scripture, divine revelation is for the sake of abiding and bearing fruit; it is for the sake of knowing God and obeying all that he has commanded. What I have shown in this chapter is

---

150. Bloesch, *Holy Scripture*, 48. A few pages later Bloesch gives us the largeness of revelation which confronts the "whole person": "The knowledge of God given in revelation has many sides. It is conceptual because it enlightens our mind concerning the nature and purpose of God. It is existential because it affects the whole human existence. It is personal because it involves a dialogue between two subjects. It is spiritual because it opens our inner eyes to transcendent dimensions of reality" (53).

151. Bloesch, *Holy Scripture*, 49. We read also in *The Ground of Certainty* that "revelation is essentially an encounter of the living Christ and the believer" (Bloesch, *Ground of Certainty*, 149).

152. Bloesch, *Holy Scripture*, 50.

153. Bloesch, *Holy Scripture*, 28.

154. Bloesch, *Holy Scripture*, 26.

that the Christian life is itself an instrument of divine revelation, but more so, it is the goal of divine revelation as well. As Bloesch claims,

> Moreover, the Spirit chooses to work and speak through human acts and means. These divinely appointed means of grace are preaching, prayer, the Bible, the sacraments and the Christian life. God acts to save us, but in conjunction with our telling the story of salvation and our living out this story in fidelity and obedience.[155]

The Christian life is both the means and the telos of the doctrines of salvation and revelation. The task of theology, as Bloesch understands it, demonstrates this governing commitment: "We begin with faith's apprehension of divine revelation and then endeavor to explore the ramifications and implications of this for daily life."[156]

In my analysis of Donald Bloesch's doctrine of revelation, I have demonstrated the distributive role of the doctrine of the Christian life as both materially presupposed in revelation and materially pervasive throughout. I have, furthermore, demonstrated the informing role that revelation plays throughout the whole of Bloesch's system, bringing with it the Christian life at every doctrinal turn. As Bloesch's formal doctrine of distribution, the doctrine of revelation is presupposed and pervasive throughout Bloesch's entire theological system. Since the Christian life is materially distributed within the doctrine of revelation, and because the doctrine of revelation influences and informs all of Bloesch's doctrinal decisions, it follows that the Christian life is materially distributed throughout the whole of his dogmatic project.

---

155. Bloesch, *Theology of Word & Spirit*, 222.
156. Bloesch, *Theology of Word & Spirit*, 59.

4

Prayer and the Christian Life

THE THEOLOGY OF DONALD Bloesch is a theology of the divine-human encounter. This encounter is a transhistorical event initiated in the past objective work of the Word and consummated in the present subjective work of the Spirit. Moored to pneumatology, the Christian life is the arena in which the human person encounters the personal God. For Bloesch, this divine-human encounter is embraced in a life of piety (personal obedience) and is expressed in an active life (social obedience). To use a biblical analogy, the vocation of the Christian is to abide in his or her encounter with God, as a branch abides in the vine, and to bear the fruit of that encounter. To be sure, Bloesch is concerned with bearing fruit, but he is insistent that abiding must come first.[1]

The focus of my project is to explicate the meaning and role of the doctrine of the Christian life in Bloesch's distinctively *evangelical* theology. Bloesch's theology of prayer offers a concrete depiction of his doctrine of the Christian life. Prayer captures the essence of biblical personalism; it makes good on the promise of the divine-human encounter. A life without prayer, on the other hand, is void of life-giving communion with God.[2] If the Christian life is the territory of the divine-human encounter, then prayer is the central hub in which that encounter occurs: "Prayer is the

---

1. "Every Christian life should be nurtured by prayer and should bear fruit in works of love" (Bloesch, *Struggle of Prayer*, 142).

2. "The worst of all afflictions is the inability to pray" (Bloesch, *Theological Notebook*, 2:57).

heart of spirituality and therefore has a certain priority over other areas," Bloesch notes.[3]

While Bloesch views prayer as the most central and critical component of the Christian life, he argues a life of personal obedience will necessarily be marked by a host of spiritual disciplines.[4] Bloesch shares the Reformation concern that spiritual disciplines can be viewed as meritorious acts in salvation, but he remains committed to their value as means of grace in the life of devotion.[5] His "respect for the ethos of Pietism" has led him to embrace the "necessity for disciplining the flesh so that we can gain freedom for obedience."[6] The "value" of the spiritual disciplines is grounded in the "secret hidden work of the Holy Spirit."[7] This embrace of the critical role of the spiritual disciplines in the Christian life is not merely theological, but personal.[8] While Bloesch commends many spiritual disciplines—meditation, study, family devotions, simplicity, fasting, chastity,

---

3. Bloesch, *Struggle of Prayer*, vii. Echoing this point, we read elsewhere, "Of all the disciplines of the spiritual life, prayer is the most necessary. It is the very soul of faith (Calvin)" (Bloesch, *Spirituality East & West*, 187).

4. For Bloesch, "personal holiness" or the life of obedience in piety is most fundamentally expressed in a commitment to the spiritual disciplines (*Crisis of Piety*, 49).

5. Bloesch, *Faith in Search of Obedience*, 64. Bloesch argues that further work of retrieval is required here for evangelical theology. The Protestant tradition as a whole has reacted against a Roman Catholic embrace of spiritual disciplines that tended toward works-righteousness. As Bloesch argues, "It is not an exaggeration to state that this is the lost dimension in modern Protestantism.... The stress today is on Christian action and social relevance rather than piety" (*Crisis of Piety*, 49). Bloesch believes the Pietist, Puritan, and Evangelical (historical) movements can provide a welcome corrective to this Protestant overreaction; but he believes constructive work must be built upon such retrieval in order to provide a robust account of spiritual disciplines that is distinctively evangelical. Following the Reformation concerns about the spiritual disciplines, Bloesch maintains amidst this retrieval work there are five temptations to be cautious of in an embrace of the spiritual disciplines: the danger of moralism, the danger of escapism, the danger of Pharisaism, the danger of perfectionism, and the danger of rigorism. Each of these temptations in the practice of spiritual disciplines are at their core a departure from "the foundation of justification by grace through faith and the call to communion with Christ" (53–55). Nevertheless, Bloesch believes this work is critical because while we cannot "merit salvation by means of spiritual exercises ... we can in this way strengthen ourselves for Christian service" (52).

6. Bloesch, *Faith in Search of Obedience*, 64.

7. Bloesch, *Essentials of Evangelical Theology*, 2:64.

8. Bloesch, *Faith in Search of Obedience*, 64–66. At the end of this spiritual autobiography Bloesch has a brief chapter on the spiritual disciplines in which he explores the importance of the spiritual disciplines in his own spiritual pilgrimage.

abstinence, Sabbath, and the Lord's Supper—he gives them thoughtful, but brief consideration in comparison to prayer.[9] As Bloesch states, "Surely prayer is the most sought-after discipline of the spirit, for it places us in contact with the reality of the living God."[10] According to Bloesch, "apart from prayer no other discipline has any spiritual or practical efficacy."[11] For this reason, prayer is the focus of the final chapter of my project.

My investigation of Bloesch's theology of prayer functions as a kind of case study in his doctrine of the Christian life. Since the Christian life is the defining doctrine of Bloesch's evangelical theology, and prayer is the defining feature of the Christian life, there is no component of Bloesch's constructive account of the Christian life more worthy of detailed analysis. Bloesch constructs his theology of prayer with two key building blocks of the doctrine of the Christian life—biblical personalism and obedience (personal and social). While I have already provided an account of these two key features of Bloesch's doctrine of the Christian life in chapter 2, an analysis of how they form Bloesch's theology of prayer provides greater depth of understanding in regard to both. Bloesch's vision of personal encounter and obedience finds concrete expression in the Christian's life of prayer.

Before I analyze Bloesch's theology of prayer, it is important to pause and acknowledge the substantial influence Friedrich Heiler's book *Prayer: A Study in the History and Psychology of Religion* has on Bloesch's thought. While Bloesch's theology of prayer is influenced by a variety of thinkers, the breadth and depth of Heiler's influence is unique.[12] Bloesch repeatedly appeals to Heiler in an effort to distinguish false notions of prayer from a properly evangelical account.[13] Heiler's project provides a grid for locating

---

9. Bloesch, *Crisis of Piety*, 56–59. While Bloesch affirms the importance of spiritual disciplines such as Scripture reading, silence, hymn singing, Sunday morning worship, service, and fasting, he gives prayer a position of priority in such lists (*Faith in Search of Obedience*, 64–66).

10. Bloesch, *Faith in Search of Obedience*, 64.

11. Bloesch, *Crisis of Piety*, 55.

12. Bloesch specifically identifies Martin Luther, Richard Baxter, and P. T. Forsyth as significant influencers of his theology of prayer (*Struggle of Prayer*, viii). Bloesch's catholic sensibility means that he is influenced by a broad spectrum of Christian theologians in regard to prayer. Nevertheless, Bloesch is uniquely influenced by Heiler in his account of prayer, which is why I give Heiler the most attention.

13. In *A Theology of Word & Spirit* Bloesch refers to Heiler's book as both "brilliant" and "controversial" (*Theology of Word & Spirit*, 97). In *The Struggle for Prayer* Bloesch states, "A book that has had a decisive influence on my understanding of prayer is Friedrich Heiler's *Prayer*, a study in the history and psychology of religion. Heiler, a convert

different accounts of prayer.[14] According to Heiler, there are six fundamental types of prayer: primitive, ritual, Greek Religion, philosophical, mystical, and prophetic.[15] Bloesch is particularly interested in the distinctions

from Roman Catholicism to Lutheranism, distinguishes between several different types of prayer, including the mystical and the prophetic" (*Struggle of Prayer*, 3). Interestingly, Bloesch references a conversation he had with Emil Brunner at his home in Zürich. Apparently, Heiler's work was so impactful to Bloesch that he deemed a discussion of the book important in the one opportunity for dialogue with Brunner:

> In my visit with him in Switzerland, I asked what he thought of the book by Friedrich Heiler titled *Das Gebert* (Prayer), which had influenced me. Brunner replied that Heiler's book was interesting but definitely deficient, theologically speaking. Karl Barth had given a similar response to this question. Heiler had been a convert from Roman Catholicism to Lutheranism, but many of his Protestant critics believed that his break with Catholicism was superficial. In my opinion, Heiler mounted a critique of Catholic spirituality that was both incisive and devastating without being dismissive. (Bloesch, *Faith in Search of Obedience*, 18)

In his article on prayer in the *Evangelical Dictionary of Theology*, we find Bloesch using Heiler's typological framework as his grid for mapping prayer (Bloesch, "Prayer," 946). Heiler continues to appear throughout his corpus as a primary informer of his understanding of prayer. See, e.g., Bloesch, *Essentials of Evangelical Theology*, 2:56–59; *Crisis of Piety*, 83; *Ground of Certainty*, 95.

14. Heiler's book is neither a theology of prayer nor even a practical guide to prayer, but it is a study of the history and psychology of prayer. Heiler's book is a phenomenological investigation of accounts and experiences of prayer across a myriad of cultures and faith traditions. Prayer is the distinguishing feature of every religion, and therefore in Heiler's mind it is the most fitting window into understanding religious differences throughout history. As Heiler notes, "There can be no doubt at all that prayer is the heart and centre of all religion. Not in dogmas and institutions, not in rites and ethical ideals, but in prayer do we grasp the peculiar quality of the religious life. In the words of a prayer we can penetrate into the deepest and the most intimate movements of the religious soul" (Heiler, *Prayer*, xv).

15. The first form of prayer that Heiler identifies is what he calls "primitive prayer." Primitive prayer is the "free spontaneous petitionary prayer of the natural man" (Heiler, *Prayer*, 1). What Heiler has in mind are those prayers that arise from tribal and animistic cultures in which there is no literature or formal structures related to religious activity. Primitive prayers of petition are "almost exclusively for things which are useful or contribute to personal happiness" (17). The second form of prayer Heiler calls "ritual prayer." In ritual prayer the spontaneity of primitive prayer gives way to formulas. Heiler remarks on this shift: "Primitive prayer expresses always a vital, mutual relation between God and man, especially a relation of kinship. But when prayer becomes formally constrained and a part of a hard-and-fast cultural system, coldness and estrangement unavoidably enter in. Instead of free and frank communion with divinity, there is a stiff ceremonial formalism" (71). Rites, rituals and sacrifices become critical in this construction of prayer. The third form of prayer is what Heiler calls "Greek Religion." Heiler identifies the Homeric poems as the first expression of such prayers. The prayer of "Greek Religion" is a more

An Evangelical Spiritual Theology

Heiler draws between mystical and prophetic prayer; Heiler's influence helps shape Bloesch's development of these two types of prayer, meriting a brief investigation of Heiler's description.[16] Exploring the differences be-

---

clarified emphasis on the notion of dependence before the gods. There is also a movement beyond the egocentric petitionary posture of prayer toward petitions focused on the cultivation of moral values. Prayer was not void of form or ritual, but such form and ritual did not undermine the genuinely personal and expressive nature of prayer. The god of Greek Religion was also distinct from primitive and ritual prayer. Heiler states, "The gods are set free from their original restrictions of nature or of place, they are strongly individualized, they are personal figures with sharply defined features" (74). For Greek Religion, prayer is directed toward gods who have some dimension of personality and character. The fourth form of prayer Heiler refers to as "philosophical." Philosophical prayer is most fundamentally marked by a note of idealism. It is a form of prayer which seeks to rationalize: "Philosophic thought tries to make ethical and rational the traditional, cultural religion by excluding eudaemonism from piety, purifying the conception of God from all the anthropomorphic features, and putting in place of acts of prescribed worship the realization of moral values in the individual and social life. This ethical, rational, ideal religion is not naïve religion, but reformed religion, born of conscious critics of naïve piety" (87–88). Philosophical prayer is grounded in a fundamental critique of that which is primitive, it is oriented by a certain conception of reality defined by rational thought and is focused on an ethical standard. Praying for more primal or base needs is rejected, as is the expression of one's desires.

16. As we survey Heiler's distinction between mystical prayer and prophetic prayer, Bloesch's voice echoes throughout. One particular section of comparative analysis offered by Heiler sounds like Bloesch in this regard:

> Mysticism is neither a Christian inheritance or a peculiarity of the Christian religion, although in this religion it has assumed its finest and most beautiful form. It has penetrated into Christianity (as also into Judaism and Islam) from the outside, from the syncretist mystery religions, later religious philosophy, especially from neo-Platonism. The Gnostics and the Alexandrians, but above all Augustine and the Areopagite, were the gates by which it entered. Mysticism has indeed lost in purity and logical quality, but has gained in depth and warmth, fervour and power, from the intermingling with prophetic religion. It is important however in an age when the value of mysticism is discovered afresh and when it is regarded as the essence of Christianity, to distinguish clearly and sharply these two greater powers of the religious life, mysticism and prophetic, biblical religion. Certainly, the ultimate psychological root and ideal conception common to the two types is the struggle for a pure life, love and blessedness, and faith in a supreme, absolute, and transcendent Being in whom this yearning is satisfied. Inarguably, the innumerable contrasts between these two types have been lessened and bridged over in history, most splendidly in Augustine and Francis, but they cannot be wholly ignored. "Personality-affirming" and "personality-denying" religion, the experience of God which values history and that which ignores it, revelation and ecstasy, propheticism and monasticism, transformation of the world and flight from the world, preaching of the

tween these two modes of prayer in Heiler's thought will illuminate the distinguishing features of Bloesch's *evangelical* theology of prayer, which I analyze in the remainder of the chapter. I first survey Heiler's account of mystical prayer and then move to prophetic prayer.

According to Heiler, "mystical prayer" emphasizes union with God rather than personal encounter. "Mysticism is that form of intercourse with God in which the world and self are absolutely denied," Heiler avers, "in which human personality is dissolved, disappears and is absorbed in the infinite unity of the Godhead."[17] Heiler goes on to state, "The goal to which mysticism aspires is the isolation and the unification of the inner life, by detachment from the world, and union with God."[18] In prayer, the mystic must die to all attachment to the natural world and to his or her own selfish desires through an attunement to his or her inner being. Such a tuning to

> Gospel and contemplation—these contradictions are too great to give us the right to assert an essential identity of both types. Mysticism and the religion of revelation are the two opposite tendencies of the higher piety which in history ever repel, yet ever attract each other. (Heiler, *Prayer*, 170–71)

It is this clear distinction which Heiler draws between mystical and prophetic "religion" and "prayer" which serves as the soil for Bloesch's argument. Mysticism here is viewed as clearly alien to the Christian conception of faith and prayer, and as such is a distortion of the real thing. It is this claim of Heiler's that apparently was met with critique, precisely because of its inherent critique of "Christian mysticism." Bloesch states:

> Heiler's analysis has often been subject to severe criticism, especially by Roman Catholic and Anglican scholars who are concerned with defending the biblical foundations of Christian mysticism. Louis Bouyer claims that Heiler fails to perceive that prophetic religion can too easily become utilitarian; it seems that we seek God only for his gifts and not for himself. Some have charged that Heiler does not do justice to the missionary zeal of many of the Catholic mystics, for he maintains that mystics seek exclusive solitude and lack missionary motivation. (Bloesch, *Struggle of Prayer*, 5)

Bloesch unsurprisingly comes to Heiler's defense. He states, "In defense of Heiler, it should be said that he is working with ideal types and freely admits that some of his examples only partially reflect the category in which they are places" (5). Bloesch goes on to state that it is also important to recognize that Heiler is tracing a phenomenology of religion and prayer, and that none of these forms of prayer Heiler identifies is truly and purely Christian. Ultimately, true Christian prayer cannot take place "apart from conscious surrender to and union with the living Christ" and are only truly Christian if the Holy Spirit is present (5).

17. Heiler, *Prayer*, 136.

18. Heiler, *Prayer*, 173. According to Heiler, while there are forms of mystical prayer that are personal, on the whole, mystical prayer tends to be depersonal. Depersonal, mystical prayer views God as a static being and is focused on an ecstatic experience that transcends comprehension or explanation.

one's inner being is for the sake of focusing upon "the infinite, the divine, the eternal."[19] Consequently, mystical prayer emphasizes the need to rise above the constraints of the material world. Prayer is the means by which one can accomplish this movement away from creaturely limitations and personal desires, toward the inner quest of union with the divine.

Heiler contrasts "prophetic prayer" with "mystical prayer," claiming that prophetic prayer is marked by personal engagement with a self-revealing God, steering clear of divine and human comingling or absorption as is sometimes found in mysticism. In prophetic prayer "God is not the immobile, infinite Unity, but the living, energizing Will, not the quiet Stillness but the active Energy, not always at rest but ever in action, not the highest Being but the supreme Life."[20] Rather than vacating God of personal attributes, prophetic prayer emphasizes personal attributes to such a degree that anthropomorphic language for God is wielded with specificity and confidence.[21] Prophetic prayer is marked by genuine reciprocity of relationship with God in which distinct and competing wills interact with one another.[22] In opposition to mysticism, prophetic prayer is marked not by escapism, but a love of the world that seeks its good.

Given Bloesch's aversion to "classical mysticism" identified in chapter 2 of my project, it is of little surprise that he views Heiler's account of mystical prayer as deviant and dangerous. For Bloesch, there are two fundamental errors of mystical prayer: first, mystical prayer is a *depersonalized* encounter and second, mystical prayer is a form of *disengagement* with the created order. Bloesch is concerned that mystical prayer, focused on union, has privileged a form of contemplation foreign to the biblical account of prayer.[23] Bloesch summarizes this concern in stating, "For the

19. Heiler, *Prayer*, 139.
20. Heiler, *Prayer*, 148.
21. Heiler, *Prayer*, 149.
22. As Heiler states, "The *prophetic* experience, on the other hand, reveals an antagonism of opposites; of dramatic strain, dualistic energy. Fear and hope, distress and trust, doubt and faith, struggle with one another; the contrast of moral worthiness and unworthiness is always alive in the prophetic consciousness" (Heiler, *Prayer*, 169).
23. Bloesch critiques "the mystical tradition of the church" for reducing prayer to contemplation and meditation alone (*God the Almighty*, 192). Bloesch identifies in mysticism a tendency to diminish the importance of petitionary prayer because prayer has ceased to be personal engagement and conversation. Bloesch states rather definitively, "In mysticism prayer becomes contemplative adoration of the infinite, and petition, if it is allowed at all, is seen as a lower or carnal form of prayer" (*Essentials of Evangelical Theology*, 2:57). In his commonly irenic and charitable fashion, Bloesch later offers some

Neoplatonists prayer is meditation and contemplation directed to the infinite ground and source of being rather than petition to a personal God who is intimately involved in the concerns and trials of his human creatures."[24] Bloesch believes the fundamental error of mystical prayer regards the doctrine of God. The personal, Triune God of Scripture is not addressed in prayer, but instead a more generic, albeit philosophically credible deity. Wielding his biblical personalism, Bloesch worries that mystical prayer is directed to a depersonalized divine being and is therefore detached from creaturely concerns, the very place where the struggle of prayer should happen.[25] In doing so, mystical prayer devalues embodied, creaturely life and consequently diminishes the importance of social holiness.

---

positive words in regard to the mystical contribution to Christian prayer. He states, "We can here learn from the mystics who despite their penchant for suprapersonal metaphors for God nevertheless often had a rich prayer life precisely because they laid hold of the freedom given by the Spirit to probe more deeply into the God-human relationships and express their love for God in multiform ways" (*God the Almighty*, 194). In contradistinction to this mystical account of contemplation, Bloesch posits a version of contemplation which is rooted in Pietism and Puritanism. For Bloesch, this tradition has much to offer by way of developing an evangelical spirituality which retains a biblical form of contemplation: "The themes of contemplation, meditation, and silence became prominent again in Pietism and Puritanism. Yet a biblical perspective generally predominated over a Platonic one. Contemplation was reinterpreted to mean living one's whole life toward the love of God. All activities should be performed in a constant awareness of God. Silence was used not to get beyond the Word (as in Neo-Platonism) but to prepare oneself for it" (*Essentials of Evangelical Theology*, 2:54).

24. Bloesch, *God the Almighty*, 231.

25. According to Bloesch, while the Christian mystical tradition adopts Platonic and Neoplatonic understandings of God and prayer, Bloesch acknowledges the tradition does so with certain cautions. However, the point at which the biblical-classical synthesis is clearly exposed within the tradition is a vision of prayer void of conceptualization, images, and words. Bloesch recognizes efforts of Christian mystics to retain a biblical understanding of prayer even amidst such accommodations to classical categories. In particular, he argues that the mystics sought to retain the value of petitionary prayer. See Bloesch, *God the Almighty*, 231–32. Furthermore, they also "generally acknowledged that contemplation is a gift from God and cannot be induced by human effort alone" (233). However, these biblical safeguards simply were not enough to uphold a biblically-faithful, evangelical vision of prayer. Bloesch helpfully names an exemplar of this deviant form of prayer. As he surveys modern theology, he identifies Paul Tillich as a modern mystic whose vision of prayer models the concerns Bloesch has articulated:

> In the twentieth century the mystical tradition, anchored as it is in the biblical-classical synthesis, is represented by Tillich, who defined prayer as "the spiritual longing of a finite being to return to its origin." This definition mirrors the Neoplatonic vision of the reunion of the soul with the eternal

Heiler's account of prophetic prayer, in contrast, aligns well with Bloesch's brand of evangelical spirituality.[26] Bloesch readily acknowledges the influence of Heiler's account of prophetic prayer on his own constructive project, stating, "Heiler's depiction of prophetic prayer is amazingly close to our own understanding of evangelical prayer."[27] What Bloesch recognizes in Heiler's development is that the two errors of mystical prayer—depersonalization and disengagement—are remedied by the emphases of prophetic prayer. Accentuating the personal nature of the divine-human encounter, prophetic prayer moves the pray-er into engagement with the world. These two areas of distinction, between mystical prayer and prophetic prayer, significantly influence Bloesch's evangelical theology of prayer. At a fundamental level, the two modes of prayer have differing teleologies. In mystical prayer, the teleology is beyond God in his self-revelation to *deity*—an abstraction that seeks to find the one behind the three. In prophetic prayer, the teleology is an active spiritual existence—life with God in reality—and is a refusal to shift grounds to a more "spiritual" location.

In what follows, I explore Bloesch's account of prayer, focusing on the two key features I have already mentioned—personalism and obedience. As demonstrated in my brief analysis of Heiler's influence on Bloesch's theology of prayer, these two key features align substantially with Heiler's "prophetic prayer." Additionally, I specify my inquiry of these two key features in Bloesch's theology by noting that, for Bloesch, prayer is a personal encounter, and prayer leads to engagement with the world. First, I argue, according to Bloesch, prayer is a personal encounter with the Triune God of Scripture. This encounter is marked by two relational dynamics—*dialogue* and *struggle*. In evangelical prayer, the pray-er encounters God in dynamic conversation. Second, I argue that, for Bloesch, prayer leads the Christian into engagement with the world. In summary, for Bloesch, *evangelical* prayer is marked by personal encounter with "a personal God, who love and cares,"[28] that must lead to social obedience.[29] As Bloesch baldly asserts,

---

through disentanglement form the bonds of the flesh. Prayer in this tradition is discovering the divine will and conforming ourselves to it. (233)

26. Bloesch, *Essentials of Evangelical Theology*, 2:57.
27. Bloesch, *Essentials of Evangelical Theology*, 2:57.
28. Bloesch, *Essentials of Evangelical Theology*, 1:31.
29. Bloesch, *Struggle of Prayer*, 131.

"The soundness of prayer is measured not by our feelings or fervor at the time but by our behavior afterwards."[30]

Prayer as Personal Encounter

If the lifeblood of Donald Bloesch's theology of the Christian life is the divine-human encounter, then prayer is the heartbeat of that encounter. As Bloesch explores the nature of prayerful personal encounter, he remains faithful to his revelatory order—God first and human beings second. He anchors his evangelical account of prayer in the objective action of the Triune God before discussing the subjective experience of the Christian. In what follows I outline the key features of Bloesch's "personal" account of prayer, following this objective-subjective order. First, I argue that Bloesch sees prayer as a personal encounter because it is an encounter before, with, and by the persons of the Trinity. Evangelical prayer emphasizes God's self-giving, gracious, and condescending revelation. It is this emphasis that distinguishes evangelical prayer from a depersonalized mystical account of prayer. As Bloesch states, "Biblical prayer is based on God in his infinite grace *reaching out* to fallen humanity. Mystical prayer is characterized by aspiring humanity *reaching up* to God in his holiness."[31] Bloesch's personal account of prayer is prayer of the human heart directed to the Triune God. It is not merely mystical contemplation or meditation, but rather a personal encounter of the Christian with God the Father, Son, and Holy Spirit. Second, I argue that a primary feature of Bloesch's vision of *personal* prayer is dialogue. Prayer is dialogical in the sense that it entails a conversation between persons.[32] Bloesch summarizes personal prayer in stating, "In biblical religion prayer is understood as both a gift and a task. God takes the initiative (cf. Ps 50:3-4; Ezek 2:1-2), but we must respond. This kind of prayer is personalistic and dialogic. It entails revealing our innermost selves to God but also God's revelation of his desire to us (cf. Prov 1:23)."[33] For Bloesch, tangible and heartfelt communication is what marks

---

30. Bloesch, *Struggle of Prayer*, 131.

31. Bloesch, *Theological Notebook*, 3:130.

32. "I basically stand in the tradition of the biblical prophets and the Protestant Reformation, which sees prayer not as *recitation* (as in formalistic religion) or *meditation* (as in mysticism) but as *dialogue* between the living God and the one who has been touched by his grace" (Bloesch, *Struggle of Prayer*, vii).

33. Bloesch, "Prayer," 947.

evangelical prayer.[34] Finally, I argue another primary feature of Bloesch's vision of *personal* prayer is struggle. Prayer is an encounter of two wills, divine and human, and as such it entails a kind of wrestling with each other. The Christian pray-er is called to persist and even resist in prayer, contending with God through petition and supplication.

The Triune Shape of Personal Prayer

In contrast to the biblical-classical synthesis of mystical prayer, Bloesch proposes an evangelical account of prayer. Such an account of prayer must be shaped by a properly construed doctrine of God. If Bloesch is right in naming the locus of error in mystical prayer as a distorted doctrine of God, then one could assume the proper corrective would be a proper doctrine of God. Bloesch argues, "Christian prayer rests upon the irreversible fact of the self-revelation of God in Jesus Christ and its confirmation in our hearts by the Holy Spirit. The holy Trinity is the basis of true prayer as well as its goal."[35] Likewise, Bloesch states,

> The Trinitarian formula—Father, Son and Spirit—must never become an idol that directs us only to words and rites as opposed to the reality that encompasses this name. On the other hand, the Trinitarian definition will always be the ruling criterion that regulates the life of worship and prayer, one that keeps us on the biblical path and prevents us from projecting on God our own vision of what God should be like.[36]

The Trinity is the ground and goal of evangelical prayer. This conviction is clearly demonstrated by Bloesch's decision to locate a discussion of prayer in the *God the Almighty* volume in his seven-volume systematic theology, *Christian Foundations*. Expectedly, for Bloesch, the Triune shape of evangelical prayer is an appeal to the economic activity of the Triune God more than it is a focus on the immanent life of God. As he states, "Belief in the Trinity has far-reaching implications for the spiritual. It means that the God we worship is not a solitary, detached being but a living, personal God who can enter into meaningful relations with us."[37] For Bloesch, evangelical prayer is shaped by the Triune God of revelation. This priority on the Trinity

---

34. Bloesch, *Spirituality East & West*, 188.
35. Bloesch, *Struggle of Prayer*, 26.
36. Bloesch, *God the Almighty*, 194.
37. Bloesch, *God the Almighty*, 191.

produces the emphasis on "personal encounter" that Bloesch is driving toward, funding Bloesch's relationally dynamic vision of prayer marked by dialogue and struggle.[38]

Bloesch's relationally dynamic evangelical prayer is anchored in a robust Trinitarianism that advocates the critical role of each person of the Triune Godhead in the act of prayer. Prayer must always be directed to the Father, with the Son, and by the Spirit. As Bloesch states, "in biblical prayer we pour out our soul before God, we entreat him and beg him for his favor and mercy. We do not merely bring our requests before God, but we struggle with God, even wrestle with God. God is over us and above us to be sure, but he is also within us and beside us."[39] God is above the Christian as Father, but He is also beside the Christian in the incarnation of Jesus Christ, and within the Christian by the indwelling presence of the Spirit. In prayer, the Christian is encompassed by the Triune God of Holy Scripture.

According to Bloesch, prayer is personal precisely because it is communion with the personal God. Grounding prayer in the Triune nature of God establishes the soil from which personal evangelical prayer can grow. Prayer is to be ordered by and directed to the Triune God, such that neither subordinationism nor tritheism could provide the kind of relational vision of prayer that Bloesch seeks to uphold.[40] The prayer of subordinationism is a kind submission to divine authority and power, thereby lacking the companionship of Jesus and indwelling presence of the Spirit. The prayer of tritheism leads to a privileging of one person over another in search of agreement or approval, circumventing the call to persistence and wrestling

---

38. Bloesch, *God the Almighty*, 191. We read elsewhere, "Evangelical prayer rests on several theological premises. One is that God is a Personal Spirit and that he hearkens to and answers our prayers. Another is that God is both all-loving to and answers our prayers. Another is that God is both all-loving and all-powerful, and therefore he is willing and able to fulfill our deepest petitions" (Bloesch, *Crisis of Piety*, 188).

39. Bloesch, *God the Almighty*, 192.

40. Bloesch's concern regarding errant doctrines of God and their detrimental impact on prayer is not limited to mysticism. Bloesch identifies other traditional heresies and the ways in which they form sub-Christian accounts of prayer. In particular, Bloesch is concerned with a form of subordinationist-monarchialism infecting the church and shaping an understanding of prayer. Here, Bloesch's concern is that the Son and the Spirit are located beneath the Father within the Godhead. Consequentially, the Christian is called to relate to God as solely Father, perhaps even to the neglect of recognizing the co-equal and co-eternal Son and Spirit. Bloesch argues that we can pray to God the Father, God the Son, and God the Holy Spirit. See Bloesch, *God the Almighty*, 191. His concerns with a rigid commitment of prayer to the Father alone is that it can push away from the genuine reciprocity essential to genuine prayer.

with God in prayer.[41] For Bloesch, only a Biblically faithful account of the Trinity can form prayer into a personal encounter of genuine reciprocity. Such reciprocity does not mean that God somehow needs or is dependent upon the pray-er, but it does mean that God is personally invested in and impacted by the encounter which occurs in the dialogue and struggle of prayer. More importantly, it means that the pray-er is invested in and impacted by the encounter with God. The pray-er is spiritually formed by the experience of the encounter with God the Father, Son, and Holy Spirit. In order to uphold this personal form of prayer, Bloesch proposes that "trinitarian Christians" ought to invoke the name of Father, Son, and Holy Spirit in their prayers.[42] The Triune shape of Bloesch's "personal" vision of prayer calls for a consideration of the role each of the Triune persons plays in the act of prayer. This will draw out and accentuate the contours of Bloesch's trinitarian vision of personal encounter.

Prayer Before the Father

According to Bloesch, evangelical prayer is before God the Father. In discussing the role of the Father in prayer, Bloesch stresses the divine attributes. Consequently, prayer before the Father is a personal encounter with God who is omnipresent, omniscient, omnipotent, transcendent, holy, and loving. Bloesch believes each of these divine attributes primarily identified with the Father come to bear on prayer, each uniquely shaping the personal

---

41. Bloesch states, "If we move toward tritheism as opposed to trinitarianism, we become prone to think of the members of the Trinity as varying in their responses to our requests. If we receive no answer to our prayers from one person of the Trinity, the temptation is then to solicit the favor of another" (*God the Almighty*, 193). Because Bloesch believes evangelical prayer is about wrestling with God, his concern lies in the circumventing of relational wrestling by the pray-er pitting the persons of the Trinity against one another in an effort to avoid persistence and patience in prayer. Here, the concern is that the Christian avoids the struggle of prayer by using another "person" of the Trinity to get around the experience of conflict or consternation in prayer. This mode of prayer grounded in a form of tritheism seeks to manipulate God in order to get what we want.

42. Bloesch, *God the Almighty*, 192. Bloesch goes on to state later in the chapter:

> We pray to the Father in the Son and through the power of the Spirit. We pray to Christ who proceeds from the Father and who is made available to us by the Spirit. We pray to the Spirit through the intercession of Christ and by the grace given to us by the Father. Because of the perichoresis (mutual indwelling), each member of the Trinity is fully present in the being and acts of the others. (193)

encounter known in prayer. Bloesch offers a detailed description of how each of these attributes shapes the encounter of prayer.

First, in reflecting on the Christian's personal encounter with God the Father in prayer, Bloesch considers God's *omniscience*. God "is closer to us than we are to ourselves (Augustine). He is not a part of us, but he is with us and for us."[43] The personal encounter of prayer is marked by God's deep knowing of the pray-er. As a result, the pray-er is infused with an assurance and confidence in coming before God in truth, as he or she recognizes that "God knows our innermost thoughts and needs."[44] Second, because God the Father is not only omniscient but also *transcendent* ("wholly other"[45]), His presence is not confined by or collapsed into the created order. Therefore, there is a legitimacy and viability to appealing to God in prayer because He is unconstrained and beyond creaturely limitations. Third, Bloesch believes an understanding of *omnipresence* focused on divine sovereignty and freedom leads the pray-er to confidently share his or her needs with God. God's capacity to answer and meet those needs in accordance with His will encourages the pray-er to petition God and nurtures the importance of dialogue with God in prayer. Fourth, the *holiness* of God the Father means that a prayerful personal encounter with God is not to be treated lightly or flippantly, but rather God is to be approached in "penitence" and "even in fear and trembling."[46] Finally, because God the Father is *loving*, personal encounter is marked by intimacy and care. As Bloesch states, "As the God of love, he is merciful, compassionate, solicitous. He will listen to us even while we are yet in our sins."[47] Furthermore, "If God is envisaged as the all-powerful and all-loving heavenly Father—infinitely concerned with the well-being of his sons and daughters—then prayer could express itself in heartfelt supplication, intercession and confession (as in biblical religion)."[48] In prayer this ought to bring human beings comfort knowing God's "power is informed by mercy and that his glory is his overflowing love, the grace that goes out to the undeserving."[49]

---

43. Bloesch, *Struggle of Prayer*, 28.
44. Bloesch, *Struggle of Prayer*, 29.
45. Bloesch, *Struggle of Prayer*, 30.
46. Bloesch, *Struggle of Prayer*, 30.
47. Bloesch, *Struggle of Prayer*, 31.
48. Bloesch, *God the Almighty*, 234.
49. Bloesch, *Struggle of Prayer*, 32.

Evangelical prayer is directed to God the Father. This directional emphasis given to the Father in the Triune economy of prayer undergirds Bloesch's decision to specifically lodge a discussion of the divine attributes in God the Father. To say prayer is shaped by the Trinity is to say that prayer is shaped by the attributes of the Triune God. Bloesch recognizes the formative power of the divine attributes on the nature of prayer itself is to be found in the Christian's encounter *before* the Father. In short, the question is who has the Son and Spirit brought the pray-er into contact with? Bloesch seeks to demonstrate that evangelical prayer is prayer *to* a certain kind of God, namely a God who is omniscient, transcendent, omnipresent, holy, and loving. These attributes *personalize* the one being prayed to and establish a set of fitting expectations for personal encounter with God.

Prayer With the Son

Prayer is a personal encounter of the Christian who has been brought before God the Father. It is the Son who has brought the believer before the Father for the sake of this encounter. According to Bloesch, the Christian, therefore, prays with Jesus who is mediator, interceder, and exemplar.[50] According to Bloesch, Jesus makes prayer possible, prays on the Christian's behalf, and faithfully models personal prayer.

Christ's mediation of the divine-human encounter in prayer is a result of his vocation as revealer, reconciler, and redeemer. As *revealer*, Jesus is the one who makes known to the believer the attributes of God, namely, his holiness and love. As *reconciler*, Jesus is the one who has "overcome the enmity between God and man by making the one sacrifice acceptable to God, a sacrifice on man's behalf."[51] In Christ's reconciling work, prayer is now made possible: "It is the sacrifice of Christ on the Cross of Calvary that makes Christian prayer possible, for we are now able to approach God on the basis of the righteousness of Christ which is imputed to us."[52] The personal encounter of prayer rests on the restoration of right relationship to God made possible in Christ's atoning work on the cross. Concerning Christ's *redeeming* role, Bloesch states, "Whereas formerly we were enslaved to powers and forces beyond our control, we have now been liberated from these powers through the cross and resurrection of Jesus Christ

---

50. Bloesch, *Struggle of Prayer*, 33.
51. Bloesch, *Struggle of Prayer*, 34.
52. Bloesch, *Crisis of Piety*, 188.

from the grave."[53] This means that human beings have been released from the tyranny of the powers of evil and set free from their bondage such that they are set free to life in God.

On Bloesch's trinitarian account of prayer, Christ serves not only as the mediator of personal encounter in prayer but also as intercessor. Christ personally prays *with* the human person praying. This emphasis on Christ's present role of intercession in the Christian life is peculiar within the logic of Bloesch's theology, in which he tends to stress Christ's past work. As I have demonstrated throughout this project, Bloesch prioritizes the past work of Christ to articulate the objective pole of revelation and stresses the Spirit's role in the present subjective experience of the Christian life. Here, Bloesch brings the work of Christ into that present subjective experience of the Christian. Bloesch states, "Christ gives our prayers form and substance in his role as Intercessor in heaven. He prays our prayers for us. He unites our prayers with his so that God hears us (cf. Rom 8:34)."[54] The Christian's prayers are received by the Father because they come before Him in the Son. The Christian has assurance that his or her prayers are heard and received in Christ.

Christ is, furthermore, with the Christian in prayer not only by mediation and intercession but also by example. The Christian pray-er is called to imitate the prayer life of Jesus. Christ is not merely an example of forms and techniques of prayer but more importantly is the exemplar of personal prayer.[55] The prayer life of Jesus demonstrates what it means to pray to the Father by the Spirit. Therefore, as the Christian prays, he or she prays with Jesus as his or her model of relational engagement. The Christian looks to Jesus as a companion demonstrating what personal encounter with God the Father by the Holy Spirit looks like.

Prayer By the Spirit

In Bloesch's account of prayer, the Holy Spirit serves a unique role in making possible the divine-human encounter. Bloesch argues, "Christian prayer is also grounded in the gift of the Holy Spirit to the church. We pray because we are prompted and enabled to do so by the Spirit."[56] If evangeli-

---

53. Bloesch, *Struggle of Prayer*, 34.
54. Bloesch, *Struggle of Prayer*, 35.
55. Bloesch, *Struggle of Prayer*, 36.
56. Bloesch, *Crisis of Piety*, 188.

An Evangelical Spiritual Theology

cal prayer is before the Father and with the Son, then it is by the Holy Spirit. Bloesch states, "Apart from the outpouring of the Holy Spirit there can be no prayer worthy of the name of Christian. Wherever the Holy Spirit makes his entry into human life, there we find the origin of Christian prayer, since it is the Spirit who moves us to pray and who instructs us in the life of prayer."[57] If the Son's mediating work makes the divine-human encounter in prayer objectively possible, then the Spirit's indwelling work makes the divine-human encounter in prayer subjectively possible.

There are several ways in which the Holy Spirit plays a definitive role in the life of prayer: The Spirit unites the person to Christ and draws him or her into communion with Him; The Spirit prays for the Christian from within the depths of his or her being; The Spirit convicts of sin in prayer; The Spirit makes known the glory and goodness of God to the Christian's inner being; and, The Spirit cultivates within the Christian new desires for God and His glory.[58] The Holy Spirit internalizes the pray-er's encounter with the Triune God. The Spirit applies the work of Christ to the believer's heart and enlivens the believer to come before God as those who are with Christ. Bloesch concludes, "True prayer is not taking place unless it is enlivened and directed by the Holy Spirit. Prayer is something more than a discourse or an address directed to God: it is the passionate crying out of our whole being for God."[59] The Spirit gives rise to the pray-er's prayers. Nevertheless, one must not presume upon the indwelling power and presence of the Spirit: "We can grieve and quench the Spirit; the Spirit can and does withdraw his aid from us if we turn again to the pathway of sin."[60]

Unsurprisingly, in Bloesch's Triune account of personal prayer, he stresses the Spirit's role. It is here that the Pietistic side of his Pietistic, Reformed evangelicalism shines through once again. Bloesch states, "Whereas Luther located the source of prayer in the command of God, and Calvin in the mediation and intercession of Christ, my emphasis is on the indwelling of the Holy Spirit."[61] For Bloesch, prayer is the locus of divine-human encounter in the Christian life, and this encounter is an internal experience wrought forth by the indwelling presence of the Holy Spirit. While it is an internal experience, it is "not so much perpetual communion with God as

---

57. Bloesch, *Struggle of Prayer*, 37.
58. Bloesch, *Struggle of Prayer*, 37–38.
59. Bloesch, *Struggle of Prayer*, 38.
60. Bloesch, *Struggle of Prayer*, 39.
61. Bloesch, *Theological Notebook*, 2:78.

lively conversation with God. It is not so much gazing on the beauty and wonder of God as struggling with God."[62] It is to these two features (conversation and struggle) of trinitarian prayer that I now turn my attention.

Prayer as Dialogical Encounter

As a divine-human encounter, prayer is dialogical at its core; prayer is about personal conversation with the Triune God.[63] In contrast with an emphasis on union in mystical prayer, Bloesch's evangelical account of prayer is marked by a "more concrete" dialogue between God and the human person.[64] Bloesch envisions dialogical prayer being a frequent, ongoing part of the Christian's life.[65] For Bloesch, prayer is not an occasional spiritual act but instead a way of life.[66] The Christian is called to a life of prayerfulness.

God takes the lead in this ongoing personal dialogue, or put otherwise, "Prayer begins in the action of God."[67] Therefore, the human side of this encounter in prayer begins with listening. The dialogue begins with the human person hearing the Word by the Spirit.[68] For Bloesch, this hearing of the Word frequently "transcends the senses and the imagination."[69] Listening, according to Bloesch, will entail waiting, but after waiting and listening, the human person is invited to speak.[70] As with prayerful listening, prayerful speaking is a Word & Spirit endeavor. The Christian's prayers are heard by the mediation of the Word and the intercession of the Spirit.[71] According to Bloesch, "The essence of true prayer is heartfelt supplication, bringing before God one's innermost needs and requests in the confident

---

62. Bloesch, *God the Almighty*, 231.

63. Bloesch, *Faith in Search of Obedience*, 64.

64. Bloesch, *Struggle of Prayer*, 50. Bloesch acknowledges an evangelical account of union in which "the emphasis is on the union of *faith*, not the ecstatic future union of perfected *love*. The foundation of this union, moreover, is the vicarious atonement of Jesus Christ, not the works of love of the believer. Our hope is anchored in the historical revelation and mediation of Jesus Christ, not in the presence of Eternity with the depths of the soul" (158).

65. Bloesch, *Struggle of Prayer*, 60–62.

66. Bloesch, "Call to Spirituality," 162.

67. Bloesch, *Struggle of Prayer*, 54.

68. Bloesch, *Struggle of Prayer*, 54.

69. Bloesch, *Struggle of Prayer*, 63.

70. Bloesch, *Struggle of Prayer*, 63.

71. Bloesch, *Struggle of Prayer*, 58.

expectation that God will hear and answer."[72] In Bloesch's vision of evangelical prayer, the pray-er is invited to speak honestly, presenting his or her mind and heart to God in truth. In this sense, prayer is a "personal, loving address."[73] The dialogue that marks an encounter with God in prayer includes complaint, challenge, and questions.[74] It is a dialogue of authenticity and of persistence.

This commitment to honest dialogue causes Bloesch to stress the value of spontaneity in prayer: "Biblical prayer, unlike ritual prayer, is spontaneous."[75] This does not mean there is no room for formal, structured, or corporate prayer, but it does mean that such prayers are for the sake of authentic personal encounter. Bloesch states,

> Prayer is not so much an address directed to God as a spontaneous outburst of praise and supplication in response to God's gracious outreach to man. Prayer will invariably take the form of structured address and of ritualized formula because man, in his weakness, desires a crutch in his relationship with the divine. But in those moments when he is impelled by the interior movement of the Spirit to cry out to God as a child to his loving father, he transcends the prayer of rote and enters into biblical or prophetic prayer, the conversation of the heart with God.[76]

72. Bloesch, *Struggle of Prayer*, 67.

73. Bloesch, *Struggle of Prayer*, 53.

74. Bloesch states elsewhere, "The one who prays can come confidently to the throne of God and make known desires and wishes that have remained hidden in the depths of the psyche" (*Paradox of Holiness*, 11).

75. Bloesch, *Spirituality Old & New*, 95. Bloesch echoes this sentiment elsewhere: "Prayer in the biblical perspective is spontaneous, though it may take structured forms" ("Prayer," 947). Bloesch strikes an expectedly balanced tone in discussing prayer in his spiritual autobiography:

> One danger in the life of prayer, as I can personally attest, is that the prayer time can become nothing more than saying prayers. To pray in the Spirit is to pray with the spontaneity of perfected loved. This is not simply a matter of practice but a gift of God's grace. We must sedulously try to avoid the pitfall of ritualism—vain repetition. But saying prayers is better than no prayer at all. If we say prayers that we have memorized, the possibility is always there that meaning will come to us from the Spirit of God. Indeed, if we cease from prayer—simply waiting until the Spirit acts—then we will sink into a prayerless existence, in which faith itself begins to erode. (*Faith in Search of Obedience*, 53)

76. Bloesch, *Essentials of Evangelical Theology*, 2:59. As Bloesch states elsewhere, "By contrast, in the biblical view prayer is the pouring out of the soul to a God who hears and acts. Prayer is crying out to God in our anguish and being set free when he answers (Ps 118:5 NIV; cf. Ps 116:1–8)" (*God the Almighty*, 231).

Here, we find Bloesch appealing directly to Heiler's language of "prophetic" when referencing this mode of personal spontaneous prayer. Interestingly, structure and formalism in prayer are viewed as necessary given humanity's fallen condition, but as ultimately and necessarily transcended by dialogical prayer. For Bloesch, spontaneous personal prayer is the heart of the divine-human encounter.

While Bloesch's dialogical account of prayer prioritizes speech (intercession and supplication), this does not mean that Bloesch has no place for silence in prayer. While he has an aversion to the mystical account of silent prayer which "transcends all conceptualization,"[77] there are two places in

---

77. Bloesch, *Struggle of Prayer*, 51. Bloesch is concerned that the mystical emphasis on reaching up to God defines prayer as a mode of transcending the knowable and verbal in order to attain to the mysterious and wordless. This movement away from conscious communication to a kind of apophatic contemplation is a key difference in between Bloesch's evangelical prayer and mystical prayer. See Bloesch, *Spirituality Old & New*, 95. The sharp contrast between evangelical (Biblical) prayer and mystical prayer is demonstrated in Bloesch's emphasis on dialogue over silence in prayer. Prayer is not transcending beyond creaturely reality to a detached yet infinite deity but is about personal communication. Prayer is not void of concepts and words but is rather filled with them. Bloesch states, "The goal is not wordless or mindless prayer, but prayer in which we make known our needs and concerns to a holy and merciful God" (*Church*, 132). The contrast between Bloesch's understanding of mystical contemplation and biblical prayer is evident here. Bloesch is so vehement in his rejection of mystical prayer and his quest to establish the uniqueness of evangelical prayer that he is willing to risk the impression being made that there is no place for silent communion or "practicing God's presence," as has been common within the Christian tradition. However, Bloesch curtails this potential overreaction: "Although the tradition of biblical or prophetic religion also holds silence in high esteem, it never excludes the spoken Word of God. Silence is to be used not to take us beyond the Word (as in Neoplatonism) but to enable us to hear the Word. It is not silence itself but the Word that breaks into our silence that brings us true knowledge and freedom" (*God the Almighty*, 232). Bloesch states elsewhere, "In the biblical view silence has a salutary role in preparing us to hear the Word of God. It does not take us beyond the Word but helps us to be open to the Word" (*Church*, 133). Bloesch echoes this in his spiritual autobiography:

> Silence itself can be a discipline of the spirit, for we cannot carry on a meaningful conversation with God if we are distracted by noise or disturbances of any kind. The eminent philosopher Alfred North Whitehead has cogently observed that religion is what we do in our solitariness. It sometimes behooves us to break away from the security of the family or from the demands of work in order to be alone with God in prayer and meditation. Retreat houses or organized retreats can be helpful in this regard. Silence does not take us beyond the Word (as in mysticism), but it prepares us to hear the Word—so long as we do not sever the course of our thoughts from Holy Scripture. (*Faith in Search of Obedience*, 65)

which a kind of silent prayer is acceptable: First, as a participation in the inner groaning of the Spirit; and, second, as the Christian "shouts" and "sings" praise to God.[78] In Bloesch's view this work of the Spirit is still a work that points toward words; ultimately, for Bloesch, "true prayer will always give rise to words."[79] In both cases the Spirit is leading us toward "meaningful language so that real dialogue can take place between God and ourselves."[80] As Bloesch notes, "Biblical spirituality makes a place for silence, yet silence is to be used not to get beyond the Word but to prepare ourselves to hear the Word."[81] The fundamental exchange of prayer is wrought through speaking and listening.

Prayer as an Encounter of Struggle

In Donald Bloesch's brand of evangelical spirituality, prayer is a dialogically-oriented personal encounter between the Triune God and the Christian. As already noted, human dialogue with God entails complaint and questioning. These aspects of conversation with God, Bloesch summarily refers to as "struggle." Evangelical prayer should be a struggle, and as a result, petition is a primary task of the evangelical pray-er. Petition, of course, is not the only form of prayer, but it is the most fundamental in personal dialogue.[82] As Bloesch states, "Prayer is not simply petition, but strenuous petition. It is not just passive surrender but active pleading with God."[83] The person praying is called to be honest; frustration, disappointment, and argument are all welcome realities in prayer. Without genuine relational vulnerability and reciprocity, actual prayer is not taking place. This is the struggle of prayer.

Bloesch turns to the biblical imagery of wrestling with God to describe the nature of struggle in prayer, appealing specifically to the story of

78. Bloesch, *Struggle of Prayer*, 51–52.
79. Bloesch, *Struggle of Prayer*, 50.
80. Bloesch, *Struggle of Prayer*, 52.
81. Bloesch, "Prayer," 947.
82. Bloesch, *Spirituality Old & New*, 94. Bloesch states elsewhere, "In the Bible petition and intercession are primary, though adoration, thanksgiving, and confession also have a role" ("Prayer," 947). Bloesch clearly anchors petition as more primary than intercession in *Spirituality East & West*: "One of the primary forms of petitionary prayer is intercession. This type of prayer was particularly emphasized by the Reformers Luther and Calvin" (*Spirituality East & West*, 189).
83. Bloesch, *Struggle of Prayer*, 72.

Jacob wrestling with God as an example of the dynamic encounter he has in mind.[84] Wrestling is marked by persistence and resistance. Such persistent and resistant wrestling with God in prayer is made possible by God himself according to Bloesch. He states, "We are able to wrestle with God because God chooses to wrestle with us."[85] A true encounter of persons is an encounter between two, sometimes competing, wills. Bloesch argues,

> True prayer is not only resignation and submission but striving with God, pleading with God, seeking to change the ways of God with his people so that his ultimate will might be more surely or fully accomplished. God's ultimate purposes are unchangeable, but his immediate will is flexible and open to change through the prayers of his children.[86]

Yet again, Bloesch distinguishes his account of prayer from that of mysticism. Rather than the focus of prayer being on surrender, the focus is on struggle. The pray-er is not called to passive submission but rather active petition. Ultimately, Bloesch argues, "biblical prayer culminates in submission to God's will," but not before the Christian struggles "to make known to God the depth of [their] predicament and need."[87] While God already knows the will of His people, He delights when they actively share their desires in prayer.[88]

Bloesch's emphasis on genuine personal encounter means that the human will is not the only will that shows up in prayer. What makes prayer a struggle is the meeting of the human and divine wills.[89] For Bloesch,

---

84. Bloesch, *Crisis of Piety*, 94.
85. Bloesch, *Struggle of Prayer*, 77.
86. Bloesch, *Essentials of Evangelical Theology*, 2:57.
87. Bloesch, *Struggle of Prayer*, 94.
88. Bloesch, *Struggle of Prayer*, 94.
89. Bloesch has clearly been influenced by P. T. Forsyth on this point. As noted in an earlier footnote at the beginning of this chapter, Forsyth is a primary source for Bloesch as he develops his theology of prayer. On this point in particular we can see Forsyth's influence. As he builds his account of struggle in prayer marked by the encounter of two wills, Bloesch affirms Forsyth's concept of "importunity" in prayer. See Bloesch, *Struggle of Prayer*, 79. This way of viewing prayer is developed by Forsyth in his work *The Soul of Prayer*. There Forsyth states, "prayer should be strenuously *importunate*. Observe, not petitionary merely, nor concentrated, nor active alone, but importunate. For prayer is not only meditation or communion. Nor ought it be merely submissive in tone, as the 'quietist' ideal is" (Forsyth, *Soul of Prayer*, 95). Forsyth adds that prayer "cannot be importunate unless it is felt to have a real effect on the Will of God" (95). Prayer, argues Forsyth, "has largely ceased to be *wrestling* for many Christians, but wrestling is the

there is an integrity to the relationality of prayer that demands an actual exchange of wills, the possibility of God changing his mind as a result of a conversation with the believer. This does not mean that somehow God is no longer sovereign, but rather that in the economy of divine action, God maintains his sovereignty by an inclusion of human engagement. This is biblical-personalism at its best, according to Bloesch. Rather than positing a God of classical mysticism or classical theism, who is unmoved and unaffected, Bloesch contends that the Triune God of the Bible reveals himself to be personally invested and impacted in relating to his people.[90] Bloesch

---

"dominant scriptural idea" regarding prayer (97). Forsyth concludes, importunate prayer is built on the fundamental belief that "prayer is an encounter of *wills*—till one will or the other give way" (97). Wakefield summarizes Forsyth's theology of prayer: "It is encounter with God in petition, importunity, wrestling. It is co-operation with the divine will, but often after a striving which may in some sense change it" (Wakefield, "Forsyth on Prayer," 67). Bloesch's emphasis on the struggle of encounter between the pray-er and God clearly echoes Forsyth.

90. In the *Paradox of Holiness*, we find an interesting passage laying the doctrinal groundwork for this view:

> The God of biblical personalism is qualitatively different form the God of classical theism. The biblical God is flexible in his judgments and is ready to alter his decisions when his people turn to him in faith. By contrast, the God of classical theism is immutable and impassible. He does not change because he is incapable of change. The God of the Bible is not "the unmoved mover" who moves by the lure of his perfections, but the Lord of hosts who faithfully responds to the cries of his children. He is characterized not by static perfection but by dynamic righteousness. He does not change in the integrity of his being, but he makes himself dependent on the petitions of his people so that he can realize his purposes in every-new ways. (Bloesch, *Paradox of Holiness*, 60)

Bloesch's concern is to uphold a personal God of the Bible while rejecting a depersonalized God of philosophy. His aversion to classical theism and its emphasis on metaphysical divine attributes can be traced back to the influence of modern theology on his thinking. According to Stephen R. Holmes there is a movement in modern theology away from viewing the "doctrine of God from a metaphysical study to a personal encounter" (Holmes, "Divine Attributes," 56). Holmes goes on to argue that this movement in modern theology is marked by several key features. First, "natural theology was excluded in principle, and there could be no general science of the divine, no metaphysics—instead only knowledge granted by direct revelation" (56). Second, a concern with the "Greek 'infection' of Christianity in its formative period" (56). Third, "The language of Greek 'infection' of biblical religion is regularly advanced as a reason to be suspicious of a certain set of traditional, metaphysical attributes of God, including simplicity, aseity . . . impassibility . . . immutability, and eternity" (57). It is clear that Bloesch has followed this reaction of modern theology in its concern regarding the God of classical theism. Holmes notes the modern theological anxiety regarding the Greek influence of

tells us that prayer, "involves not only submission to the will of God but seeking to change his will."[91] Prayer has "a definite impact on both of the parties involves."[92]

This does not mean that God's ultimate will and purposes can be changed by our petitions, but rather, "God has chosen to work out his purposes in cooperation with his children."[93] The evangelical pray-er endeavors "to change what appears to be God's will so that his greater will might be fulfilled."[94] While God does not alter his "final purpose," he "does alter his method for realizing this purpose."[95] Bloesch states, "In biblical religion God's ultimate will is unchangeable, but the method by which He implements His purposes in the world can be altered by the prayers of the faithful."[96] The Christian petitions, struggles, wrestles with God, believing that God includes such prayers in the accomplishment of His sovereign will and purposes. God is not somehow coerced or controlled in this relationship of reciprocity; rather, struggle, wrestling, and contending are welcomed. God has graciously chosen to relate to His people in His sovereign freedom and His holy love.

While true prayer necessitates reciprocity—a genuine give and take—this does not mean that the Christian is somehow seeking to overcome God. "In our striving with God in prayer," Bloesch claims, "we do not defeat God. As we prevail, so does he. We prevail in and through God."[97] In this sense, Bloesch argues the Christian is ultimately called to surrender to God's

---

early Christianity has been historically debunked, but this line of concern has "left a strangely resilient legacy in dogmatics" (57). Bloesch's perspective appears to be evidence of Holmes's claim.

91. Bloesch, *Struggle of Prayer*, 72.
92. Bloesch, *Struggle of Prayer*, 73.
93. Bloesch, *Struggle of Prayer*, 74.
94. Bloesch, *Struggle of Prayer*, 94.
95. Bloesch, *Struggle of Prayer*, 74. We read elsewhere, "Evangelical prayer is based on the view that a sovereign God can and does make himself dependent on the requests of his children. He chooses to realize his purposes in the world in collaboration with his people. To be sure, God knows our needs before we ask, but he desires that we discuss them with him so that he might work with us as his covenant partners toward their solution" (Bloesch, *Essentials of Evangelical Theology*, 2:58).
96. Bloesch, *Struggle of Prayer*, 144.
97. Bloesch, *Struggle of Prayer*, 74.

will, trusting that He will act in the proper way and proper time. However, Bloesch argues that such surrender does not come as a result of passive resignation, but rather active struggle. It is only through the struggle that we come to genuinely surrender to God's will.[98] As Bloesch states, "Prayer is both a pleading with God to hear and act upon our requests and a trusting surrender to God in the confidence that he will act in his own time and way. But the confidence comes to us only through the struggle."[99] Ultimately, this wrestling with the will of God is for the sake of being conformed to His will. As Bloesch states,

> Prayer . . . is not a passive resignation to God's will but a wrestling with God so that one might discover the best way in which His will can be fulfilled. In biblical religion God's ultimate will is unchangeable, but the method by which He implements His purposes in the world can be altered by the prayers of the faithful.[100]

It is a movement of prayer by which we are transformed by the renewing of our mind. Bloesch states, "In this restricted sense prayer may be said to change the will of God. But more fundamentally it is sharing with God our needs and desires so that we might be more fully conformed to his ultimate will and purpose."[101] It is through genuine wrestling with God that the Christian comes to pray truly "thy will be done on earth as it is in heaven." It is only through the clash of wills, the cry of the heart, and the embrace of honest dialogue that this occurs. The Christian is transformed by true prayer, but this transformation is challenging because it exposes one's true

---

98. Bloesch, "Prayer," 947. As Bloesch states elsewhere, "It is incumbent on us to struggle with God in prayer in order to discern his will for our lives" (*Faith in Search of Obedience*, 64).

99. Bloesch, *Theological Notebook*, 3:289. We read elsewhere,

> Evangelical prayer, in contrast to mystical prayer, consists not in passive resignation to the will of God, but in wrestling with the divine will. We do not simply submit ourselves to God's will; rather we seek to change his will. We finally surrender to God's will only after much agony and tribulation. This kind of prayer is testimony to the freedom of both God and man. God in his graciousness makes himself dependent upon the supplications of his children. He sanctions petitions that seek to change what is his will temporarily, so that his ultimate will might be done. Moreover, in questioning what appears to be God's will for the moment, we are led to discover what is his final will for us and for others. (Bloesch, *Spirituality East & West*, 190)

100. Bloesch, *Ground of Certainty*, 143–44.

101. Bloesch, "Prayer," 947.

heart before God.[102] The exposure of the heart in the pray-er's wrestling with God means that the Christian is called to wrestle not only with God but likewise with him or herself in prayer.[103]

Bloesch anchors the struggle of dialogical prayer in the prayer life of Christ Himself. As I have already noted, Bloesch views Jesus not only as mediator and interceder in prayer, but also as exemplar. Regarding Christ's prayer life, Bloesch states, "He wrestled with God in prayer and did not surrender until he had undergone the agony and joy in the struggle of prayer."[104] Bloesch looks to Christ's prayer in the Garden of Gethsemane as an example of struggle and a picture of the human person's strenuous petition. In Christ's prayer, Bloesch identifies the kind of pleading with God and honest expression of the will that he envisions as central to the divine-human encounter of the Christian life.

In the prayer life of Jesus, we also see that the struggle of prayer involves spiritual warfare. Jesus models for the Christian what the struggle between God's will and the pray-er's will looks like in the Garden of Gethsemane, so too Jesus models what the struggle with demonic powers looks like in His wilderness temptation. While Bloesch's account of struggle in prayer is primarily focused on the divine-human encounter of wills, it is important to note that his notion of struggle also includes the Biblical notion of struggling with principalities and powers of darkness. In prayer the Christian is called to be discerning and vigilant of demonic temptations and distractions. Ultimately, the struggle of prayer is an active wrestling with God that never forgets its true enemy—the devil.[105]

Bloesch's understanding of prayer as an arena of spiritual battle is oriented by his theology of "two-kingdoms."[106] While "two-kingdom" the-

---

102. Bloesch, *Spirituality East & West*, 190. Pulling together several threads of his argument, Bloesch summarizes things nicely for us in *The Crisis of Piety*:

> Prayer in prophetic religion consists essentially in supplication. Adoration and thanksgiving are seen as elements of petitionary prayer (Karl Barth). Prayer is wrestling with God, not meditating upon God. It is an attempt to change God's will, not simply a passive resignation to God's will. It entails not the total renunciation of one's desires but the offering up of one's desires to God in the hope that they may be fulfilled in God's own way and time. It is the pouring out of the heart before God more than a lifting up of the mind to God. (*Crisis of Piety*, 94)

103. See Bloesch, *Struggle of Prayer*, 133.

104. Bloesch, *Struggle of Prayer*, 36.

105. See Bloesch, *Struggle of Prayer*, 133–34.

106. We can trace some of the historical-theological background to Bloesch's

An Evangelical Spiritual Theology

ology is common within contemporary Reformed circles, Bloesch's use of the concept denotes something other than what is commonly derived in contemporary Reformed thought. Bloesch, in fact, derides the classical Lutheran notion of "two-kingdom" theology, arguing that its distinction between the "spiritual and temporal" can result in an "interiorized religion" in which the Christian life is not meaningfully worked out in the public sphere.[107] Bloesch is not only critical of the classical Lutheran view but also a "modern theology" notion of two kingdom theology:

> A different kind of error can be discerned in certain strands of modern theology (Barth, Tillich, Cullmann, Bonhoeffer) that includes both church and state in the kingdom of Christ or the Spiritual Community. This position loses sight of the truth that God's kingdom is fundamentally eschatological and that the forces of evil still exert real power in this world.[108]

Seeking to avoid these two errors, Bloesch offers his own particular account of "two-kingdom" theology, namely that "the history of salvation has been seen . . . in terms of a conflict between the Kingdom of Christ and the kingdom of the devil."[109] Bloesch's "two-kingdom" theology assumes a demonology in which demonic forces are not demythologized, but given

---

constructive work here in *Jesus Christ*. In his chapter "The Lordship of Christ in Theological History" we are given a historical overview of kingdom theology. Bloesch maps a two-kingdom thread of theology from Augustine to Luther to Calvin, which has clearly influenced his own position.

107. Bloesch, *Crisis of Piety*, 43. Bloesch states,

> The Christian is a member of both spheres, and this means that he owes duties to each. This distinction is legitimate (cf. Rom 13:1-7), but if it is pushed too far it tends to foster interiorized religion. It becomes particularly suspect when the temporal sphere is conceived of as a separate kingdom rather than the arena in which the Christian works out his salvation. Then the Christian is placed under two different standards of morality, a private and a public. (43)

108. Bloesch, *Crisis of Piety*, 43. In response to this view Bloesch states, "God's kingdom is not simply the rule of God but also the realm where his rule is acknowledged" (43).

109. Bloesch et al., *Christian Spirituality*, 171. Bloesch echoes this definition of his two-kingdom theology in *Essentials of Evangelical Theology*: "Biblical religion speaks of two kingdoms in irrevocable conflict with one another—the kingdom of God and the kingdom of the world, also known as the kingdom of Satan. This dualistic vision runs throughout the Scriptures, though the two kingdoms go under many different names" (*Essentials of Evangelical Theology*, 2:131). He continues, "This idea has had important implications for the life of devotion" (Bloesch et al., *Christian Spirituality*, 171).

personal agency.[110] While "the demonic powers have been dethroned by the cross and resurrection victory of Christ" they "continue to wage war."[111] These "hostile spiritual forces opposed to the rule of Christ" have been "mortally wounded but not yet vanquished."[112] On Bloesch's account, the ongoing work of the demonic in this world is under the sovereign permission of God, and yet the demonic remains in firm opposition to God's will and plan. The dark kingdom produces "disorder" and "anarchy" in culture, and it is the "fulcrum of inhumanity" as it "denigrates and defaces the human."[113]

110. Bloesch states,

> There is a real devil and there are real demons, though not as animistic thought describes them but as divine revelation redescribes them. . . . The language of poetry and myth is the best available tool to delineate the cosmic warfare between Christ and Satan, which concerns not inner conflicts of the soul but invisible conflicts in objective history. In this discussion I am reaffirming orthodoxy but at the same time recognizing that narrational language is best for describing realities that transcend the reach of discursive reason. Just as God himself is not myth but fact, so the angelic adversary of God is not the product of human imagination but the embodiment of realities objective to the observer. (*Holy Spirit*, 221)

Bloesch states elsewhere,

> We are presently confused concerning the mission of the church because we have demythologized the demonology of the Bible, and, as Kallas rightly points out, when demonology is cast aside eschatology soon follows. Indeed, demonology is an integral part of eschatology. We cannot speak of the culmination of God's victory unless we understand the meaning and purpose of this victory. The triumph of the kingdom of God is unintelligible if it does not entail the destruction of the kingdom of evil. The concepts of the church militant and the church triumphant lose their meaning if Christians are not engaged in a battle with the world rulers of this present age. (*Crisis of Piety*, 48)

111. Bloesch, *Crisis of Piety*, 43–44.

112. Bloesch, *Crisis of Piety*, 43–44.

113. Bloesch, *Freedom for Obedience*, 234. Here, Bloesch demonstrates an appreciation for both Luther and Calvin. And yet, it is Bloesch's belief in the similarity between his view and Barth's that stands out the most:

> Yet we are not being fair to Barth if we fail to take seriously his belief that the demonic kingdom of darkness, which spawns anarchy and disorder, is still very much alive. Though it has been divested of its power ontologically, it still wields power through deception. This is why he can refer to the lordless powers that continue to rule as rebels and usurpers. Christ has indeed demolished the demonic powers that have held the world in subjection, but until this fact is generally recognized they will continue to wreak havoc. Barth can speak at the same time of a world fully reconciled to God in Jesus Christ and of a "still unredeemed world." (237)

An Evangelical Spiritual Theology

The fight between the demonic realm and God is properly understood as a battle between light and dark. The world, already in the grips of darkness, is the battleground of this fight, where Christians are enlisted to engage in the fight.[114] The operation of demonic forces in this fallen world can be overcome only in the location of Christ's reign—the church. In this battle the church is on the offensive, while the demonic is "on the run."[115] The final destruction of the kingdom of darkness will come in the fullness of the kingdom—the second advent of Christ.[116] The Christian life, according to Bloesch, is a battle between light and dark, one that necessitates a sober-minded recognition and discernment of the spiritual battle Christians are called to engage during this present evil age. It is a battle that is fought within the walls of the church, just as it must be engaged in worldly structures and systems.[117] Bloesch concludes, "This biblical perspec-

---

114. Bloesch states,

> The world is depicted in the Bible as a battleground between these two kingdoms, light and darkness. Both church and state are imperiled by the power of darkness, and only by looking to Jesus Christ can men save themselves from idolatry and bondage. Because it is only through the Word proclaimed in the church that men are liberated from the hold of the tyrants, the world outside the church is more or less in the grip of demonic power. (Bloesch et al., *Christian Spirituality*, 171)

Bloesch uses this language in *Essentials of Evangelical Theology* as he discusses his "two-kingdom" theology. There we read, "The church is an island of light in a sea of darkness, but its light is spreading. The holy catholic church is not on the defensive but on the offensive. Through the word that it proclaims it evicts the demons from their strongholds" (Bloesch, *Essentials of Evangelical Theology*, 2:134). We hear echoes of this language in a lengthy appendix on demonology and spiritual warfare in Bloesch's *Holy Spirit*: "In a world of darkness Christ by his Spirit has established islands of light, centers of Christian renewal, that testify to the coming of a new kingdom that is basically in the future but whose power and impact can already be felt and whose eventual victory is completely assured" (*Holy Spirit*, 220).

115. Bloesch, *Holy Spirit*, 221.

116. Bloesch et al., *Christian Spirituality*, 173. In *Essentials of Evangelical Theology*, Bloesch states,

> We are told that at the end of the age Satan will again be loosed to persecute the saints and deceive the nations . . . but his final attack will be to no avail, for his doom has already been assured. The "great city" of the world . . . will ultimately be overthrown, and the "beloved city" of God . . . will reign triumphant. In the last days the city of God will be surrounded by the forces of wickedness . . . but because God has made the cause of the saints his own, they shall persevere and gain the victory. (*Essentials of Evangelical Theology*, 2:134)

117. Bloesch, *Crisis of Piety*, 44.

tive reminds us that the church is essentially an army, and that its mission is to drive out the demons from the lives of individuals and nations. Yet this warfare is spiritual, and our weapons are perforce spiritual."[118] Prayer is the primary spiritual weapon wielded by Christians in this fight.

Prayer as an Encounter Leading to Engagement

In the evangelical spirituality of Donald Bloesch, the Christian is called to a life of obedience. Such obedience has two poles—personal and social. Bloesch believes a life of personal obedience, or piety, should lead to a life of social obedience, or activism.[119] The heart of personal obedience is personal encounter with God in prayer. Personal encounter with the Triune God in prayer is for the sake of personal encounter with other human beings. In his ordering of obedience from piety to activism, Bloesch is consistent in giving prayer the place of primacy.[120] It is prayer that is the most fundamental to a life of obedience in piety and consequently to a life of obedience in engagement with the world. As Bloesch states, "All creative action in the world (mission, service, social reform) is ultimately grounded in the discipline of prayer—adoration, thanksgiving, personal petition, and intercession."[121] Devotion to the Triune God must precede service in the name of the Triune God.

The act of prayer is *itself* an act of social obedience, and it is an act that *leads to* social obedience. As an act *of* social obedience in itself, evangelical prayer is to be marked by intercession and supplication for one's neighbor. As an act *leading to* social obedience, evangelical prayer gives rise to other acts of love and service toward one's neighbor. The Christian's life of holy

---

118. Bloesch, *Crisis of Piety*, 44.

119. As Bloesch states, "The goal of the Christian life is not simply personal holiness but social holiness" (*Faith in Search of Obedience*, 52). He states elsewhere, "Creative action has its roots in contemplation—prayer, study, and disciplined reflection on the revelation of God in Jesus Christ" (*Crumbling Foundations*, 132). Bloesch goes on to say, "Our commitment to social justice will be self-defeating if it is not grounded in works of piety, which serve to deepen our relationship with God: worship, prayer, meditation, devotional reading, fasting" (135).

120. Bloesch states, "Evangelical religion emphasizes the inward over the outward, though it does not dispense with the latter as does radical mysticism or spiritualism" (*Essentials of Evangelical Theology*, 2:257). He goes on to say, "It believes that personal transformation takes priority over social reformation, though it strongly supports efforts toward a more just or equitable society" (2:257).

121. Bloesch, *Crumbling Foundations*, 136.

and loving service is the fruit of abiding in God's holy-loving presence in prayer. Bloesch's vision of social obedience is a call to proclamation of the gospel and evangelism classically understood, but it is also a call to works of mercy and justice. In short, the Christian life of obedience is a life committed to love of neighbor, a bearing witness to the power of the cross.[122] In what follows I explore Bloesch's vision of prayer as an act of social obedience and as an act leading to social obedience. In so doing, I provide a concrete picture of Bloesch's evangelical brand of the Christian life.

Prayer as Social Action

According to Bloesch, the wrestling of evangelical prayer is a struggle of two wills regarding not only the pray-er's particular needs or desires but also for the sake of the needs and desires of others. For Bloesch, prayer entails a wrestling with God on behalf of others. Intercession is a key part of the struggle of prayer.[123] In this sense, prayer is an act of social action. It is a divine-human encounter for the sake of one's neighbor.[124] This personal encounter between God and the pray-er should ordinarily and consistently include personal prayer for others. Bloesch states, "How does one pray the prayer of intercession? Evangelical piety has generally advocated mentioning people by name and praying for solutions to specific needs in the world."[125] For Bloesch, this personal emphasis upon others in prayer stands in stark contrast to mystical prayer. The emphasis on ineffable experience and focusing on God alone in the mystical prayer tradition displaces care for other human persons from the life of prayer. In contradistinction to mysticism's view of intercessory prayer as in some manner a lower form of prayer, Bloesch argues that evangelical prayer (prophetic prayer) places intercessory prayer in high regard.

The call of evangelical prayer is to pray for the world by praying for both the advancement of the kingdom of God and for social justice.[126]

---

122. Bloesch, *Crumbling Foundations*, 131–34.

123. Bloesch, *Struggle of Prayer*, 86.

124. Bloesch states, "Prayer has reference both to God and to the world. It proceeds in two ways—*upward* to God in adoration and supplication, and *outward* to the world in intercession. One might say that prayer is a vertical relation with a horizontal awareness" (*Struggle of Prayer*, 131).

125. Bloesch, *Struggle of Prayer*, 88.

126. Bloesch, *Struggle of Prayer*, 158–61.

These are the two critical spheres of socially active prayer to the glory of God. Prayer for the advancement of the kingdom is evangelistic in nature. It is prayer for the salvation of the world. Prayer for social justice is prayer for "civil righteousness."[127] It is prayer for the well-being of one's neighbor. The Christian is called to pray for the salvation of others, to pray for a hurting world, and to pray for all the needs of a broken and fallen world. The Christian is called to pray for other human persons, and, in so doing, the Christian engages in the "highest form of action."[128]

Prayer Leading to Social Action

Prayer is meant to lead the Christian into other forms of social obedience. Personal encounter with God should drive the Christian into personal encounter with other human beings. In prayer the Christian encounters a Triune God of love, and that encounter of love motivates the Christian to love his or her neighbor.[129] The Christian is called to a life of love shaped by the love of God, known objectively on the cross and known subjectively in prayer by the Holy Spirit.[130] If prayer does not lead the Christian in love toward his or her neighbor, then something has gone wrong. As Bloesch states, "The soundness of a prayer is measured not by our feelings or fervor at the time but by our behavior afterwards."[131] For Bloesch, contemplation must lead to action.[132] As he argues,

> Christian prayer will invariably give rise to activity that seeks the fulfillment of the prayer request. We do not pray in earnest if we do not commit ourselves to do our best to bring about what we

---

127. Bloesch, *Struggle of Prayer*, 161.

128. Bloesch, *Struggle of Prayer*, 131.

129. Bloesch, *Freedom for Obedience*, 34. Bloesch places a particular emphasis on love. As Bloesch states, "Christian obedience is characterized not by exhibiting virtue but by radiating love" (81). As Bloesch goes on to argue, "Evangelical Christianity does not denigrate the life of virtue, but it insists that virtue is not enough. Virtue and knowledge are to be fulfilled in love (2 Pet 1:5–7), and love (agape) is something that happens to us before it is exercised by us" (82).

130. Bloesch states, "What characterizes the . . . Christian life is not gaining the good of this world, whether by diligence or piety, but dying to the world" (*Freedom for Obedience*, 18). He goes on to argue, "Ethics in the general sense refers to the attempt to understand the meaning of the good. Christian ethics, on the other hand, means the attempt to live the Christian life, a life reflecting the passion and victory of Jesus Christ" (21).

131. Bloesch, *Struggle of Prayer*, 131.

132. Bloesch, *Struggle of Prayer*, 137.

hope and pray for. There is no prayer without risk. We must take the risk of becoming involved in the action of prayer. We cannot, for example, pray for racial peace without extending the hand of friendship to members of a minority race and also supporting legislation that insures their civil rights.[133]

Social obedience is the necessary fruit of personal obedience. For Bloesch, the proper relation of a prayerful life of devotion and an active life of service and love is embraced by identifying the two competing errors—quietism and activism. Quietism tends to view the Christian life as spiritual, internal, and ascetic, to the exclusion of social obedience.[134] Activism on the other hand views the Christian life as ethical, political, and service oriented, to the exclusion of personal obedience.[135] In activism, prayer "becomes a means for getting things done."[136] Activism calls into question the integrity of prayer and its fundamental purpose of encounter with God. In opposition to these two errors, Bloesch casts a vision of prayer guided by biblical personalism in which devotion and action are both ingredients to a faithful Christian life.

As I just identified in the previous section, the life of social obedience that is the fruit of a prayerful life of devotion is expressed in two fundamental forms—"social justice" and "kingdom righteousness."[137] Social justice is the Christian duty of love expressed in care, advocacy, protection and compassion toward all people, in particular the poor, marginalized, and vulnerable.[138] Social justice is expressed in good deeds of care for one's neighbor, in political engagement and conscientious civic participation. Kingdom righteousness (kingdom of God) is the work of calling "people

---

133. Bloesch, *Struggle of Prayer*, 138.

134. Bloesch, *Freedom for Obedience*, 107, 150. See also Bloesch, *Crumbling Foundations*, 131.

135. Bloesch, *Crumbling Foundations*, 158–59. In response to these errors Bloesch states, "Against world-denying mysticism and radical pietism, the Christian faith calls for active involvement in the great social issues and problems of the world. Against humanitarianism or ethicism, the Christian faith upholds not mere service but the cure of souls, offers not simply a helping hand but a sacrificial spirit" (157–58).

136. Bloesch, *Struggle of Prayer*, 148.

137. Bloesch, *Freedom for Obedience*, 83. Later, Bloesch refers to these two vocations of Christian obedience as "spiritual and cultural mandates" (156). For Bloesch, the goal is always to point people to their need for God, and thus the cultural mandate is in service of the spiritual mandate.

138. Bloesch, *Freedom for Obedience*, 83–84.

to walk in the light of the gospel of redemption."[139] The work of the kingdom is focused on evangelism and the proclamation of the good news of the gospel. The work of social justice can be a sign and witness of the kingdom of God, but ultimately the goal of a Christian's love for neighbor is to fulfill the great commission.[140] While social justice focuses on the fair treatment of one's neighbor, kingdom righteousness focuses on a kind of love in which the Christian has "an infinite preference for our neighbor's welfare."[141] Ultimately, the Christian called to a life of holiness must embrace an active life of justice and love.[142] This life of social obedience, bearing the fruit of personal obedience in prayer, is a life that by the work of the Spirit demonstrates the Word.[143] Bloesch states,

> The church has a spiritual mission with far-reaching political and cultural implications. Its principal concern is to bring people into a right relationship with God through the power of the Word and Spirit, but it will also be involved in teaching people to be agents of justice and righteousness in a basically unjust society. Its spiritual mission takes precedence over its cultural mandate, since being in Christ has priority over acting in Christ.[144]

For Bloesch, embracing this twofold life of social obedience is certainly interpersonal, but it is also public and political.[145] In both the interpersonal and public/political spheres discernment is required in order to obediently love the world with the love the Christian has received. Once again, the critical role of prayer comes to the forefront. For Bloesch, the location of this discernment is the life of prayer.[146] Expectedly, Bloesch balances this Spirit driven mode of prayerful discernment by upholding the authority of the Word in the process of discernment. Rohrer correctly notes, Bloesch "insists that Christians must self-consciously subject their own positions to judgment and correction by the holy Word of God."[147] The Christian's call

---

139. Bloesch, *Freedom for Obedience*, 83–84.
140. See Bloesch, *Freedom for Obedience*, 85.
141. See Bloesch, *Freedom for Obedience*, 90.
142. See Bloesch, *Freedom for Obedience*, 98.
143. Bloesch, *Freedom for Obedience*, 154.
144. Bloesch, *Church*, 64.
145. See Bloesch, *Freedom for Obedience*, 156–57.
146. See Bloesch, *Freedom for Obedience*, 63.
147. Rohrer, "Donald Bloesch as a Social Prophet," 171–72.

to obedient engagement with the world requires wisdom. Such wisdom is the fruit of Word & Spirit; the ripening of that fruit is in a life of prayer.[148]

Conclusion

Donald Bloesch's theology of prayer is built with the machinery of the doctrine of the Christian life. Prayer is a personal encounter with the Triune God of Scripture because the Christian life is defined by biblical-personalism. Prayer is for the sake of engagement with the world because the Christian life is a life of obedience—personal and social. The divine-human encounter of revelation and salvation is subjectively experienced in prayer. If the Christian life is the arena of salvation, the location in which the Christian fights for and retains his or her salvation, then prayer is the frontline of that battle. As we have seen through an analysis of Bloesch's theology of prayer, the subjective experience of the divine-human encounter is marked by dialogue and struggle. The encounter between the Christian and God is an encounter of conversational reciprocity in which the Christian is called to share his or her heart in spontaneous supplication and petition. Likewise, it is an encounter marked by struggle. The struggle of the Christian life occurs in and through this ongoing dialogue with God. As the Christian cries out to God in honesty and vulnerability, there is a meeting of wills. This meeting of wills calls for the Christian to persist and resist in prayer.

A study of Bloesch's theology of prayer provides a concrete example of his brand of evangelical spirituality. His constructive theological interest in prayer itself demonstrates his abiding interest in the doctrine of the Christian life. For Bloesch, evangelical theology is distinguished by a particular emphasis on the Christian life, and the Christian life finds its primary expression in prayer. By the power of the Spirit, the Christian subjectively experiences the divine-human encounter objectively known in the life of Jesus Christ. As a transhistorical event, the divine-human encounter is consummated in the prayer life of the Christian. Evangelical theology, according to Donald Bloesch, is a theology of the Christian life, and a theology of the Christian life is a theology of prayer.

---

148. Bloesch, *Freedom for Obedience*, 60.

Conclusion

The corpus of Donald Bloesch occupies substantial shelf space in the library of twentieth-century evangelical theology. Nevertheless, not a single monograph specifically engages Bloesch's work as a whole. This project has engaged the entirety of Bloesch's work with a particular interest in one critical aspect of his theology—the Christian life. Through a close analysis of Bloesch's evangelical theology, I have endeavored to highlight an often-ignored resource, raising questions concerning the nature and task of what a *distinctively* evangelical theology involves. Bloesch's evangelical identity, catholic sensibility and hopeful disposition make him a unique conversation partner in the contemporary dialogue concerning evangelical theology.

Bloesch's *evangelical identity*, mutually informed by the streams of Reformed and Pietistic theology, distinctively positions him to be a resource for current evangelical theology. As I demonstrated in chapter 1, the formative influence of both the Pietistic and Reformed traditions on Bloesch's theological identity can make it difficult to locate him on the landscape of evangelical theology. Bloesch is content to dwell in the land of evangelicalism absent a specific tribal allegiance; opting instead for an evangelical identity marked by unity in diversity. It is this commitment to unity in diversity, embodied in the theology of Bloesch, that makes him a useful resource on the contested landscape of contemporary evangelical theology. This is demonstrated by the recent appreciation of and engagement with his theological work by both Reformed and Pietistic evangelical theologians.[1]

---

1. On the Reformed side we find engagement with Bloesch's project by theologians such as Vanhoozer, "On the Very Idea of a Theological System." On the Pietism side we

Bloesch's *catholic sensibility*, implicitly demonstrated throughout this project, positions him as an instructive resource amidst an ongoing emphasis on catholicity within evangelical theology.[2] Throughout Bloesch's corpus we encounter a sustained commitment to interact with a broad spectrum of current theological positions and to retrieve the broad-church tradition with an eye toward constructive appropriation. Bloesch's catholic sensibility has been recognized and appreciated by recent evangelical theologians, as for example in Michael Allen and Scott Swain's volume *Reformed Catholicity*.[3] Allen and Swain argue their proposal for Reformed catholicity is nothing new. To prove this point, they provide several examples of catholicity in recent Protestant theological history, including Bloesch. Regarding Bloesch's catholic disposition they state,

> Donald Bloesch, the late United Church of Christ theologian, addressed the Protestant mainline church with the promise of what he called "consensual Christianity." Bloesch published a multivolume systematic theology entitled "Christian Foundations," and the title is meant to connote the basic firmament of Christian faith and practice, derived from Holy Scripture and developed in the course of the church's witness. In a context where the Protestant mainline church was pulled in directions of revision and pluralism, Bloesch spent his career pointing to the apostolic gospel and the deep consensus of Christians across the centuries and over denominational divides regarding its nature and implications.[4]

Allen and Swain appreciate Bloesch's commitment to irenic engagement with the church catholic and his faithfulness to the "apostolic gospel." In

---

find engagement with Bloesch's project by theologians such as Olsen and Collins Winn, *Reclaiming Pietism*.

2. Bloesch's disposition of theological catholicity was recognized by his peers. Avery Dulles states, "Donald Bloesch is a man of peace and conciliation, a moderate who has read widely and appreciated the wisdom embedded in a great variety of traditions. He intends to be firmly evangelical but at the same time broadly catholic" (Dulles, "Donald Bloesch on Revelation," 61). Dulles astutely observes that in part it is this irenic and catholic posture of Bloesch that actually leads him into debates with other theologians. In effect, because Bloesch does not identify himself with one tribe, all tribes are open to corrective engagement. In recent evangelical theology this emphasis on catholicity echoes Bloesch's own disposition. For example, Kevin Vanhoozer argues, "*Catholic* and *evangelical* belong together. To be precise: 'catholic' qualifies 'evangelical.' The gospel designated a determinate word; catholicity, the scope of its reception" (Vanhoozer, *Drama of Doctrine*, 27).

3. Allen and Swain, *Reformed Catholicity*, 5–6.

4. Allen and Swain, *Reformed Catholicity*, 5–6.

Bloesch, they find an example of theological catholicity which supports their own constructive vision.

Bloesch is not only a resource for current evangelical theology because of his catholic sensibility but also because of his *hopeful disposition*. Interestingly, despite its ongoing factions and divisions, there are concurrent signs of resurgence in evangelical theology.[5] Three examples of this resurgence are Graham McFarlane's *A Model for Evangelical Theology*, Michael Bird's *Evangelical Theology*, and Dan Trier's *Introducing Evangelical Theology*. Evangelical theologians like McFarlane, Bird, and Treier, who are committed to articulating a comprehensive vision for evangelical theology despite its continued tensions and factions, will find Bloesch's hopeful disposition an encouragement in furthering their work. In the foreword to Bloesch's *The Future of Evangelical Christianity*, published in 1983, Mark Noll writes, "The most remarkable thing about this book is that Bloesch is optimistic about the future of evangelical Christianity."[6] Amidst growing pessimism regarding the future of evangelicalism, Bloesch's optimism was grounded not in a naïve confidence but rather a sober-minded faith. In his own day, Bloesch recognized deviant forms of evangelicalism—both right (fundamentalism) and left (liberalism)—which posed a real threat to the future of properly "evangelical theology."[7] Nevertheless, Bloesch remained

---

5. One diagnostician of the current state of evangelicalism notes:

> In its current mode, evangelicalism contains an amalgam of theological views, partisan political debates, regional power blocks, populist visions, racial biases, and cultural anxieties, all mixed in an ethos of fear. No wonder it can be difficult to know whether one is still evangelical. The impression of many on the evangelical left is that the good news of Jesus Christ has been taken hostage by a highly charged, toxic subculture on the evangelical right that—in the name of God—expresses steely resolve to have its own way in the public square. From the evangelical right, the critique is that Christian America is at war with any and all liberalism—evangelical or otherwise—and is in serious danger of losing its conservative virtues and spiritual practices. The Bible may be quoted in various ways, but arguments on all sides often seem more ideological than biblical. (Labberton, *Still Evangelical?*, 3–4)

Noting these divisions within evangelicalism Michael Bird argues, "The various subgroups within evangelicalism articulate and prioritize things like doctrine, mission, and social justice in different ways. There is a genuine risk that the evangelical movement in the West could splinter into factions with each headed in a different direction" (Bird, *Evangelical Theology*, xxvii).

6. Bloesch, *Future of Evangelical Christianity*, x.

7. Bloesch hopes his theology will speak to both the right and the left: "I hope that

An Evangelical Spiritual Theology

committed to "spell out a centrist evangelical theology, not in the sense of occupying a middle-of-the-road position but in the sense of reclaiming the dynamic center of biblical and apostolic faith—God's self-revelation in Jesus Christ."[8] Bloesch believed evangelical theology to be the truest and purest form of theology and, as such, a vital and enduring work of God to renew the church.[9]

Here, in the conclusion, I present Bloesch's *catholic* and *hopeful* evangelical theology of the Christian life as a resource for contemporary evangelical theology. First, I provide a brief summary of my thesis *in toto*. Second, I interact with two recent projects in evangelical theology—Michael Bird's *Evangelical Theology* and Dan Trier's *Introducing Evangelical Theology*. My engagement with these two projects highlights the ways in which they both explicitly engage Bloesch's work and offers my own reflections on how Bloesch might interact with their respective approaches to evangelical theology. Lastly, I offer recommendations for continued research and analysis of Bloesch's own project. I provide two suggestions for further research in Bloesch studies more broadly, and I offer two suggestions for advancing my own research in particular.

Thesis Summary

The fundamental argument of my thesis is that the doctrine of the Christian life is the distinctive emphasis of Bloesch's particular practice of evangelical theology. The Christian life decisively shapes Bloesch's theological identity and work. For Bloesch, the Christian life is a materially distributed doctrine that is presupposed throughout the whole of his theological system. This instinct is fundamental to Bloesch's evangelical commitments, expounded through relentless focus on Word & Spirit, and proves also to be the heart of his attempt to be a prophetic voice against reductive tendencies.

In chapter 1, *Bloesch As Evangelical Theologian of the Christian Life*, I demonstrated how the doctrine of the Christian life is central to Bloesch's identity as an evangelical theologian. While acknowledging the complexity

---

my theology will appeal to two groups: those coming out of fundamentalism in search of a biblical alternative to liberalism, and those who have become disillusioned with liberalism and sense the need to recover the transcendent truth of the gospel kept alive in church tradition by the Spirit of the living God" (*Jesus Christ*, 12).

8. Bloesch, *Jesus Chris*, 11.

9. Bloesch, *Future of Evangelical Christianity*, 5.

and challenge involved in positing a definition of evangelicalism, I affirmed Bebbington's Quadrilateral, the most commonly agreed upon definition. According to Bebbington, there are four primary tenets of evangelical identity—conversionism, activism, crucicentrism, and biblicism. With Bebbington's Rule as a rubric for evangelical identity, I demonstrated that while Bloesch aligns with Bebbington's definition, he adds his unique emphasis on the doctrine of the Christian life. This emphasis is particularly informed by Bloesch's pietistic background which leads to his affirmation that a specific type of spirituality is an essential feature of what it means to be an evangelical. Consequently, as an *evangelical* theologian, Bloesch maintains an abiding concern for the doctrine of the Christian life in his constructive theological work.

In chapter 2, *Defining the Christian Life,* I analyzed the material content of Bloesch's distinctively evangelical account of the Christian life. To map this material, I surveyed Bloesch's primary terminology for the Christian life—devotion, piety, spirituality, and biblical-personalism. While Bloesch uses all four of these terms to talk about the Christian life, he ultimately prefers biblical-personalism as his leading concept. For Bloesch, "biblical-personalism" articulates the heart of the Christian life as a divine-human encounter between the triune God and the Christian. This divine-human encounter is known and expressed in a life of personal and social obedience. The Christian's life of *personal* obedience is marked by piety, devotion, and prayer, and the Christian's *social* obedience is marked by ethics, action, and mission.

Rather than treating the Christian life at a distance from doctrinal material, or as mere application of already developed doctrine, Bloesch weds his constructive account of the Christian life to soteriology. The Christian life, therefore, while distributive, is also necessarily integrated with the doctrine of salvation. His goal here is to avoid two errors: separating the Christian life from salvation, on the one hand, and grounding salvation in the Christian life on the other. Bloesch argues the Christian life is the arena in which the believer fights for and retains his or her salvation. While the Christian life is not a means of earning salvation, it plays a vital role in the preservation and demonstration of salvation. According to Bloesch, every facet of the *ordo salutis*—predestination, justification, sanctification, glorification—must be subjectively appropriated in a life of active obedience if it is to find its fulfillment. Here, the material pressure applied by the doctrine of the Christian life begins to show up in Bloesch's constructive work.

Traditionally objective, historical aspects of the *ordo salutis*, e.g., justification, are for Bloesch brought to completion in and through the subjective experience and enactment of the Christian life.

At the close of this second chapter, I provided an analysis of Bloesch's concern with mysticism, in order to contrastively highlight the distinctive features of Bloesch's account. Throughout Bloesch's corpus he regularly identifies mysticism as a competing view of spirituality. According to Bloesch, there are two forms of mysticism that threaten a properly evangelical vision of spirituality in the church: what he styles classical mysticism and new mysticism. While both forms of mysticism have specific features troubling to Bloesch, his central concern regarding both is their rejection of that biblical-personalism he considers central to gospel faith. Both forms of mysticism disorder and depersonalize the divine-human encounter at the heart of the Christian life. The personal identity and primary agency of God central to the biblical witness are lost, and as a result the nature of true Christian spirituality is distorted.

In chapter 3, *Distributing the Christian Life,* I showed how Bloesch's account of the Christian life is materially distributed across the whole of his theological system in and through his doctrine of revelation. In Bloesch's dogmatic project the doctrine of revelation formally distributes the Christian life. While the doctrine of the Christian life is materially presupposed within his doctrine of revelation, revelation formally influences and informs all of Bloesch's doctrinal decisions. The fact that Bloesch presupposes the Christian life within revelation means that the Christian life pervades Bloesch's dogmatic work: we might say that the doctrine of revelation is something of a vehicle that delivers the material interest in the Christian life throughout the whole of his theological system, ordered as it is by Word & Spirit. Therefore, the material distribution of the Christian life shows up unexpectedly in a variety of doctrinal loci, such as the doctrine of God and the doctrine of the atonement.

The material influence of the Christian life on Bloesch's doctrine of revelation itself shows up in Bloesch's description of revelation as a divine-human encounter. For Bloesch, this encounter is a transhistorical event that has happened *objectively* in the incarnation, but which continues to happen in the believer's *subjective* communion with Christ by the Spirit. In his mature theological work Bloesch refers to this subjective-objective dialectic of revelation as a theology of Word & Spirit. Bloesch uses this construct to avoid the two errors of rationalistic-objectivism and mystical-subjectivism.

For Bloesch, revelation has objectively occurred in the history of God's self-disclosure, particularly in the incarnation of Christ, and revelation *subjectively* continues to occur in the Spirit-driven obedience of the Christian life. Therefore, I argue that for Bloesch, the subjective-Spirit pole of revelation *just is* the Christian life.

In chapter 4, *Prayer and the Christian Life*, I explored Bloesch's theology of prayer as a case study in his evangelical theology of the Christian life. I focused on Bloesch's theology of prayer because, according to Bloesch, prayer is the heart of the practice of the Christian life. Prayer is the primary location of personal encounter between the Christian and the Triune God of Scripture; it is the fundamental practice in the Christian's vocation of personal and social obedience. In prayer, the Christian fights for and retains his or her salvation. Prayer is the location in which the Christian fights the good fight of faith against the kingdom of darkness. It is in prayer that the Christian comes to know and experience the divine-human encounter through dialogue and struggle in a life open to the Word and seized by the Spirit. This encounter is marked by conversational reciprocity—speaking and listening—and is marked by the meeting of two wills, calling the Christian to pray with persistence and resistance. By exploring Bloesch's theology of prayer I provided a concrete example of his distinctively evangelical vision of the Christian life.

Bloesch and Contemporary Evangelical Theology

As I have noted throughout this project, there has been only minimal engagement with Bloesch's corpus in contemporary evangelical theology. A secondary result of the focus of this project is that it can serve to introduce him as a resource to contemporary evangelical theology. Having said that, there are some evangelical theologians currently writing who have in fact recently begun to engage with Bloesch's work. In what follows I explore two leading examples of such engagement: Daniel J. Treier's *Introducing Evangelical Theology* and Michael F. Bird's *Evangelical Theology: A Biblical and Systematic Introduction*. My engagement with these two single-volume systematic texts is not for the purpose of providing a detailed or critical review but rather simply to help to locate Bloesch on the current landscape of evangelical theology. Therefore, my interaction with these two volumes follows a basic threefold structure. First, I provide a brief overview of the nature and goal of each project by noting its distinguishing structural and methodological features. Second, I highlight the ways in which Treier and Bird explicitly engage Bloesch in their constructions of what a distinctively evangelical theology entails. By noting their use of Bloesch in constructing their own account of what "evangelical" necessitates, we get a sense of how Bloesch has been recently understood, invoked and utilized. Second, with reference to the argument of my own thesis, I analyze formal and material decisions by both Treier and Bird with reflections on how Bloesch would potentially affirm and critique. In doing so, I seek to cast a vision for how Bloesch's voice could be heard in the ongoing conversation of evangelical theology.

Engaging with "Introducing Evangelical Theology"

Daniel J. Treier's one-volume evangelical theology *Introducing Evangelical Theology* provides readers with a foundational understanding of the nature and content of evangelical theology. Treier seeks to introduce a "theological vocabulary and grammar that will help students to embrace an ecumenically orthodox and evangelical heritage."[10] His objective is not to offer a sectarian account of evangelical theology but rather a congenial account that will be met with broad appreciation within the evangelical movement. Treier utilizes the Nicene Creed and organizes his project according to its three articles (i.e., Father, Son, and Holy Spirit). He sets the course for this Trinitarian approach to evangelical theology with a catechetical emphasis: the Creed, the Lord's Prayer, and the Ten Commandments. This catechetical triad represents an integrated vision of evangelical theology. According to Treier, "Christian teaching integrates beliefs with belonging and behavior. While the Creed focuses on beliefs, the Ten Commandments and the Lord's Prayer focus on behavior and belonging."[11] For Treier, evangelical theology necessarily entails not only doctrinal formation, but moral and spiritual formation in the body of Christ.[12]

Treier's engagement with Bloesch is restricted to his doctrine of God. In chapter 5, *The Character of Providence,* Treier appeals to Bloesch as a resource in developing his *evangelical* account of the divine attributes. He directly cites Bloesch four times.[13] His account of the divine attributes is

---

10. Treier, *Introducing Evangelical Theology*, 3.
11. Treier, *Introducing Evangelical Theology*, 35.
12. See Treier, *Introducing Evangelical Theology*, 2–3.
13. Treier cites Bloesch four separate times in this short section (Treier, *Introducing Evangelical Theology*, 106–10).

divided into two categories: the "preeminent divine perfections" and "other perfections of the holy one."[14] The manner in which he divides his list of attributes into two groups appears to be informed by a concern shared with Bloesch, namely, that attributes which are biblically more explicit are given priority in articulating the character of the Triune God.[15] The "preeminent divine perfections" are power, wisdom, love, and holiness. This fourfold list mirrors exactly Bloesch's own fourfold list of the divine attributes.[16] The direct influence of Bloesch is made all the more explicit here when Treier follows Bloesch's coupling of these four attributes, connecting power with wisdom and love with holiness.[17]

While the only direct engagement with Bloesch's work is found in Treier's account of the divine attributes, there are many features of his introduction which Bloesch would undoubtedly affirm. First, Bloesch would affirm the overall catechetical vision of Treier's project. As demonstrated throughout my project, Treier's emphasis on the importance of prayer (Lord's Prayer) and obedience (Ten Commandments) echo similar areas of emphasis for Bloesch. Treier's emphasis on the Christian life, furthermore, is not a brief and inconsequential affirmation of its importance. He demonstrates the meaningful role the Christian life plays in evangelical theology by dedicating considerable time in developing a substantive account of both the Lord's Prayer and the Ten Commandments. Second, Treier's posture of catholicity would certainly be commended by Bloesch. Treier retrieves the tradition broadly and charitably, infusing contemporary evangelical concerns with ecumenical sensibility. Third, Treier acknowledges the evangelical heritage to be found in both the Reformed and Pietistic traditions, and he seeks to account for this in the tone and content of his project.[18] While this recognition of the two streams that inform evangelical theology may not inform his project in the same manner, his concern not to collapse evangelical identity into one tradition or the other reflects the same concerns of Bloesch in his work. Finally, Treier's doctrine of revelation

---

14. Treier, *Introducing Evangelical Theology*, 104–13. In the category of "other perfections of the holy one," Treier lists omnipresence, necessity, aseity, simplicity, eternality, immutability, impassibility, and glory.

15. Treier, *Introducing Evangelical Theology*, 104–5.

16. As a reminder, the third volume of Bloesch's seven-volume systematic theology is focused on the doctrine of God. The title of the volume is *God the Almighty: Power, Wisdom, Holiness, Love*.

17. Treier, *Introducing Evangelical Theology*, 106–9.

18. Treier, *Introducing Evangelical Theology*, 6.

strikes very similar notes to that of Bloesch. Treier argues for a doctrine of revelation focused on God's self-disclosure by Word and Spirit for the sake of encounter.[19] Treier states,

> Special revelation meets our need for redemption without nullifying human freedom. The Word and the Spirit make spiritual seeking meaningful, fulfilling our search for divine Light. Once we have encountered the Triune God in Jesus Christ, the Spirit uses the Scripture to shine further light on our spiritual path.[20]

Treier's commitment to revelation by Word & Spirit, while upholding the integrity and participatory role of the human person in receiving divine revelation, echoes Bloesch's commitments.

I think Bloesch would be extraordinarily affirming of Treier's project on the whole. It, in many ways, represents the vision of evangelical theology that Bloesch himself sought to articulate. That being said, there is perhaps one particular feature of Treier's project that Bloesch would critique. While Treier argues for a Word & Spirit account of divine revelation, Bloesch would find the Spirit side of that account under-developed. For Bloesch, revelation is an open-ended event, one which has an objective starting point but which finds its fulfillment in the subjectivity of the Christian life. While Treier upholds the importance of subjective experience in the Christian's encounter with God, the Christian life is not considered a domain of revelation itself or treated as such. Treier stresses the idea of integration regarding theology and the Christian life, but such integration does not have the same material impact on the content of his doctrinal work as it does for Bloesch. As robust as his treatment of the Lord's Prayer and the Ten Commandments are, the ethical and devotional features they represent are not materially returned to elsewhere in his project. Treier seeks to give real *formal* weight to the catechetical and subjective by beginning with this reflection, but it does not appear to have real weight *materially* throughout

---

19. Treier, *Introducing Evangelical Theology*, 15. Treier repeatedly articulates a Word & Spirit account of revelation, which stresses the goal of encounter: "In this saving announcement—a Word that God literally speaks in person—we encounter the Logos . . . which holds together all creation (John 1:1–18; Col 1:15–20). The Spirit prompts us to express our faith by seeking theological understanding, wanting to know more fully the God who first loves us" (1). Once again, Treier argues, "Because seeing is not yet fully believing, to know the True Way of Life we must listen to God's Word, led by God's Spirit" (15). Lastly Treier states, "The church's understanding of its faith, as we have seen from the beginning, is a response to God's self-revelation through the Word and Spirit" (79).

20. Treier, *Introducing Evangelical Theology*, 21.

the corpus. Whereas Treier explicitly reminds his readers that the Christian life must not be forgotten in the doing of evangelical theology, Bloesch implicitly ensures his readers do not forget it by diffusing it as a materially salient factor throughout the doctrinal content of his systematic theology.

Engaging with "Evangelical Theology: A Biblical and Systematic Introduction"

Like Treier's one-volume introduction to evangelical theology, Michael F. Bird's single-volume work *Evangelical Theology* is a "textbook for Christians that represents a biblically sound expression of the Christian faith from the vantage point of the evangelical tradition."[21] Like Treier, Bird affirms Bebbington's Quadrilateral as an apt definition of evangelicalism. Adding his own particular emphasis to Bebbington's definition Bird states, "I take it as proven that *evangelicalism* refers to the constellation of movements where there is a commitment to a gospel-centered orthodoxy, a gospel-soaked piety, and gospel-promoting activities."[22] For Bird, evangelicalism is gospel-centered. As such, the prolegomena of evangelical theology is the *gospel*. Therefore, the goal of Bird's volume is to "lay out what a theology driven and defined by the gospel looks like."[23] Bird defines the gospel as "the announcement that God's kingdom has come in the life, death, and resurrection of Jesus of Nazareth, the Lord and Messiah, in fulfillment of Israel's Scriptures. The gospel evokes faith, repentance, and discipleship; its accompanying effects include salvation and the gift of the Holy Spirit."[24]

Bird's primary engagement with Bloesch is connected to his doctrine of Scripture.[25] Bird clearly affirms elements of Bloesch's account of the doc-

21. Bird, *Evangelical Theology*, xxv.

22. Bird, *Evangelical Theology*, xxviii.

23. Bird, *Evangelical Theology*, xxix. Bird offers six reasons why the gospel is the "evangelical prolegomena" (see Bird, *Evangelical Theology*, 21–29). He states, "In the end, evangelical theology is the *theologia evangelii*, a theology of the gospel. The scarlet thread running through an evangelical theology is the gospel of Jesus Christ. The gospel comprises the beginning, center, boundary, and unifying theme for all theology. It is also the interpretive grid through which our reading of Scripture takes place" (28).

24. Bird, *Evangelical Theology*, 37.

25. At times, in secondary literature, engagement with Bloesch's doctrine of Scripture has been critical. Here, Bird turns to Bloesch's doctrine of Scripture as a positive resource in developing his own account of Scripture and revelation. Another recent example of positive engagement with Bloesch's doctrine of Scripture is found in Graham McFarlane's book *A Model for Evangelical Theology*:

trine of Scripture.[26] He argues that Bloesch holds to a "dynamic theory" of inspiration, which Bird himself affirms.[27] Bird states, "This view sees the combination of divine and human elements in the process of writing Scripture. The Spirit of God directed writers' thoughts and concepts while allowing their respective personality, style, and disposition to come into play with the choice of words and expressions."[28] In a discussion of the doctrine of inerrancy, Bird states that he "prefers stating the truthfulness of the Christian Bible in positive terms as *veracity*."[29] He affirmingly quotes Bloesch's own position regarding the truthfulness and veracity of Scripture, suggesting a direct influence of Bloesch on his own position. Bird does not exclusively engage Bloesch regarding the doctrine of Scripture but also briefly appeals to his Word & Spirit theology of revelation. Echoing Bloesch, he argues that revelation is a personal encounter between the Triune God and the human person.[30]

Beyond these direct appropriations of Bloesch's theology, I believe there are several features of Bird's evangelical theology that Bloesch would also affirm. First, Bird's emphasis on the gospel would undoubtedly be commended by Bloesch. Bloesch consistently expresses the centrality of the gospel in providing a distinctively evangelical account of theology. Second, like Treier, Bird embraces a disposition of catholicity in the construction of his theology. He explicitly stresses catholicity as a necessary ingredient of evangelical theology and ecclesiology.[31] Lastly, Bird's emphasis on the gospel as the prolegomena of evangelical theology results in a methodological emphasis on the divine

> Can you see, then, that Scripture does not contain deposits of knowledge that we excavate at will, but rather invites our engagement in order that its truth can be unlocked and we can experience what it reveals to us? Donald Bloesch defines this as "revelationalism," which he describes as "the living God personally addressing us in the moment of decision." Thus, Scripture demands of us a particular stance, what Bloesch calls "fideistic revelationalism"—where, as he puts it, "the decision of faith is as important as the fact of revelation in giving us certainty of the truth of faith." (McFarlane, *Model of Evangelical Theology*, 89)

While McFarlane quotes Bloesch a handful of times throughout his project, this use of Bloesch marks the most substantial engagement with Bloesch's project in his monograph.

26. Bird, *Evangelical Theology*, 54.
27. Bird, *Evangelical Theology*, 712–18.
28. Bird, *Evangelical Theology*, 712.
29. Bird, *Evangelical Theology*, 722.
30. Bird, *Evangelical Theology*, 261.
31. See Bird, *Evangelical Theology*, 805–6.

economy over God's life *in se*. Bird argues that "theology should not begin with the metaphysics of theism, an account of divine perfections, or even with God's immanent being (i.e., God-in-himself, his inner life, and mysterious being). Instead, our knowledge of God derives from the divine economy (i.e., God's actions, God as known by what he does, what God shows us of himself in redemption)."[32] This emphasis on God's economic action over the doctrine of God's immanent life in setting the course for evangelical theology is remarkably similar to Bloesch's own approach.

As with Treier's project, Bloesch would affirm much of what Bird is up to. That said, there is one likely critique Bloesch would have of Bird's evangelical theology. While Bird emphasizes God's action in the economy of redemption as the formal organizing principle of his theology, he is less inclined to emphasize the appropriation of God's work in Christ in the life of the believer by the Spirit. While Bird stresses the ethical implications of the gospel in the Christian life, he does not give material priority to ethics throughout his volume.[33] Bird stresses the Spirit's work of transformation in his outline of the *ordo salutis*, but he mutes this interest throughout other aspects and elements of his account of evangelical theology.[34] Bird's account advocates a material minimalism concerning the Christian life, evidenced in his concise account of the themes of the doctrine of the Christian life—prayer and obedience.[35] Bird does discuss prayer and obedience, albeit briefly. Nevertheless, both themes are located within ecclesiology rather than the Christian life appearing as a locus of its own. Prayer is primarily considered as a corporate practice of the body of Christ; obedience as part of the church's vocation in accomplishing the great commission.[36] Similarly to Treier's project, Bloesch would express concern that Bird has not placed a strong enough emphasis on the critical role of the Christian life in evangelical theology.

---

32. Bird, *Evangelical Theology*, 23.

33. See Bird, *Evangelical Theology*, 24.

34. See Bird, *Evangelical Theology*, 595. For Bird, "transformation" is the "subjective and inward change to the believer" (595).

35. See Bird, *Evangelical Theology*, 176–77.

36. See Bird, *Evangelical Theology*, 859.

Continuing Research

One intention of the present project is to inspire further research and engagement with the theology of Donald Bloesch. There is a need for continued work to be done in two distinct areas. First, the whole of Bloesch's dogmatic project demands robust analysis and interaction. The expansiveness of his corpus necessitates numerous lines of inquiry. Second, there is further work to be done by way of advancing my project specifically. While I have provided an account of Bloesch's doctrine of the Christian life and its relation to his theological system, there are areas of further consideration that merit dedicated research and analysis.

Further Bloesch Studies

Bloesch's project was appreciated and engaged by his theological peers, and yet his project has been minimally present in recent theological discourse.[37] The sparse academic engagement that Bloesch's work has received has often sought to position him alongside other theologians for the sake of mapping one particular doctrinal debate.[38] Furthermore, until now, no single-volume monograph has been done with a singular dedication to Bloesch's entire completed theological corpus. While my project is an attempt to fill this gap, it is merely one contribution toward that end. Further analysis and exposition of Bloesch's wider dogmatic work is needed. To that end, I propose two distinct lines of continued research and work in Bloesch studies.

---

37. Elmer M. Colyer's *Evangelical Theology in Transition* is the only monograph that substantially engages with Bloesch's project. *Evangelical Theology in Transition* demonstrates the significance of Bloesch's project in that it is a rigorous engagement with his constructive work from notable peer theologians. The volume includes contributions from theologians such as Avery Dulles, Thomas Torrance, Stanley Grenz, and Millard Erickson. Each theologian engages a particular doctrinal locus in Bloesch's thought, and in turn Bloesch provides a brief reply to their critical interaction.

38. James Emery White engages the theology of Bloesch in *What is Truth?* White's project is a comparative study of Bloesch alongside Cornelius Van Til, Francis Schaeffer, Carl Henry, and Millard Erickson. As a result, White engages Bloesch's thought in a very limited manner, and for the sake of broader engagement with other thinkers. The result is limited analysis of Bloesch's project. There is one other volume that engages Bloesch's theology which is a collection of essays in his honor from a distinctively Asian perspective: *From East to West*, edited by Daniel Taylor. This collection of essays is not designed to be a focused treatment of Bloesch's theology but instead a project of diverse, constructive advancements from a collection of scholars who appreciate Bloesch's work. As a result, this volume provides little rigorous engagement with Bloesch's project.

First, further work needs to be done in regard to Bloesch's doctrine of God. As I have argued throughout my project, Word & Spirit are epistemological categories more than they are ontological for Bloesch. In his account, to speak of Word & Spirit together is first and foremost to refer to the saving knowledge that results from the divine economy of Son and Spirit. As a result, Bloesch does not treat the doctrine of God *in se* until the third volume of his seven-volume dogmatic magnum opus. He is also resistant to speaking of God in the language of classical theism. Bloesch focuses instead on the God of biblical-personalism who has and continues to move toward humanity for the sake of a redeeming and formative encounter. This methodological decision governs Bloesch's dogmatic project and invites further critical engagement in conversation with current debates surrounding the doctrine of God in Christian theology.

Second, further research needs to be done regarding Bloesch's doctrine of Scripture. This is one area that Bloesch has been more engaged than others, and it is for just that reason that I believe further work is warranted. In my judgment, Bloesch's doctrine of Scripture has been too quickly critiqued and not patiently analyzed and understood. Much of the critical engagement his doctrine of Scripture has received came in the midst of narrow debates regarding the doctrine of inerrancy. Bloesch was often heard in light of certain cautions and anxieties that are no longer as prominent, in particular, among evangelical theologians. In light of the burgeoning interest in the theology of Karl Barth among American evangelicals and the creative work being done in the doctrine of Scripture by evangelical theologians like Kevin J. Vanhoozer and J. Todd Billings, I believe a renewed and robust engagement with Bloesch's project will prove fruitful.[39]

Advancing My Project

The focus of my research and analysis of Bloesch's project was on the doctrine of the Christian life. I provided an account of Bloesch's distinctively evangelical emphasis of the Christian life, and I demonstrated how this emphasis informed the whole of his theological work. I offered a thorough treatment of the primary contours of his doctrine of the Christian life along with a focused case study on how this doctrine is expressed in a theology of prayer. However, there are facets of Bloesch's doctrine of the Christian

---

39. I have two particular monographs in mind here. See Vanhoozer, *Is There a Meaning in This Text?*; Billings, *Word of God for the People of God*.

life that my research could not focus on in detail. In light of that, I propose two particular areas of further investigation into Bloesch's theology of the Christian life which I believe will advance the work I have begun here.

The two areas I believe would be most fruitful for further research are: social obedience and spiritual practices. First, further exploration of Bloesch's understanding of social obedience would prove fruitful, especially considering how social action remains a point of continued division within evangelical circles. Given the current dialogue in Christian theology, and more specifically evangelical theology, regarding the relationship of the gospel and justice as they specifically come to bear on an account of social justice, further exploration of Bloesch's theology of social obedience would help to situate Bloesch amidst this conversation. Second, investigation and analysis of Bloesch's understanding of the role of spiritual practices in the Christian life is worthy of greater consideration. In recent years there has been a flurry of interest in this area, in particular regarding ecclesial practices, and an exploration into Bloesch's understanding of spiritual practices would help to situate him within contemporary theological discourse.[40] I now consider these two directions in turn.

The Christian Life and Social Obedience

While Bloesch's full understanding of social obedience was not within the purview of this project, I briefly outlined Bloesch's theology of social obedience in my chapter *Defining the Christian Life*. The breadth of his writing on the subject coupled with the relevance of the topic in contemporary evangelical theology demands further research and analysis. For Bloesch, a focus on social action is central to a properly evangelical understanding of the Christian life.[41] While Bloesch discusses social obedience in a variety of locations throughout his corpus, there are four primary monographs in which he develops his theology of social obedience—*Freedom for Obedience, The Reform of the Church, The Invaded Church,* and *Crumbling*

---

40. One example is James K. A. Smith's series of Cultural Liturgies books: *Imagining the Kingdom*; *Desiring the Kingdom*; and *Awaiting the King*.

41. "The older evangelicals were not averse to social action so long as it served not clerical control but the correction of grave social abuses. It is well to note that evangelicals were the main arm of the movement for the abolition of slavery in both England and America. It has also been evangelical Christians who have been chiefly responsible for securing legislation designed to control gambling, pornography, dope peddling and alcoholism" (Bloesch, *Reform of the Church*, 168).

Foundations.⁴² *Freedom for Obedience* is a particularly important work because it is there that Bloesch offers his evangelical ethics, to which his understanding of social obedience is moored.

There are a few specific lines of inquiry that I believe would be important for further research into Bloesch's account of social obedience. First, an investigation of Bloesch's account of social obedience would need to engage the manner in which Bloesch relates evangelism and social justice. As I stated in chapter 2, Bloesch believes social obedience is rightly ordered first to evangelism and then to social justice. Further investigation of Bloesch's account of social obedience would require an analysis of this ordered relationship and the impact that it has on the nature of the Christian life. Second, an adequate account of Bloesch's theology of social obedience demands a detailed analysis of Bloesch's distinctively evangelical understanding of social justice. Bloesch states, "The secular conception of justice is giving each man his due; the biblical understanding of justice is to bring people into right relationship with one another. It both fulfills and transcends the secular conception."⁴³ With this in view, Bloesch does not shy away from directly addressing specific social injustices that must be met with biblical justice.⁴⁴ An investigation of what these issues are and how Bloesch envisages a Christian's call to action regarding these issues

---

42. While Bloesch's theology of social obedience is focused in these four volumes, one can find it spread across his corpus in a variety of locations. For example, Bloesch also explores the topic in *Spiritual Old & New* and vol. 2 of *Essentials of Evangelical Theology*.

43. Bloesch, *Invaded Church*, 59. Bloesch echoes this in *God the Almighty* where he states, "Yet social justice as a viable possibility in a fallen world is not to be confounded with divine holiness—the impossible possibility realized only through grace. In the former the claims of wronged individuals are rightly adjudicated; in the latter persons are accepted and loved as brothers and sisters. A just society by human standards falls drastically short of the ideal of love exemplified in the life and death of Jesus Christ" (*God the Almighty*, 153). Bloesch refers to secular justice in *Faith and Its Counterfeits* as "humanitarians." Regarding humanitarianism he states, "Humanitarianism seeks to have *morality* (service to one's neighbor) without *piety* (submission and surrender to God). The problem is that morality bereft of the fear of God often degenerates into attempts to manipulate one's neighbor for one's own ends. True piety invariably leads to moral action on behalf of others. Moral action may or may not lead to piety" (Bloesch, *Faith and It's Counterfeits*, 53). He goes on to state, "The object of humanitarianism is not to identify with the world in its shame and affliction (Jas 1:27), nor to permeate the world with the leaven of the gospel, but to remold the world in the image of enlightened humanity" (47–48). He succinctly concludes, "The goal is the great happiness of man, not the glory of God" (48).

44. For example, Bloesch dedicates an entire section in *The Reform of the Church* to "Moral Issues of Our Time." See Bloesch, *Reform of the Church*, 169–74.

merits serious consideration. Third, a thorough understanding of Bloesch's vision of social obedience must consider how Bloesch relates prayer to social action in the Christian life. Bloesch argues, "Seeking the will of God in prayer should precede works of loving-kindness and mercy. The fruit of faith is good works; the soul of faith is prayer."[45] A consideration of how Bloesch practically relates the life of prayer (as a form of personal obedience) to the works of mercy and love (as the outworking of social obedience) would prove to be instructive. Fourth, to properly understand Bloesch's account of social obedience one must carefully consider whether Bloesch understands this call to active obedience for the Christian to be an individual or a corporate reality. Bloesch argues that the church as an institution engages in social obedience indirectly "by means of its proclamation of the Word of God in the form of the Law," while "Christian laymen may at times act corporately in facilitating social justice."[46] It appears that Bloesch believes social obedience is a vocation for individual Christians that does not necessarily provide a mandate for the institutional church as such. The distinctions Bloesch seems to draw here need to be fleshed out in more detail. Lastly, a rigorous investigation of Bloesch's understanding of social obedience would involve a consideration of how the Christian's call to social obedience informs the political dimension of his or her life. For Bloesch, social action entails "deeds of personal kindness" and social service in "charitable works," but it is also expressed in "political action."[47] Bloesch argues that an embrace of the gospel "entails not only taking up the cross in service to the unfortunate in society but also engaging in political programs for social change."[48] More work needs to be done here to understand the individual versus ecclesial reality of this political dimension of social obedience for Bloesch.

The Christian Life and Spiritual Practices

In chapter 4 of my project, I provided a detailed analysis of Bloesch's primary spiritual practice of the Christian life—prayer. I briefly noted that

45. Bloesch, *Faith & Its Counterfeits*, 52. With practical consideration for the life of the church Bloesch states, "Churches that encourage prayer groups should also encourage social action groups, since communion with God must never be divorced from service to our neighbor" (*Theological Notebook*, 1:214).

46. Bloesch, *Invaded Church*, 56.

47. Bloesch, *Invaded Church*, 103.

48. Bloesch, *Essentials of Evangelical Theology*, 1:168.

Bloesch advances a variety of spiritual practices/spiritual disciplines built on the foundation of prayer which ought to play a critical role in the Christian's life of obedience. When Bloesch discusses the spiritual practices throughout his corpus he is sometimes referring to personal disciplines—fasting, solitude, and devotional reading of Scripture, and at other times he is referencing ecclesial practices—the Lord's Supper and baptism. Bloesch's discussion of personal spiritual disciplines is primarily developed in his monographs focused on evangelical spirituality such as *Spirituality Old & New* and *The Paradox of Holiness*. He develops a theology of ecclesial practices with specific interest in the sacraments in his more doctrinal works: *The Church* and *Essentials of Evangelical Theology: Volume 1*.[49]

There are a few key aspects of Bloesch's account of personal and ecclesial spiritual practices that demand further research in an effort to more robustly articulate his distinctively evangelical account of the Christian life. First, a thorough inquiry into the role Bloesch envisages the spiritual practices play in the divine-human encounter of the Christian life. For Bloesch, the Christian life is most fundamentally an ongoing personal encounter between the Triune God and the Christian. An investigation of Bloesch's theology of the spiritual practices can help provide some specifics regarding the *when* and *how* of such an encounter. Second, further research would need to reflect on how Bloesch's theology of Word & Spirit informs his understanding of the role of spiritual practices. Following the Reformed tradition, Bloesch argues that spiritual practices are "means of grace" in the Christian life.[50] Bloesch states,

> It is our view that there are certain designated means of grace by which God encounters us and also infuses his energy into us. This energy is not an impersonal force but the Spirit of power. The Holy Spirit is not tied to these means of grace, but we are so bound to them, since they were commanded by Jesus Christ. God ordinarily works through the means of grace, but in extraordinary circumstances he may well pour out his Spirit upon people apart from the

---

49. Bloesch also provides an account of the sacraments in his essay in *Spirituality East & West* and his early monograph *The Reform of the Church*.

50. "Evangelical catholic theology speaks not only of the gift of grace but also the means of grace.... God does not work directly or immediately upon the soul but through certain external channels including the Gospel, the Bible, and the sacraments. It is these means of grace that comprise the church" (Bloesch, *Essentials of Evangelical Theology*, 1:208).

external means of grace, though no one will come to a saving faith in Christ apart from a knowledge of the Gospel.[51]

As we would expect, Bloesch is careful not to imbue the "means of grace" with a power that properly belongs to the Spirit. He orders the means of grace through a robust account of Word & Spirit, grounding whatever power they have in God himself rather than human action.[52] Further exploration of how Bloesch's theology of Word & Spirit shapes his understanding of disciplines as "means of grace" would shed light on the nature of the divine-human encounter. Lastly, a specific inquiry into the role of the sacraments as means of grace in the divine-human encounter of the Christian life would prove to be fruitful. Bloesch identifies several important ecclesial means of grace such as hymn singing and preaching.[53] However, he views baptism and communion as the only two ecclesial means of grace that are *sacraments*.[54] For Bloesch, unsurprisingly, the sacraments are ultimately the media of divine-human encounter.[55] As one would expect, a theology of Word & Spirit shapes the nature of this personal encounter.[56] Bloesch names two temptations that always lie before Christians regarding the ecclesial means of grace: first, a detachment from religious structures into a

---

51. Bloesch, *Essentials of Evangelical Theology*, 1:210.

52. Bloesch, *Essentials of Evangelical Theology*, 1:211.

53. Bloesch, *Struggle of Prayer*, 123.

54. Bloesch, *Essentials of Evangelical Theology*, 1:210. Bloesch's criteria for sacraments is twofold—outward symbol and commanded by Christ.

55. For example, Bloesch writes:

> The holy communion that takes place in the Lord's Supper should be conceived not in terms of mystical assimilation into Christ but of confrontation with the living Jesus Christ, crucified and risen. I propose a biblical personalistic view of the eucharist, as opposed to a mystical view, on the one hand, in which we inwardly commune with the all-encompassing Spiritual Presence, and a rationalistic view, on the other hand, in which we rethink what has happened in the past. What takes place is not simply a remembrance of a past occurrence in history but the experience of the impact of this event in the present. What occurs is a divine-human encounter in which we are given both a realistic intimation of Christ's suffering and death and a foretaste of his coming glory. (*Church*, 163)

56. Bloesch, *Church*, 156. According to Bloesch, God is not bound to encounter human persons in the sacraments but chooses to by grace. He states, "From my perspective, only God himself is divine, only his Word and Spirit are filled with divine power. Even the preaching and hearing of the gospel does not automatically convey sacramental reality and power. The preached word and sacraments are signs and tokens of divine action in history, but they are not vessels that hold divine energy" (174).

kind of privatized piety, and second, an overly optimistic view of religious practices that voids the necessity of encounter with the living God himself.[57] Further investigation of Bloesch's understanding of ecclesial means of grace and his particular account of the sacraments will help to shed light on the role of the *church* in the Christian life.

Conclusion

I believe Bloesch would be encouraged by the attention given to the doctrine of the Christian life in recent theological discourse. This contemporary theological interest in the Christian life is perhaps most prominently on display in current Anglican theology. Bloesch would be heartened by the work in the vein undertaken by theologians such as Rowan Williams, Mark McIntosh, Sarah Coakley, and Ashley Cocksworth. These theologians have not only focused their work on specific themes of the Christian life but are seeking to do theology with an abiding attentiveness to the Christian life. More specifically, within contemporary evangelical theology there is serious interest in the doctrine of the Christian life. In recent evangelical theological work four figures stand out as particularly helpful examples of this interest—Todd Billings, Julie Canlis, Kelly Kapic, and Kyle Strobel. All four of these evangelical theologians have recently completed monographs focused on various themes of the Christian life. While all four draw upon the resources of the Reformed tradition, they also all seek to be catholic in their research and writing. In many ways, these are Bloesch's kind of evangelical theologians: dedicated to rigorous and creative doctrinal work, but ever concerned with how doctrine is shaped by and informs the Christian life.

---

57. Bloesch, *Theology of Word & Spirit*, 51–52. Bloesch expresses skepticism regarding what he calls the "liturgical movement," which has sought to answer the crisis of piety by emphasizing the importance of "the services of worship and making the Eucharist central again in the lives of people" (*Crisis of Piety*, 29). He believes that there is merit in the agenda of the movement, and that a renewed emphasis on the importance of ecclesial means of grace is to be commended. However, he is skeptical that this is the fundamental solution to the crisis of piety as he identifies it. He argues, "The church today needs liturgical reform, but the answer to the problem of declining piety does not lie in formal prayers and litanies as such. People cannot be said to have personal devotion to Christ until they preach and testify with power and conviction and sing and pray from their hearts" (29). Summarizing his view Bloesch declares, "As catholic evangelicals we wish to retain the sacraments but avoid sacramentalism. We desire to uphold the preaching of the Word as the primary means of grace, but to eschew the vice of verbalism. With the Pietists we desire to make a real place for the Christian life as a means of grace, but to avoid slipping into heresy or moralism" (*Essentials of Evangelical Theology*, 1:211).

While much of this increased interest in the doctrine of the Christian life in contemporary theology does not explicitly trace its roots to the theology of Donald Bloesch, the implicit connection is noteworthy. Bloesch stands as one of the few Protestant theologians of the twentieth century who emphasized the Christian life in the manner currently pursued.[58] Bloesch's commitment to the Christian life was demonstrated not only in the distributive role he afforded the doctrine within his systematic work, but also in focused constructive work on the doctrine—*The Christian Life & Salvation*, *The Crisis of Piety*, *The Struggle of Prayer*, *Spirituality Old & New*, and *The Paradox of Holiness*. This emphasis on the Christian life made Bloesch's approach to evangelical theology unique in its time. Contemporary theologians (especially evangelical theologians) interested in producing spiritually robust theology would be served well in retrieving the work of this forefather in spiritual theology.

---

58. One evangelical theologian of Bloesch's generation who demonstrated a similar interest in the doctrine of the Christian life was J. I. Packer. Packer completed several monographs with a definitive focus on the Christian life: *Knowing God*; *A Quest for Godliness*; *Praying: Finding Our Way Through Duty to Delight*; *Praying the Lord's Prayer*; and *Keep in Step with the Spirit*. For Packer, it was the heritage of Puritanism, rather than Pietism, which gave rise to this sustained theological interest in the doctrine of the Christian life throughout his career.

Bibliography

Allen, Michael, and Scott R. Swain. *Reformed Catholicity: The Promise of Retrieval for Theology and Biblical Interpretation*. Grand Rapids: Baker Academic, 2015.

Asselt, Willem J. van. "The Fundamental Meaning of Theology: Archetypal and Ectypal Theology in Seventeenth-Century Reformed Thought." *Westminster Theological Journal* 64 (2002) 319–35.

Aumann, Jordan. *Spiritual Theology*. New York: Continuum International, 2006.

Balthasar, Hans Urs von. *Word and Redemption: Essays in Theology 2*. New York: Herder and Herder, 1965.

Barrett, Matthew. *Reformation Theology: A Systematic Summary*. Wheaton, IL: Crossway, 2017.

Barth, Karl. *The Christian Life*. New York: Bloomsbury T&T Clark, 2017.

———. *The Doctrine of the Word of God*. Vol. 1.1 of *Church Dogmatics*. Edited by G. W. Bromiley and T. F. Torrance. Peabody: Hendrickson, 2010.

Bauder, Kevin T., et al. *Four Views on the Spectrum of Evangelicalism*. Edited by David Naselli and Collin Hansen. Grand Rapids: Zondervan, 2011.

Bavinck, Herman. *Reformed Ethics*. Edited by John Bolt. Grand Rapids: Baker Academics, 2019.

Bebbington, David W. *Evangelicalism in Modern Britain: A History from the 1730s to the 1980s*. Ada: Baker, 1992.

———. "Response." In *The Advent of Evangelicalism: Exploring Historical Continuities*, edited by Kenneth J. Stewart and Michael A. G. Haykin, 417–32. Nashville: B&H Academic, 2008.

Billings, J. Todd. *Union with Christ: Reframing Theology and Ministry*. Grand Rapids: Baker Academic, 2011.

———. *The Word of God for the People of God*. Grand Rapids: Eerdmans, 2010.

Bird, Michael F. *Evangelical Theology: A Biblical and Systematic Introduction*. 2nd ed. Grand Rapids: Zondervan Academic, 2020.

Bloesch, Donald G. *The Battle for the Trinity: The Debate Over Inclusive God-Language*. Eugene, OR: Wipf & Stock, 2001.

BIBLIOGRAPHY

———. "A Call to Spirituality." In *The Orthodox Evangelicals: Who They Are and What They Are Saying*, edited by Donald G. Bloesch and Robert E. Webber, 146–65. Nashville: Thomas Nelson, 1978.

———. *Centers of Christian Renewal*. Philadelphia: United Church, 1964.

———. *The Christian Life and Salvation*. Grand Rapids: Eerdmans, 1967.

———. "The Christian Life in the Plan of Salvation." *Theology and Life* 5.4 (1962) 299–308.

———. *The Christian Witness in a Secular Age: An Evaluation of Nine Contemporary Theologians*. Eugene, OR: Wipf & Stock, 2002.

———. *The Church: Sacraments, Worship, Ministry, Mission*. Downers Grove, IL: InterVarsity, 2002.

———. *Crumbling Foundations: Death & Rebirth in an Age of Upheaval*. Grand Rapids: Zondervan, 1984.

———. *Essentials of Evangelical Theology*. 2 vols. San Francisco: Harper and Row, 1978, 1979.

———. "Evangelical Rationalism and Propositional Revelation." *Reformed Review* 51.3 (1998) 169–82.

———. *The Evangelical Renaissance*. Grand Rapids: Eerdmans, 1973.

———. "Evangelicalism." In *A New Handbook of Christian Theology*, edited by Donald W. Musser and Joseph L. Price, 172. Nashville: Abingdon, 1992.

———. *Faith & Its Counterfeits*. Downers Grove, IL: InterVarsity, 1981.

———. *Faith in Search of Obedience*. Peabody: Hendrickson, 2016.

———. *Freedom for Obedience: Evangelical Ethics for Contemporary Times*. San Francisco: Harper & Row, 1986.

———. *The Future of Evangelical Christianity: A Call for Unity Amid Diversity*. Garden City: Doubleday, 1983.

———. *God the Almighty: Power, Wisdom, Holiness, Love*. Downers Grove, IL: InterVarsity, 2006.

———. *The Ground of Certainty: Toward an Evangelical Theology of Revelation*. Vancouver, BC: Regent College, 2002.

———. *Holy Scripture: Revelation, Inspiration and Interpretation*. Downers Grove, IL: InterVarsity Academic, 2005.

———. *The Holy Spirit: Works & Gifts*. Downers Grove, IL: InterVarsity, 2000.

———. *The Invaded Church*. Waco, TX: Word, 1975.

———. *Is the Bible Sexist?: Beyond Feminism and Patriarchalism*. Eugene, OR: Wipf & Stock, 2001.

———. *Jesus Christ: Savior & Lord*. Downers Grove, IL: InterVarsity, 1997.

———. *Jesus Is Victor!: Karl Barth's Doctrine of Salvation*. Eugene, OR: Wipf & Stock, 2001.

———. "Justification and Atonement." In *The Oxford Handbook of Evangelical Theology*, edited by Gerald R. McDermott, 222–35. New York: Oxford University Press, 2010.

———. *The Last Things: Resurrection, Judgment, Glory*. Downers Grove, IL: InterVarsity, 2004.

———. *The Paradox of Holiness and Faith in Search of Obedience*. Peabody: Hendrickson, 2016.

———. "Prayer." In *Evangelical Dictionary of Theology*, edited by Walter A. Elwell, 946–47. Grand Rapids: Baker, 2001.

———. *The Reform of the Church*. Grand Rapids: Eerdmans, 1970.

———. "A Response to Frank Macchia." *Journal of Pentecostal Theology* 10.2 (2002) 18–24.
———. *Spirituality Old & New: Recovering Authentic Spiritual Life*. Downers Grove, IL: IVP Academic, 2009.
———. *The Struggle of Prayer*. Colorado Springs: Helmers & Howard, 1988.
———. *Theological Notebook*. 5 vols. Colorado Springs: Helmers & Howard, 1989, 1991; Eugene, OR: Wipf & Stock, 2005, 2008, 2014.
———. *A Theology of Word & Spirit: Authority & Method in Theology*. Downers Grove, IL: InterVarsity, 1992.
———. *Wellsprings of Renewal: Promise in Christian Communal Life*. Grand Rapids: Eerdmans, 1974.
Bloesch, Donald G., and Vernard Eller. "'Evangelical': Integral to Christian Identity? An Exchange Between Donald Bloesch and Vernard Eller." *Theological Students Fellowship Bulletin* 7.2 (1983) 5–10.
Bloesch, Donald G., et al. *Christian Spirituality East & West*. Chicago: Priory, 1968.
Brand, Chad Owen. "Donald George Bloesch's Contribution to Theological Method." PhD diss., Southwestern Baptist Theological Seminary, 1998.
Brunner, Emil. *The Christian Doctrine of God*. Vol. 1 of *Dogmatics*. Philadelphia: Westminster, 1950.
———. *The Divine-Human Encounter*. London: SCM, 2012.
Canlis, Julie. *Calvin's Ladder: A Spiritual Theology of Ascent and Ascension*. Grand Rapids: Eerdmans, 2010.
Chan, Simon. *Spiritual Theology: A Systematic Study of the Christian Life*. Downers Grove, IL: InterVarsity, 1998.
Collins, Kenneth J. *The Evangelical Moment: The Promise of an American Religion*. Ada: Baker Academic, 2005.
Colyer, Elmer M. "Donald G. Bloesch & His Career." In *Evangelical Theology in Transition: Theologians in Dialogue with Donald Bloesch*, edited by Elmer M. Colyer, 11–17. Downers Grove, IL: InterVarsity, 2008.
———, ed. *Evangelical Theology in Transition: Theologians in Dialogue with Donald Bloesch*. Downers Grove, IL: InterVarsity, 2008.
Colyer, Elmer M., and John Weborg. "Bloesch's Doctrine of the Christian Life." In *Evangelical Theology in Transition: Theologians in Dialogue with Donald Bloesch*, edited by Elmer M. Colyer, 149–68. Downers Grove, IL: InterVarsity, 2008.
Dayton, Donald. "Some Doubts About the Usefulness of the Category 'Evangelical.'" In *The Variety of American Evangelicalism*, edited by Donald W. Dayton and Robert K. Johnston, 245–51. Knoxville: University of Tennessee Press, 1991.
Dorrien, Gary. *The Remaking of Evangelical Theology*. Louisville: Westminster John Knox, 1998.
Dulles, Avery. "Donald Bloesch on Revelation." In *Evangelical Theology in Transition: Theologians in Dialogue with Donald Bloesch*, edited by Elmer M. Colyer, 61–76. Downers Grove, IL: InterVarsity, 2008.
———. *Models of Revelation*. Maryknoll, NY: Orbis, 1992.
Ford, David F. "Introduction to Modern Christian Theology." In *The Modern Theologians: An Introduction to Christian Theology Since 1918*, edited by David F. Ford, 1–16. Malden: Blackwell, 2005.
Forsyth, P. T. *The Soul of Prayer*. Vancouver, BC: Regent College, 2002.
George, Timothy. "Evangelical Theology in North American Contexts." In *The Cambridge Companion to Evangelical Theology*, edited by Timothy Larsen and Daniel J. Treier, 275–92. New York: Cambridge University Press, 2007.

———. "If I'm an Evangelical, What Am I." *Christianity Today*, August 9, 1999, 62.
———. "Reshaping Evangelical Theology." *Christianity Today*, June 20, 1994, 37–38.
Greggs, Tom. "Introduction—Opening Evangelicalism: Towards a Post-Critical and Formative Theology." In *New Perspectives for Evangelical Theology*, edited by Tom Greggs, 1–13. New York: Routledge, 2009.
Grenz, Stanley. "Fideistic Revelationism." In *Evangelical Theology in Transition: Theologians in Dialogue with Donald Bloesch*, edited by Elmer M. Colyer, 35–60. Downers Grove, IL: InterVarsity, 2008.
Hasel, Frank Michael. "Scripture in the Theologies of W. Pannenberg and D. G. Bloesch: An Investigation and Assessment of Its Origin, Nature, and Use." PhD diss., Seventh-Day Adventist Theological Seminary of Andrews University, 1995.
Heiler, Friedrich. *Prayer: A Study in the History and Psychology of Religion*. London: Oneworld, 1997.
Henry, Carl. "Who Are the Evangelicals?" In *Evangelical Affirmations*, edited by Kenneth S. Kantzer and Carl F. H. Henry, 69–94. Grand Rapids: Zondervan, 1990.
Holmes, Stephen R. "Divine Attributes." In *Mapping Modern Theology*, edited by Kelly M. Kapic and Bruce L. McCromack, 47–66. Grand Rapids: Baker Academics, 2012.
Hütter, Reinhard. "The Christian Life." In *The Oxford Handbook of Systematic Theology*, edited by John Webster et al., 285–305. Oxford: Oxford University Press, 2007.
Jensen, Peter. *The Revelation of God: Contours of Christian Theology*. Downers Grove, IL: InterVarsity, 2002.
Johnson, Robert K. "American Evangelicalism: An Extended Family." In *The Variety of American Evangelicalism*, edited by Donald W. Dayton and Robert K. Johnston, 252–72. Knoxville: University of Tennessee Press, 1991.
Jones, Cheslyn. "Mysticism, Human and Divine." In *The Study of Spirituality*, edited by Cheslyn Jones et al., 17–23. Oxford: Oxford University Press, 1986.
Kidd, Thomas. *Who Is an Evangelical?: The History of a Movement in Crisis*. New Haven: Yale University Press, 2019.
Kierkegaard, Soren. *Fear and Trembling* and *Repetition*. Edited and translated by Howard V. Hong and Edna H. Hong. Princeton: Princeton University Press, 1983.
Labberton, Mark, ed. *Still Evangelical?: Insiders Reconsider Political, Social, and Theological Meaning*. Downers Grove, IL: InterVarsity, 2018.
Lane, Anthony N. S. "Justification by Faith." In *Dictionary for Theological Interpretation of the Bible*, edited by Kevin J. Vanhoozer, 416–18. Grand Rapids: Baker Academic, 2005.
Larsen, Timothy. *Cambridge Companion to Evangelical Theology*. Cambridge: Cambridge University Press, 2007.
———. "The Reception Given to Evangelicalism in Modern Britain." In *The Advent of Evangelicalism: Exploring Historical Continuities*, 21–36. Nashville: B&H Academic, 2008.
Levering, Matthew. *Engaging the Doctrine of Revelation: The Mediation of the Gospel Through Church and Scripture*. Grand Rapids: Baker Academic, 2014.
Louth, Andrew. "Deification." In *The Westminster Dictionary of Christian Spirituality*, edited by Philip Sheldrake, 229. Louisville: Westminster John Knox, 2005.
Lovelace, Richard. "Where Is Renewal?" *Charisma* 9.9 (1984) 18.
Macchia, Frank. "Toward A Theology of the Third Article in a Post-Barthian Era: A Pentecostal Review of Donald Bloesch's Pneumatology." *Journal of Pentecostal Theology* 10.2 (2002) 3–17.

Magill, Kevin, et al. *Christian Mysticism: An Introduction to Contemporary Theoretical Approaches*. Burlington: Ashgate, 2009.

Malone, Kelly Scott. "The Kingdom of God and the Mission of the Church in Contemporary Evangelical Thought: George Eldon Ladd, Donald George Bloesch, and Howard Albert Snyder." PhD diss., Southwestern Baptist Theological Seminary, 1995.

Marsden, George M., ed. *Evangelicalism and Modern America*. Grand Rapids: Eerdmans, 1984.

———. "Fundamentalism and American Evangelicalism." In *The Variety of American Evangelicalism*, edited by Donald W. Dayton and Robert K. Johnston, 22–35. Knoxville: University of Tennessee Press, 1991.

McDermott, Gerald R. "The Emerging Divide in Evangelical Theology." *The Journal of Evangelical Theological Society* 56.2 (2013) 355–77.

McFarlane, Graham. *A Model for Evangelical Theology*. Grand Rapids: Baker Academic, 2020.

McGinn, Bernard. *The Foundations of Mysticism: Origins to the Fifth Century*. New York: Herder & Herder, 1991.

McGrath, Alister. *Evangelicalism & the Future of Christianity*. Downers Grove, IL: InterVarsity, 1995.

McIntosh, Mark A. *Mystical Theology: The Integrity of Spirituality and Theology*. Malden: Wiley-Blackwell, 1998.

McKim, Donald M. "What Is the Best Systematic Theology for a Pastor or Lay Person?" *Christianity Today*, March 2, 1984.

Muller, Richard A. "The Covenant of Works and the Stability of Divine Law in Seventeenth-Century Reformed Orthodoxy: A Study in the Theology of Herman Witsius and Wilhelmus à Brakel." *Calvin Theological Journal* 29.1 (1994) 75–100.

———. *Prolegomena to Theology*. Vol. 1 of *Post-Reformation Reformed Dogmatics*. Grand Rapids: Baker Academics, 2003.

Noll, Mark. "Defining Evangelicalism." In *Global Evangelicalism: Theology, History and Culture in Regional Perspectives*, edited by Donald M. Lewis and Richard V. Pierard, 17–37. Downers Grove, IL: InterVarsity Academic, 2014.

———. *The Scandal of the Evangelical Mind*. Grand Rapids: Eerdmans, 1995.

Olson, Roger E. *Christian Scholar's Review* 10.1 (1980) 85–86.

———. "Locating Donald G. Bloesch in the Evangelical Landscape." In *Evangelical Theology in Transition: Theologians in Dialogue with Donald Bloesch*, edited by Elmer M. Colyer, 18–34. Downers Grove, IL: InterVarsity, 2008.

———. "Pietism: Myths and Realities." In *The Pietist Impulse in Christianity*, edited by Christian T. Collins Winn et al., 3–16. Eugene, OR: Pickwick, 2011.

———. *The Westminster Handbook of Evangelical Theology*. Louisville: Westminster John Knox, 2004.

Olson, Roger E., and Christian T. Collins Winn. *Reclaiming Pietism: Retrieving an Evangelical Tradition*. Grand Rapids: Eerdmans, 2015.

Perry, Ronald Mark. "A Holistic Model of Church Renewal in Light of a Critical Evaluation of the Contributions of D. Elton Trueblood, Donald G. Bloesch, and Lenardo Boff." PhD diss., New Orleans Baptist Theological Seminary, 1992.

Peters, Greg. *Reforming the Monastery*. Eugene, OR: Cascade, 2014.

———. "Spiritual Theology." In *Reading the Christian Spiritual Classics*, edited by Jamin Goggin and Kyle Strobel, 79–94. Downers Grove, IL: InterVarsity Academic, 2013.

Pinnock, Clark H. "Evangelical Essentials." *Sojourners* 8.8 (1979) 31–33.

———. "The Holy Spirit in the Theology of Donald G. Bloesch." In *Evangelical Theology in Transition: Theologians in Dialogue with Donald Bloesch*, edited by Elmer M. Colyer, 119–35. Downers Grove, IL: InterVarsity, 2008.

Ramm, Bernard. "Pioneering Theology: Review of *Essentials of Evangelical Theology: God, Authority and Salvation* (Vol. 1) by Donald G. Bloesch." *Eternity* 29.10 (1978) 46–47.

Rohrer, James R. "Donald Bloesch as a Social Prophet." In *Evangelical Theology in Transition: Theologians in Dialogue with Donald Bloesch*, edited by Elmer M. Colyer, 169–82. Downers Grove, IL: InterVarsity, 2008.

Sanders, Fred. "Saved by Word and Spirit: The Shape of Soteriology in Donald Bloesch's *Christian Foundations*." Midwestern Journal of Theology 13.1 (2014) 81–96.

Schleiermacher, Friedrich. *The Christian Faith*. Edited by H. R. Mackintosh and J. S. Stewart. Edinburgh: T & T Clark, 1960.

Schwanda, Tom. *Soul Recreation*. Eugene, OR: Pickwick, 2012.

Sheldrake, Phillip. *Spirituality and Theology: Christian Living and the Doctrine of God*. Maryknoll, NY: Orbis, 1998.

Thompson, Andrew C. "From Societies to Society: The Shift from Holiness to Justice in the Wesleyan Tradition." *Methodist Review* 3 (2011) 162. https://www.methodistreview.org/index.php/mr/article/view/56.

Torrance, Thomas F. "Bloesch's Doctrine of God." In *Evangelical Theology in Transition: Theologians in Dialogue with Donald Bloesch*, edited by Elmer M. Colyer, 136–48. Downers Grove, IL: InterVarsity, 2008.

Treier, Daniel J. *Introducing Evangelical Theology*. Grand Rapids: Baker Academic, 2019.

Vanhoozer, Kevin J. *Drama of Doctrine: A Canonical Linguistic Approach to Christiasn Theology*. Louisville: Westminster John Knox, 2005.

———. *Is There a Meaning in This Text?* Grand Rapids: Zondervan Academic, 2009.

———. "On the Very Idea of a Theological System: An Essay in Aid of Triangulating Scripture." In *Always Reforming: Explorations in Systematic Theology*, edited by A. T. B. McGowan, 125–82. Downers Grove, IL: InterVarsity Academic, 2006.

Wakefield, Gordon S. "Forsyth on Prayer." In *Justice the True and Only Mercy: Essays on the Life and Theology of Peter Taylor Forsyth*, edited by Trevor Hart, 67–76. Edinburgh: T&T Clark, 1995.

Walsh, Sylvia I. "Paradox." In *A New Handbook of Christian Theology*, edited by Donald W. Musser and Joseph L. Price, 346–48. Nashville: Abingdon, 1992.

Webster, John B. *God and the Works of God*. Vol. 1 of *God Without Measure: Working Papers in Christian Theology*. London: T&T Clark, 2018.

———. *Holy Scripture: A Dogmatic Sketch*. Cambridge: Cambridge University Press, 2003.

———. "'It Was the Will of the Lord to Bruise Him': Soteriology and the Doctrine of God." In *God of Salvation: Soteriology in Theological Perspective*, edited by Ivor J. Davidson and Murray A. Rae, 15–34. Surrey: Ashgate, 2011.

Wells, David F. "The Bleeding of the Evangelical Church." *Religion in Life* 49.1 (1980) 119–20.

Wesley, John. *The Works of John Wesley*. 3rd ed. Vols. 13–14. Grand Rapids: Baker, 2002.

White, James Emery. *What Is Truth?* Nashville: B&H, 1994.

Yong, Amos. *The Future of Evangelical Theology: Soundings from the Asian American Diaspora*. Downers Grove, IL: InterVarsity Academic, 2014.

www.ingramcontent.com/pod-product-compliance
Lightning Source LLC
Chambersburg PA
CBHW070255230426
43664CB00014B/2542